Repenters

By Peter Dugulescu

Originally published in Romanian language under the title:
"They Scheduled My Death"

Repenters

By Peter Dugulescu

ISBN: 0-9760196-0-4

Copyright 2004, Peter Dugulescu
Translator: Dorothy Elford
Editor: Kathleen Tsubata
Cover Design: PierAngelo Beltrami
Culture Design Inc.
Published by Jesus the Hope of Romania

Contact: isr@mail.dnttm.ro

Acknowledgements:

Deepest thanks my wife, Mary, my children, Ligia, Cristina, Chris and Eunice, who shared my persecution and paid the price for my ministry.

Also for Richard Wurmbrand, and his wife, Sabina, who have been an inspiration for me and encouraged me to stand fast for the Lord and to write this book.

For Dr. Peter Kuzmic, a professor at Gordon Cromwell Seminary in Massachusetts and founder of Evangelical Seminary in Osciek Seminary in Croatia, who invited me to give the commencement address in 2001, where during a walk through war-torn Vucovar, Croatia, he urged me to give voice to the message that God had been giving in my life, as a testament for future generations.

I thank my fellow pastors, who accompanied me on the stony path of faith through hard times, as well as the faithful members of my congregation of First Baptist Church of Timişoara, who endured and who sustained my family and myself through many difficult times.

I want to thank Dorothy Elford, who translated the manuscript from Romanian, Kate Tsubata who edited, and PierAngelo Beltrami, who designed, the English version of the book.

And finally, to the martyrs and the brave people of Timişoara, who risked the guns and the bullets of the brutal forces of darkness, to come to the streets to chant "God Exists! God Exists!" and knelt and prayed the Lord's Prayer. I pray that their blood and tears will extend the freedom of God to every nation, and that the revolution will continue in the hearts of all mankind.

Pastor Peter Dugulescu

Foreword:

"When measured against eternity, the span of a human life is but the blink of an eye. What Peter Dugulescu teaches us is to focus less on the length of our lives, but instead, to fill our lives with meaning. Although Peter's remarkable life story spans the historic transformation of Romania from a communist state to a democratic one, it is the role that he played and his work with street children, orphans, handicapped and the sick that will continue to inspire us."

Congressman Frank R. Wolf, R-Virginia

"Peter Dugulescu's amazing life's story, his experiences at the time of the Romanian revolution during the country's communistic regime, the events in Timişoara, his creation of the organization, Jesus Hope of Romania, his ministry with the street children, and his founding of the Onesimus Brothers orphanage, his ministry to the elderly, handicapped and sick, and his training programs—all illustrate that Pastor Peter Dugulescu is an extraordinary man with a great vision and heart."

Congressman Joseph R. Pitts, R-Pennsylvania

Prelude

It was a beautiful, early autumn day in Timişoara, Romania. My wife and daughter Cristina and I were departing from this city, on our way back to Haţeg, the small town where we still lived. I had been called to a church in Timişoara, and after much prayer, had decided to obey God's call, even though the communist authorities had threatened me with dire consequences if I took this new job.

We were driving through the intersection of Mărăşeşti Street and Lazăr Street when my wife suddenly screamed. A bus was hurtling towards us, full speed, aimed at my driver's side door. The impact was enormous. We were tossed around the car, as it was picked up and carried sideways by the speeding bus. When it finally came to a halt, we were injured, but alive.

Although we did not know it at that moment, we had just survived a planned assassination attempt. It was not the first, nor the last, just one in a series of attempts by the forces of those who hated God to end the life of one simple pastor. Many years later, the entire story would come out in an unusual way: a personal letter to me by my would-be executioner. So astounding was God's grace that even this revelation brought with it the chance to bring yet one more lost soul to forgiveness.

My story is only one of many faithful men and women of God who strove to keep the knowledge of God alive in Romania, despite the fullscale assault of the athiestic state. It is a story of modern day miracles and of the triumph of truth over falsehood, and faith over dispair. It culminates in the toppling of the very regime that sought to destroy God, using only weapons of prayer, brotherhood, and sacrifice.

It is the story of a victory no less amazing than the fall of Jericho, or the triumph of Gideon's forces over the 10,000, or the exodus from Egypt with Pharoah's army perishing in the waters of the Red Sea.

I set this story down for two reasons. First, to record the true history of how Christianity survived under the despotic regimes of communism. Second, to testify to the awesome power of God's love and protection, despite the best efforts of the enemy.

But I have a third, and more compelling reason, as you will see at the end of this book. I believe that this story will enable the faithful people of other nations to avert the destruction of their own nations' blessings of freedom, prosperity and human rights.

I hope you will feel, as I have tried to show here, that we are endowed with our inalienable rights by our Creator for a purpose, and that we must live up to the privilege and the responsibility of fulfilling that purpose. No matter what nation we are called to serve, we must realize that God is the origin of all nations, and of all people. Only when we uphold the laws of God will our nations be truly blessed.

A final word: in my nation, people who embraced the Gospel were called "Repenters." I myself tried to turn my back on God, just as many others have done. When I realized my mistakes, and willingly gave my life to God, I became, as my early classmates had called me, "Peter the Repenter." I have since learned the power of being a repenter, of being someone who forsakes worldly honor and seeks only God's will. I hope that this simple story will enable others to become "Repenters" as well.

A Village by the Mureş

"From one man he made every nation of men, that they should inhabit the whole earth; and he determined the times set for them and the exact places where they should live. God did this so that men would seek him and perhaps reach out for him and find him, though he is not far from each one of us." (Acts 17:26-27)

My story begins in the poor, unheard of village of Chelmac in Romania, a village whose poor and equally unheard of inhabitants had been since ancient times, one of a string of villages that watch over the River Mureş as it winds its unhurried way through the hills towards Arad.

The name *Dugulescu,* which is found only in Chelmac and Belotinţ, belonged to my ancestors – charcoal-burners by trade – when they moved to the Mureş Valley from Oltenia at the beginning of the 17th century. Later on, they switched to farming and cattle-raising. The land, which they cultivated assiduously, lay partly in the fertile river-meadows and partly on the hillsides where they planted orchards of apples, plums and dessert grapes.

It was in this village that my father, Petru Dugulescu, was born on May 26, 1907. On July 20, 1937 he married Irina Gruici, who had been born into a family of Baptist believers at Chizdia on March 26, 1916. Most of the inhabitants of the village lived peacefully and supported themselves and their families from the small plots of land that they possessed. Some of them also occupied themselves with fishing and hunting, or more precisely, with poaching since they had no permits. For them, it was not a sport but a necessity to feed the family.

My parents had about three hectares of land, inherited from my paternal grandparents. According to village gossip, my grandfather Nicolae, who died before my father came back from the war, was a very bad man. By contrast, my grandmother Maria, whom we called "Mama Cuța," was a small, bent woman with a heart of gold. As my mother was always out working in the fields, Mama Cuța looked after us. She loved me more than any of her other grandchildren and when her son Ion from Belotinț, my father's brother, came to see us and left her some sweets or gingerbread buns, she would hide them under her pillow and give them to me secretly. Once, when I was being beaten with a long implement as a punishment for misbehavior, Mama Cuța picked me up to protect me, thus taking some of the blows upon herself.

When I was 12 years old, Mama Cuța became very seriously ill and everyone thought that she did not have long to live. I loved her so much that I felt I would not be able to survive if she died. I used to go into the garden or the attic to pray for her: "Lord Jesus, don't take Mama Cuța away from me! Please help her to stay alive and look after us." Perhaps God heard the heartfelt prayer of a child, because she did not die until years later.

The people of Chelmac had been of the Eastern Orthodox faith for generations, until a new revival movement began in Sibiu in Transylvania in 1923. My father was inspired by this revival movement, the Lord's Army, and by the Orthodox priest, Iosif Trifa, who was preaching repentance and drawing pilgrims from all over the country. Trifa spoke strongly against sin, alcohol and sexual immorality, and formalism in religion. He was excommunicated by the Orthodox Church and defrocked, but his movement spread all over the country. This evangelical movement within the Orthodox Church was founded on Paul's Letters to Timothy: "Endure hardship together with us as a good soldier of Christ" (2 Timothy 2:3), and "Remember the covenant you made before many witnesses." (1 Timothy 6:12) Therefore, whenever someone confessed his sin and received Jesus Christ as Lord and Saviour, he was not rebaptized, but rather, that person made a covenant in front of the body of believers.

This movement's significance becomes clear only now, some 80 years later:

"It is interesting to note that the cradle of this movement was the Romania of the 1920s, the years when the Communist Party was formed. The Romanian Pentecostal movement began in the same year too. What secret spiritual forces were moving among our people in those days? And which of them won? Was it the ideology of darkness, which branded the Lord's Army as illegal, which conquered? What would have happened in our history if the Romanian Orthodox Church had not rejected the opportunity God gave it to make itself ready, through the Lord's Army revival, for the great confrontation with militant Communist atheism? In His unbounded Grace, God prepares a refuge before the storm breaks. The Lord's Army movement provided such a window of opportunity towards victory. Many people wonder why the Romanian Orthodox Church is not similar to the Catholic Church in Poland in its relationship with the Communist state. May it not be that the opportunity was lost when the Lord's Army was put down?"

P. Lascau: *Steps towards the Light*

When Father Trifa died in 1939, his disciples dressed his body in a surplice and wanted to show respect for his memory by holding a funeral service at which he was given full honours. But the Romanian Orthodox Patriarchate sent a delegation of priests who stripped him of his priestly vestments and dishonoured him in every way. Marini, the teacher, composed a special song for Father Trifa's funeral which the members of the Lord's Army were still singing many years later: "*Magic bird who sang for us / And made us kneel in the shadow of the Cross / You have gone to heaven, you have left us orphaned / Alone to face persecution and surrounded by foes.*"

Two people who were prominent in this movement: the poet Traian Dorz and the teacher Ioan Marini, were very soon to be arrested and who spent years of suffering in prison. Despite the persecution, those touched by this spiritual awakening within the Romanian Orthodox Church later joined the Baptist and Pentecostal churches. Some of the most beautiful songs sung by these churches came from the Lord's Army, and have something characteristically Romanian in their tone.

Another spiritual renewal movement was to shake the Orthodox and the Baptist churches of the Mureş valley before spreading right across the country: the Pauliş Pentecostal Movement which took its name from the place it originated. Pauliş is a prosperous community on the other side of the Mureş, about 30 kilometers from my native village.

My father joined the army to do his national military service already committed to Christ; one of the photos he was most proud of showed him in his frontier guard's uniform with his New Testament in his hand. Returning from his military duty, my father, who was constantly searching for a deeper spiritual life, met the founders of the Pauliş Pentecostal Movement. After receiving the gift of the Holy Spirit, he gave himself to the Lord Jesus in baptism in the the waters of the River Mureş, in the summer of 1929.

Wounded from fighting in the Russian Caucasus in the Second World War, he returned in time for the birth of his third daughter, Maria. Two daughters, Cornelia and Lidia were already born. On November 18, 1945, his long-held desire for a son was fulfilled with my birth, and my father gave me his own name, Petru.

After me, Ion, Vasile, Mili and Tania were born. Born onto the earth floor of our home – as was customary in poor village homes of that time to preserve the bedding – my brother Ion suffered an inflammation of the brain, became disabled, and was never able to attend school. At the age of nine, he died of tetanus after cutting himself on some dirty broken glass in the road.

I myself contracted double pneumonia at the age of six months, not surprising in the circumstances of poor housing conditions and sleeping in a wooden trough on the floor. Our parents, Mama Cuța, and all of us children were crowded into a two-room house with a floor of packed earth. And, in post-war Chelmac, there was no medicine, nor medical personnel of any kind. Even when my uncle, Ioan Dugulescu, from Belotinț, wanted to take me to a doctor, my parents refused, placing their trust instead in the healing power of God: "I am the God who heals you" (*Exodus 15:26*).

Because I had an extremely high temperature and was becoming more ill with every hour, they asked all the brothers and sisters in the village to come to our house and pray for me. While the brothers were praying fervently for my healing, my mother vowed to God: "Lord, if You will touch this child and save his life, I will worship You forever, and I pray that You will make him Your servant." As soon as she made this promise, my temperature began to fall and my breathing, which had been becoming more and more labored, became normal once more. My mother never forgot this sacred vow, and prayed always for my life to be of service to the Lord.

In the little church where I grew up, many of the sincere members sought after the gifts of the spirit. For this reason, the church in the village was sometimes called a Pentecostal one and at other times Baptist, and there was some disagreement. My father only exercised these gifts in his private devotions and in family prayer meetings based on the Apostle Paul words to the Corinthians about the exercise of such gifts in the church: "Our God is a God of order as in all the churches of the saints" (*I Corinthians 14:32,33*).

A Nation's Fall

Communism was a surrogate religion, a lie, a political and philosophical system based on a lie, an empire of falsehood, because its author was Satan, the Adversary of God, the Father of Lies. The supreme goal of the Communist system was one and the same all over the world: the denial of God and the formation of the New Man who was "atheos" – (Greek for: "without God")

On August 23, 1944, a year before my birth, the Red Army occupied Bucharest. The Romanian Communist Party, a tiny group of less than a thousand factory workers and uneducated people, seized power with the support of the Russian tanks and the forces of Joseph Stalin. Divisions of the Red Army set up their military bases in different places throughout the country. One unit of motorized troops and infantry established its headquarters at Lipova, a peaceful little old town 18 km down the Mureş from Chelmac and another at Radna, a little town made famous by the novels of Ioan Slavici (*Mara* and *The Lucky Mill*), and known for the Roman Catholic convent of Sfânta Maria (Saint Mary) which stood at the foot of the hill.

The Communists dissolved the convent soon after they came to power, threw all the nuns out and turned the building into an old people's home, but the August celebration 15th of St. Mary's Day continued to be a festival to which pilgrims came, a tradition beloved both by Orthodox Romanians and by those of other confessions, who would come even from distant villages and towns. The Swabians, an ethnic German group, also came to the festival from the villages of Banat. Their brass bands, with people walking behind in procession, would travel on foot for a whole week in order to arrive at Radna on 15th August.

Besides attending the religious services held in the huge, imposing cathedral, a Baroque building dating from the 16th century, families and their children also came to visit the open-air markets and the stalls which sold all kinds of goods. These extended right along the tree-shaded area below the convent and all through the town. With the small amounts of money our parents gave us, we bought balls made of crepe paper and elastic called *lopte,* and treats like gingerbread and sugar candy. There, I tasted my first ice cream. The price was one leu for a scoop, and I thought it was delicious.

The whole town swarmed with Soviet troops. I was a child and was attracted by their motorcycles and armaments. I even liked their uniforms. It seems as though I can see them now, wearing those khaki tunics, which were called *rubashka*, and their caps with the five-pointed star on the front. The pavements were covered with the stubs of Russian cigarettes (which were long and flat in the middle). The soldiers laughed at the country people heading towards the convent church and yelled "Bog-nyet!" (God doesn't exist). That phrase was to change my homeland beyond recognition.

Persecution Begins

Around Christmas in 1948, all kinds of rumors reached our village: that all the Uniate churches (Greco-Catholic churches linked with Rome) had been closed; that their land was to become state property; their buildings, priests and members were to be compulsorily integrated into the Romanian Orthodox Church. In the neighboring village, Belotinț, there was a Greco-Catholic church as well as the Orthodox. In spite of the protests of the priest and the villagers, this was closed on the very next Sunday. In the months that followed, all the bishops and most of the priests of this church were arrested. They were subjected to unimaginable tortures to force them become Orthodox and renounce the head of their church, the Pope in Rome. Among those who were imprisoned and, in come cases, martyred were Vasile Astenie, Alexandru Rus, Ioan Balan, Iuliu Hossu, Ioan Suciu, Tit Liviu Chinezu, Valeriu Traian Frenţiu.

To the Communists, control was the issue. Whereas the Romanian Orthodox Church was autocephalous and headed by the Patriarch in Bucharest, who could be appointed by a decree of the Council of State as a reward for his loyalty to the Communist regime, the Pope in Rome could not be controlled by the regimes in Bucharest and Moscow. He represented the West, "stinking capitalism" and imperialism. Over time and under constant duress, the members of the Uniate churches of Transylvania and Banat were forced to become Orthodox so that their children could be baptized and married, and in order to have a priest to bury them.

Another rumor that troubled our little village was that King Mihai had abdicated. Glancing nervously towards the windows of our house that looked out on the lane, neighbors told my father that the king had signed the Act of Abdication with Petru Groza's pistol held to his head. Petru Groza was prime minister and head of the first Communist government, which had taken office on March 6, 1946.

The young King Mihai of Hohenzollern was loved by the Romanians. He had come to the throne in September 1940. He often used to visit the Săvârşin hunting lodge, flying his own plane, and the local villagers could relate all kinds of escapades of the young monarch from the time when he used to wander through the hills and forests of that region.

Once, the King's German sports car got stuck in a muddy valley. A farmer coming home from work in the fields found some stranger struggling to put stones and pieces of wood in front of the wheels so that he could extricate himself. Asked to unyoke his oxen from the cart and help tow the car out of the stream, the peasant helped him, but not before treating him to a piece of his mind and a couple of Romanian oaths: "What the devil possessed you to come out here from the town and drive that posh car of yours into this ravine?" Once freed of the mud, the king thanked him and gave him the address of the hunting lodge so that he could go there and be paid for his trouble. The poor peasant didn't know how on earth he was going to ask forgiveness for swearing at His Majesty King Mihai!

But now, the 100 lei coins with the young king's image were no longer worth anything. Our parents gave them to us to play with, and we could find them lying in the street.

In the Spring of 1949, Party activists from the Lipova, Arad and Timişoara came to Chelmac to enlighten the people into joining the Collective. They told us how, in the Great Fatherland of the Soviets, the farmers were grouped into these *kolkhozes,* and were reaping the best harvests ever, happy under the wise leadership of "Little Father Stalin." Beginning with the poorest people in the village, they gave their pitch and signed people up. My parents, who had only three hectares, signed the application form and were among the first members of the Chelmac "New Times" Collective. At the first general meeting, my father was made auditor.

But when the teams of Party activists went to the doors of the more well-to-do, the people were unwilling to sign a document which said that they were handing over all their land to the Collective "willingly and joyfully" nor did they agree to the confiscation of the horses in their stables, their cattle and all their farming equipment. Aunt Marta and Uncle Budoni, had two cows and a cart, a plow, harrows and seed drills. They were allowed to keep their cows – only the oxen and horses being confiscated – but when the party activists seized the cart and its harness, Aunt Marta started pulling the cart back with all her strength, imploring her husband to do the same, shouting at the top of her voice: "Thieves, bandits, they've come to rob us! Don't let them Pepi!" Some people went mad or hanged themselves. Those not willing to sign were taken away at night by the "black van" of the Securitate, and beaten until they gave in, and were brought back and left in front of their houses. Some kept up their resistance and returned home only after eight or ten years in prison--or never came home at all.

The manor house that formerly belonged to Cicio Pop became the headquarters of the Chelmac "New Times" collective farm. I am ashamed to admit that only after the December 1989 Revolution I discovered that Cicio Pop of Arad was far from the grasping landlord, the oppressor of the people, the hostile element that we were taught in school! I learned that he had been a great Romanian who had loved his country and had made a vital contribution to the Great Union of December 1, 1918. He owned much land in Chelmac and the surrounding villages. The Communists confiscated all he owned: the orchard of "La Nuci" with its prime varieties of apples and plums where the schoolchildren used to go fruit-picking, the castle at Conop, on the opposite side of the Mureş, which was turned into a school and boarding house where all the children from Chelmac and the neighboring villages attended school. Cicio Pop left our homeland, poor and slandered.

The first president of the Chelmac "New Times" Collective was Petru Drăgoescu, a distant cousin of my father and a minor celebrity in the Communist newspapers, because the "New Times" collective farm was – along with the one in Lenauheim – among the first in the country. I remember the "general meetings" of villagers that were held in the Cultural Centre on Saturday followed by a free film, usually attended by Party activists from Lipova or Timişoara; it was embarrassing that Petru Drăgoescu, collective farm president and national deputy, was invariably drunk. These general meetings were often accompanied heavy drinking sessions involving both the local Party appointees and the important people who used to come to the headquarters of the collective farm.

As early as 1954, the village streets, the collective farm headquarters, the primary school and the Cultural Centre were supplied with electric light from a diesel generator located in the collective headquarters. Our kindergarten teacher used to tell us

Lenin's slogan: "Communism means collectivization plus electricity."

Russian films glorifying soldiers who fought against the Germans in World War II were shown in the village: "The Young Guard" and "Vaska Trubaciov's Detachment" and others. Fascinated by these films, I risked punishment at home because my parents believed that a real repenter must not attend film shows.

In 1950, a summer kindergarten was opened in the village to care for the children during the period when the adults had to go and work in the "united fields of the Collective." The kindergarten was open all day from morning till evening and we were given three meals a day plus a snack. Being one of the eight children of a poor family, I was always hungry, so I was glad of the kindergarten food – much better than what we had at home. But before each meal, in place of the traditional family prayer or, our teacher asked us to express our gratitude to Stalin. We all stood up and turned to face the large picture of the man with the big mustache and chanted:
"Stalin, Stalin, Stalin and the Russian people
Have brought us freedom
Stalin, Stalin, glory to Stalin!"

Next, we would turn to face the picture of Romania's first Communist leader, Gheorghe Gheorghiu Dej, and those of the "atheist apostles" who made up the Executive Bureau of the Central Committee of the Romanian Communist Party and chant:
"Ana Pauker, Gheorghiu D
Terrify the bourgeoisie!
With the Party to the fore
We will triumph evermore!"

Not only was Communism an ideological system founded on the denial of God and actively hostile to God, but it sought through hatred to achieve the results that Jesus Christ effects in people's lives through love.

In a parody of Christianity, Communism had its own "trinity, dogmas and saints." Portraits of Karl Marx, Friedrich Engels and V.I. Lenin were everywhere: in classrooms, in kindergartens, in offices, in universities and on the facades of official buildings. The members of the Executive Bureau of the Central Committee of the Romanian Communist Party were the "apostles," while the party activists who swarmed everywhere were "missionaries".

In Communist countries, the cult of the leaders' personality became an aspect of everyday life. Initially, the cult of Stalin dominated: later, smaller local deities were to appear. They all demanded praise, worship and unconditional obedience: Mao Zedong, Nicolae Ceaușescu, Kim Il Sung, Nikita Khruschev et al. Marx's *Das Kapital* was the "Old Testament" of Communist doctrine; the speeches of various national leaders were the "national gospels" of these countries and were considered infallible. Anyone who had the courage to criticize them openly had to face the "Holy Office" of the Secret police – the Securitate, the pitiless Inquisition of Communist regimes, rooted out heresy and meted out suitable punishment to the apostates.

The idea of Communism itself was stolen from the New Testament, from the first chapters of the Acts of the Apostles, where it is recorded that the first Christians sold their lands and possessions and shared out the money to everyone according to each person's need (Acts 2:45). But the Communists ignored the fact that what brought about this perfect organization in the first Christian community in Jerusalem had been the transformation of their hearts through God.

"When the people heard this, they were cut to the heart and said to Peter and the other apostles, "Brothers, what shall we do?" Peter replied, "Repent and be baptized, every one of you, in the name of Jesus Christ for the forgiveness of your sins. And you will receive the gift of the Holy Spirit" (Acts 2:37-38).

Waiting for America

If there ever comes a day of repentance among nations, the American government will have to confess this sin among others: that by the Treaty of Yalta, Romania and the other countries of Eastern Europe, which had made a vital contribution to the Allies' victory over Nazi Germany, were turned over to Stalin's Great Soviet Empire. There, millions of people were killed outright and even the survivors were reduced to poverty and deprived of liberty for almost fifty years.

"The Americans are coming!" I frequently heard these magic, forbidden words, whispered by my father's friends or at the home of my Aunt Marta, a dressmaker in Arad. Her husband, Uncle Budoni, had been in the police force in Timișoara under the previous regime and bitterly hated the Communists. Since he was not a repenter, he cursed the Communists frequently.

Oppressed and frightened by the brutality of the new regime, people clung to the illusion that the Americans were coming. The Cold War had just begun; people were making radios with headphones (called "galene") so that they could listen to the *Voice of America* and the BBC.

One of our neighbors across the street, Uncle Traian, had made one of these headphone radios. My father very often took me with him in the evening to listen to the news because the Romanian radio merely parroted "the triumph of socialism in the towns and villages" and newspapers did nothing but print photos of Gheorghe Gheorghiu Dej and the other "beloved leaders." One single hope still warmed the crushed hearts of our unfortunate people: "The Americans will not leave us in the hands of the Russians. They believe in God, they believe in freedom and in private property; they will surely come and liberate us."

The belief that the Americans were coming was a powerful one and was kept alive by the rumors that kept going around that

American spies had been parachuted into Romania from high altitude planes under the cover of darkness to send back information and to prepare for the decisive attack. Some of the villagers even reported seeing a suspicious civilian dressed in black on the nearby hills. Even the authorities fueled the rumors by ruling that anyone who saw such a person must report this at once to the militia headquarters.

In the Făgăraş and Caransebeş mountains, former military men and civilians, retreated to the forests and formed a "resistance army," taking arms and munitions from the depots. From their hiding places, they scanned the skies saying: "Why this delay? When are the Americans coming?"

Many of the bravest and most valiant sons of our people died this way. They had to come down into the villages from time to time to get supplies, and were spotted or betrayed by some of their neighbors or acquaintances. Tracked back to their hideouts by the militia and then the battle would begin. The People's Army was led by poorly educated men with no training, promoted overnight solely on the grounds that they had joined the Romanian Workers' Party. The Communist regime branded the fugitives as "bandits," and "enemies of the people," who must be wiped out "to the last man." But the soldiers sent to fight the ill-equipped resistance were described as national heroes, and the photos of the dead were displayed in national and local newspapers and in public places.

A top secret report, *The Trial of the Caransebeş Mountains subversive group led by Spiru Blănaru, Petru Domasneanu,* reached me. All of these men were condemned to death by the Timişoara Military Tribunal and shot in the Green Forest outside Timişoara. Their deaths were hidden for years. After the 1989 Revolution a monument was erected on the spot where they had been executed, proclaiming them as fighters for the anti-Communist resistance movement and as heroes of the Romanian people. They were among many who courageously opposed a totalitarian, godless regime and trusted that the Americans would not tolerate the oppressive Russian occupation of a country like Romania, which had played a decisive role in ending the Second World War and defeating Hitler. Yet, they met their deaths scanning the sky for American planes which never came.

Instead, one million Russian soldiers invaded Romania, destroying the economy, stealing and looting everything. My mother told me that she had to hide when she saw Russian soldiers coming along the street. They would stick their bayonets into haystacks, looking for new girls to rape. They imposed Communism upon us by force; deported hundreds of thousands of our people to Siberia; constructed dozens of prisons and filled them with clergymen, anti-Communists, and anyone who they saw as a threat.

Peter the Repenter

"You would not look for Me if you had not already found Me."
(Pascal)

I was in the second grade when the first "pioneer unit" was founded at my school, complete with two trumpets, two drums and a flag. Modeled on the military system, promotion earned symbols of higher rank: a red stripe for platoon commander, two stripes for a detachment commander, three stripes for a unit commander.

Despite my childish desire for these distinguishments, they eluded me, perhaps because my family attended the "meeting of the repenters" on Sundays. In school, I was nicknamed "Peter the Repenter."

In Romania, those who belong to Evangelical Protestant denominations which take the Bible seriously are labeled 'repenters.' During Atheistic Education lessons, the teacher would ask those who were the children of repenters to stand up so the others would laugh at them and make fun of them. For me, the nickname Peter the Repenter was a shameful stigma that I did not know how to get rid of. When I was 13, I told my parents that I did not want to go to church any more as it was boring and only for old people. I also told them that I did not want to read the Bible any more because "comrade teacher" had told us that the Bible was not true. Throughout the country, an extremely vigorous campaign was being waged against "mysticism and the superstitions of religion," but nowhere was it more fervently waged than in the schools.

I liked reading. I used to read whatever came into my hands, but everything had to pass through the strict ideological censorship of the atheist state. Books were my only enjoyment, but were filled with only what the Party allowed.

Meanwhile, we were learning other lessons. In the first year in which people worked on the Collective, the share of the crops each family received – calculated according to how many days they had worked – was very good. My father was pleased and congratulated himself on having joined the Collective. Besides wheat and maize, we also received sugar, honey, cheese and fruit from Cicio Pop's orchards. I later that this initial bounty was part of the scheme, in order to attract people. After the first year, despite my parents working harder each year, they received less and less, not enough to feed their eight children. The system of harvest quotas had been imposed in order to pay war reparations and to send support to the Great Fatherland of Soviets. Every day, entire trains loaded with grain, wine and all kinds of foodstuffs headed towards the Soviet Union. Or, Russian soldiers stationed in Lipova came to the village in trucks, went straight to the vegetable farms on the banks of the Mureş, loaded their trucks full and left without paying.

This injustice provoked its mirror: the practice of stealing from the collective became widespread. But while the Party officials used carts and trucks to carry out their thefts unimpeded, the ordinary people who, convinced that they were only taking the fruit of their own labor, would be arrested with a bagful of corncobs on them, put on trial and sent to prison. My uncle, a former policeman and strong anti-Communist, used to recite: "Envy Greater Romania style! The people who have are the ones who steal!"

My father was no longer able to support his family by working for the collective farm, so he found work loading logs at Calăci (Nadăş), along with other men from the neighboring villages. They crossed the Mureş in a skiff, or in winter by holding onto a rope stretched across the frozen river, and walked seven kilometers each way to work, with their food in leather bags over their shoulders. Every Saturday they were given fat bacon, jam and tins of fish on credit from the stores of this timber company. The food was cheaper that way. After rising early to gather kindling in the summer, we would have breakfast: a mug of herb tea or chicory with milk plus a fried or a boiled egg each, or a slice of bread and jam, or, best of all, a slice of wholemeal bread with fish paste.

Our food was always portioned out to us, and the portions were extremely precise. That fish paste on bread was so good, but shared out very strictly. My idea of worldly success was to grow up and buy a whole can of fish paste and eat the entire thing myself.

Then, we set off to to work in the fields, or to graze our cow and Aunt Marta's two cows. We rushed those poor cows shamelessly, so that we could go swim and fish in the Mureş, occasionally earning a beating. Unable to afford real hooks, I fished with a bent pin. When I caught a fish and pulled it out of the water, it would not stay on the pin but fell onto the bank. I had to hurl myself on it to hold it, or it would leap back into the Mureş. With this fishing method, I always had cuts and bruises on my elbows and knees!

In autumn 1956, I started the fifth grade in the boarding school at Conop, in Cicio Pop's former castle. I set out on foot on Monday mornings, crossing the Mureş by boat; on Saturday afternoons I came back. That autumn, the Hungarian Revolution began in Budapest. The Communist empire was under threat from one of its tiny members, and we were to witness the response. The railway that ran from Bucharest to Budapest lay right beside our school. Night and day the long trains went by, full of Russian soldiers, tanks, big guns and military vehicles.

The Lipova motorized unit was mobilized speedily to help crush the popular revolt in Budapest, which was described in the Romanian news as "the Hungarian counter-revolution." Since we were near the border with Hungary, we could see the night sky lit up with rockets and explosives, which frightened us.

At Timişoara, students of the Polytechnic and the Faculty of Medicine, emboldened by the Hungarian effort, gathered to protest the Soviet occupation and the Communist dictatorship. The same thing happened on a larger scale in Budapest and still the Americans did not come. The leaders of the protests were very soon arrested, tortured and thrown into prison for terms of between five and seven years. The popular liberation movement was aborted, and we sank back into oppression.

An Odyssey Begins

Within this larger struggle that was consuming the nation, I was experiencing my own inner revolution. I was almost twelve years old and was searching but could find no answer. The little church in my native village no longer held my interest. I didn't like reading the Bible but immersed myself in the books from the school library. While I was living in the boarding house, I used to go for evening walks under the pines and look up at the starry sky and ask myself: "Who created the Universe? Does God exist? What am I to believe? Do I accept what my parents have told me, although they are less well-educated, or what my schoolteachers have taught me?"

Though I was still a child, I was going through a genuine crisis. I very much wanted to go to high school and study languages and literature at university. I loved Romanian and world literature and I had started to write my first poems when I was still in the fifth grade. My Romanian teacher sympathised with me and advised me to go to a military high school where everything was provided free, even clothing. My parents felt that military career and faith in God were incompatible, and that I might lose my soul in such a school. So, in September 1959, my older sister Cornelia took me to Orțișoara, where I enrolled in the Agricultural Engineering Vocational School, for three years from 8th to 10th grade.

Despite my family's efforts, my spiritual crisis deepened dramatically in Orțișoara. Living far from my family, the others boys' way of life influenced me develop bad habits of vocabulary and swearing, of smoking, drinking and lying. When former comrades said to me: "What's all this? Do repenters smoke and swear?" I used to reply in fury: "I am not a repenter anymore! My parents are! I smoke with you, drink with you, swear with you. I am no longer a repenter!" But in spite of my protests, they still mocked me with the hated name 'Peter the Repenter.'

Every summer I did work study, driving a tractor in my home village. After graduating in June 1962, I was assigned to SMT Neudorf (near Lipova) to work in the tractor brigade on the farmland belonging to the Chelmac collective farm. I did not like this job at all. When the Russian tractors first appeared in our village in 1952, we had run after them in crazy enthusiasm, but now they made my life miserable, as they were forever breaking down. I was just sixteen, struggling to repair that wreck of a tractor, all by myself in the fields under the scorching summer sun. My mother used to bring my lunch out to the fields to wherever I was, only to find me covered with oil and diesel, wretched and depressed, and would cry when she saw me. My tractor broke down so often that I was unable to fulfill my quota, so I was paid very little. Still, I used that first salary to buy a kilogram of sausages and a kilogram of cheese to bring home on a Saturday evening, proud of being a wage-earner.

Alienation

Psalm 38; Isaiah 54:7; Hebrews 11:25; Psalm 81:12

During the month of October 1962, just before my seventeenth birthday, I desperately told my oldest sister: "Cornelia, I can't go on like this any longer. Please help me! You were the one who took me to that school; you've got to get me out of here, because otherwise I have no future!"

Cornelia was married to a Securitate officer and had moved from Lipova to Timişoara. Through her contacts in the Agricultural Administration, she succeeded in having me transferred to SMT Freidorf in Timişoara, where I worked as a mechanic in the repair shop. In February 1963, I became a repair mechanic in the Romanian Railways Carriage Maintenance Workshop, fixing the brake system of railway carriages.

The desire to go to high school had not left me, but my parents were unable to help me attend daytime school. In autumn 1962, I enrolled in the extramural courses of First High School and the following year, transferred to evening classes. From September 1963 onwards, I studied Theatre and Acting in a class taught by the actress Geta Angheluţă and the greatly-respected artist Ştefan Iordănescu in the Popular Arts School, and the theater became my passion. I no longer attended church at all; instead I would go to the theatre or the opera every Sunday. I would watch the same production of the same show dozens of times and knew biographical details about all the most popular actors in Timişoara, Bucharest and other Romanian theatres. They were my idols, my role-models. As soon as I joined the staff of Romanian Railways, I threw myself with enthusiasm into the Railway Club drama group, one of the most famous groups in Timişoara. I was also acting and reciting in the propaganda brigade, which was not only enjoyable for me, but had the distinct advantage that I was often excused from work and, of course, paid for taking part in the rehearsals and performances. The fact that I was living in my sister Cornelia's home made it easier for me to smoke and drink openly, since she and her husband did the same.

On 23rd August 1964, to celebrate the twentieth anniversary of "the freeing of our fatherland from the Fascist yoke by the glorious Soviet army," we performed a mammoth show in Timişoara's Rose Park. The artistic brigade of the Romanian Railway Club and the Electromotor Choir rehearsed for several months and I was excused from work for many weeks. I still remember one of the songs we sang:

> "August the 23rd we glorify you with our toil
> No foes upon this earth
> Our ascent can spoil
> In our hearts a passionate song you sow
> And 'neath the Party flag
> Onward we go!"

Against the musical background of these choruses, we recited poems in honour of the Romanian Communist Party.

> "Dominions come, then fade away
> But Communism's here to stay
> Kings and Emperors are passing things"
> and then everyone on the stage responded in unison:
> "Here forever the People are King"

Ceauşescu had taken the leadership in the spring of the next year, after the death of Gheorghe Gheorghiu Dej. Ironically, Ceauşescu accused his dead predecessor of fostering a cult of personality, so the praise given to Ceauşescu himself was pretty restrained in comparison to the excesses of later years.

The excitement of the performances was inevitably followed by parties in restaurants, at which I used to drink and smoke excessively. But always, just when I thought I was enjoying myself and feeling at home in those surroundings, an inner voice would say to me: "Your place is not here. You are the son of repenter parents, you grew up in the church. Your parents are praying for you now". There, in the midst of the general jollity, my face would cloud over and I would begin to feel very lonely. I knew that my parents were praying for me and it made me angry. I felt that their prayers were dogging me and that there was an unseen hand which always prevented me from getting the full enjoyment from these fleeting pleasures.

One Sunday night I returned home from a performance, reeking of drink and cigarettes, unaware that my mother had come to town and was waiting for me in my sister's apartment. Shocked at my state, my mother burst into tears saying, "Petru darling, I can't believe it! Do you really like the life you're living? Do you believe that it was for this that God preserved you from death when you were little?"

"When that happened I dedicated you to the Lord to be his servant. Petru darling, why don't you want to repent? If the Lord Jesus was to come tonight, would you be ready for the Rapture or would you be left down here? I am praying that you won't end up in the flames of hell but will be in heaven with Lord Jesus."

I felt such shame—of her, and of myself. I attempted to excuse my behavior, and insist that she and my father had to understand me because I belonged to a different generation and that my dream was to become a professional actor. I told my mother that after I had finished high school, I wanted to take the entrance exams for the Bucharest Academy of Theatre, Art and Cinema. My mother said that if I became an artist I would lose my soul and that she and my father were praying that I would repent.

My heart was hardened and I would not listen. And yet I became more and more alienated from the world I loved, although I tried with all my might to conform to its standards. That inner voice never left me alone and constantly whispered to me: "You do not belong to this way of life; your parents are praying for you."

My parents had bought a plot of land in Ciarda Roşie – an area of Timişoara – built a small house and moved there in order to be nearer, but I still lived at my sister Cornelia's and went home very rarely. I remember one Sunday, I went to a restaurant with my colleagues after a performance given by the Romanian Railways Club theatre group and was drinking heavily. From there, I went to my parents' home, where the whole family was eating after church.

My mother asked me: "Petru darling, where have you come from?"

I replied: "From the Cosmos, and if you go on getting at me I shall leave."

"Where will you go?"

"To the Moon," I replied.

Arrogantly, I told my parents that I wanted to be an intellectual, not a bigot like them, and that only old men, grannies and fools went to church. I said that I wanted to be free and enjoy life. Ignoring their questions or advice, I walked out of the house and went into town, through the park behind the Cathedral, smoking cigarette after cigarette. I gazed at the starry sky and asked myself what the real meaning of life was. Beyond the stars and the firmament, did God exist? What would happen to my soul when I died? Would I go on thinking, feeling, existing?

My best friend at the time was a colleague in the acting class at the Popular Arts School and in the Romanian Railways Club theatre: Biţă Murgu. His parents lived in Anina, but he was staying with his grandparents. What drew us together was an intense love of the theatre. We used to go together to rehearsals and performances at the theatre and the opera, with girls or by ourselves, and to the bar called 'The Pit' on the Eminescu Terrace, with its ever-flowing beer. My entrance exams for the Bucharest Academy of Theater, Art and Cinema involved reciting a poem, so I was working very hard on memorizing George Topîrceanu's 'May Night'. Biță would listen to me and correct me.

One day, Biță asked me: "D'you know what those people called repenters are? My grandparents are Baptists and they go to First Baptist Church on Romulus Street." I didn't want him to know that my parents were repenters too, and than they went to Second Baptist Church, where my sister Maria's father-in-law was a deacon, so I gave an evasive reply: "I'm not interested in that. Let's talk about something else."

But, from that moment on, I did not smoke in my friend's grandparents' house, and everytime my eyes met theirs, I felt ashamed.

Conversion

For it is by grace you have been saved, through faith – and this not from yourselves, it is the gift of God. (Ephesians 2:8)

One Saturday afternoon at the Romanian Railways Club rehearsal, Biță said, "Peter, I'm meeting a girl this evening."
"Good for you" I returned.
"But do you know where?" he prodded me. "At First Baptist Church on Romulus Street, where my grandparents go. Do you want to come with me? You'll see a lot of pretty girls there – nice sensible ones too."

I accepted his invitation only to please my friend and to see some pretty girls, and went to church with him that September evening in 1965. I had a cigarettes in my pocket and thought that two hours would be rather a long time to be in church and not smoke. I had not the slightest wish to listen to the sermon. My friend had informed me that the pastor who served that church was the most famous pastor in Romania, that he was very much persecuted by the Communist authorities and that he preached sermons that were of great interest to students and young people.

I went up to the balcony with my friend and managed with difficulty to find a place. The meeting house had been roughly converted from a former mill about twenty years earlier, after the war. The benches to the right were reserved for men and those on the left for sisters. The balcony and choir section were filled with young people. I first tried to sit in the part that was reserved for girls, but my friend warned me that this was not allowed.

I was first impressed by the appearance of the pastor in the pulpit, before he had spoken a single word. He was a slim man, small in stature, with a long pale face showing a depth of inner peace and goodness. He had a high, thoughtful forehead, and his brown eyes shone, mild and penetrating at the same time. He seemed to look through you and see everything. He was much given to prayer and fasting. When he was preaching, the brothers would sometimes say of him: "Look, he's melting like a candle!"

This man was Pastor Pitt Popovici, and that Saturday evening, he was just starting his famous series: *Is the Bible true?* It was a courageous evangelistic initiative that was quite new in the political and ideological context of that era. The balconies were crowded with students from the University and the Polytechnic. In this introductory sermon, he announced that every Saturday evening he would present arguments and proofs drawn from one particular area of knowledge: astronomy, biology, mathematics, history, archaeology.

The moment he began his sermon, I forgot that I was there to see pretty girls. I was first impressed, then afraid. The pastor in the pulpit was preaching to me, to me alone. I wondered if anyone could have told him about me, and how he knew me so well, because I had the impression that he was reading my soul. When he shook hands with me at the end, and asked me where I was from and what I did, I stammered a few words and tried to escape quickly. I was not prepared to tell him too much about myself and, besides, when he looked at me I had the impression that he knew everything about me.

I found myself troubled and confused, saying: "This man seems to believe what he says and is sure that what he proclaims is true. If he is right, it means that I have got to change direction and follow a new path in life." I felt the need to hear more of his sermons, sermons that were full of grace and inspiration. I started coming every Saturday evening and Sunday morning, except on the days when I had rehearsals or performances. I was convicted by every sermon I heard, but I struggled. Every message was one more blow of a hammer, striking the stone walls of my heart: "The ruins of the cities of Ninevah and Babylon are proof that the Bible is true!" Or: "Scientists agree that the Flood happened." I struggled with the implications for my own life.

One Sunday morning, the sermon was about the prophet Jonah and the repentance of the Ninevites. I will never forget that sermon, for it was then that the powerful hammer of the Word dealt its final blow to my hardened heart. Pastor Pitt had an exceptional gift as a storyteller. That morning he described the architecture of the buildings of Ninevah, the symmetrical street plan and the sinful state of the inhabitants of the city at the time of the divine judgement: "Yet forty days and Ninevah will be destroyed!" I could see it all.

In the streets, people collected around the travelling preacher, tore their clothes and repented. In front of the great library of Ninevah, some scholars with papyrus scrolls under their arms also stopped and listened to Jonah's message. They began to look up to heaven and cry out: "God, forgive us!" They began to tear their clothes and to repent. The message reached the palace of the king. There, the king dressed in sackcloth over his royal robes and he and his advisors began beating their breasts and repenting.

"But I want to tell you that there is Someone here today who is greater than Jonah. It is Jesus Christ, the Son of God, the One who died on the cross for your sins, who rose from the dead for your justification and who is alive forever and ever. He says: "Here I am! I stand at the door and knock. If anyone hears my voice and opens the door, I will come in and eat with him and he with me." (Revelation 3:20). You must make a personal decision today about your salvation. He wants to forgive you today. He wants you to receive Him today!"

His voice shaking with tears of sorrow for those lost, Pastor Pitt made the plea. The church choir was softly singing, "Come to Jesus now, He forgives you now, He receives you now…" At that moment, I could not resist the call any longer. I had known that this was the right way, but until that moment, I felt that the things I would have to give up were too precious to me. Not act any more? Abandon the idea of becoming a professional actor? Be called "Peter the Repenter" by my colleagues again? All this had kept me bound until that Sunday, when I went forward with two other young people. It was the first time I really prayed. I acknowledged my sins and invited Jesus Christ into my heart. For the first time I was weeping for my sins, aware that these tears were bringing me to salvation. The pastor prayed for me, and I felt happier than I had ever felt before. I set off to catch my tram, but I felt as if I was flying. I was joyfully humming the song which the whole church had sung after the sermon and which had touched my heart:

> *"O, if I had a thousand tongues*
> *A thousand lips to speak his praise*
> *A thousand tunes to sing my songs*
> *To the Holy One of endless days*
> *I'd thank him still for what he's done*
> *For me, a lost and prodigal son."*

I went straight to my parents in Ciarda Roşie and told them what had happened that morning. They wept for joy.

On December 18, 1965, I was baptized. I had turned twenty on November 18, and I considered the covenant I had made with the Lord in baptism to be the greatest present I had ever been given.

But something unexpected happened at that baptism service. In that period, all lists of candidates for baptism had to be approved by the Inspector of the Banat Region Religious Denominations Department. Any candidate who was not from a Baptist family or who was a student was automatically crossed off the list. All eight of us candidates were young, and three were students. As the pastor was giving us the final technical instructions about the baptism, this Inspector arrived, absolutely appalled, and tried to persuade all of us, but especially the three who were students, to change our minds.

Someone said that he had come to fulfill Scripture. "What Scripture?" I asked. "Job 1:6," was the reply: "The sons of God came one day and appeared before the Lord. And among them Satan also came."

My good friend who had taken me to church that Saturday evening refused to come to my baptism, preferring to go to the Opera with his girlfriend. I was very sad and prayed earnestly for him and spoke to him about the Lord. Finally, a year later, he too gave his heart to Jesus

After my baptism, I gave up tobacco and alcohol but I couldn't surrender the dream of my teenage years: acting. I tried to reconcile my faith in God with my passion for the stage and continued going to rehearsals.

I was playing the part of a young man called Mişa in a Russian play. My role involved trying to persuade my girlfriend to leave her husband and perform a patriotic act by coming with me to a young people's construction site in Siberia. She refused to come without him, and my line was: "Let him come too, the devil take him!" Before my conversion, I was able to say this line without the slightest problem at all the rehearsals and performances. Now I suffered pangs of conscience after saying it.

I struggled all night, and finally decided to cut off from the Club. They tried many times to contact me by telephone and the colleague who played the role of my girlfriend tried to persuade me to return. When I refused, she asked, "Why? You haven't been converted, have you?" I told her I had. She said that she was sorry for me wasting my youth in religion, superstition and mysticism, concluding,"It's a sin and a shame that you've been converted!"

I told her that what I was doing was not sinful; Sin was the condition in which I had lived before, when I did not know God.

"Have you converted Biţă too?" she asked. By this time, Biţă too had decided to follow the Lord.

"I haven't converted him; he has repented in obedience to God's command."

"A sin and a shame," she said once more, "because I have lost the best people in the group."

After letting go of the thing I had feared most, from that moment on, I was free.

In the state of grace in which I was living my new life, I experienced great joy. I had never known that there could be so much liberty and so much wonder in a relationship with God that was based on love and submission. I had finally learned the meaning of "repentance," a word that had sounded so repellant to me before. I realised that repentance means "metanoia" – the renewal of the mind – that my value system had changed. Things which had previously seemed to me to be unattractive and boring, like prayer, fasting, reading the Bible and going to church, were now becoming so enjoyable and vital, while things that had been attractive and normal before were now sinful.

I realised that repentance was not the stigma of ignorant, uncultured "sectarians" in a mainly Orthodox country, but rather the only proper response of sinful man to a Holy God. Soon I discovered what my spiritual gift in the Body of Christ was. I now felt the desire to express my love for the Lord in poetry: I began to write and recite poems such as *Lord, you are so Great* and *The Bible* at Pastor Pitt's Saturday evening services. They were followed by *At Your Cross*, *It Will Be Late*, *Truth*, and others. These poems, typed or copied out by hand, spread at lightning speed among all the evangelical churches in Romania

Now, not only my poetic talent but also my dramatic skills became useful in the work of the Kingdom. I began teaching other young people to recite poetry and organised a group of young people with whom I used to go on mission visits to small village churches. There we were welcomed with great warmth and joy. At these churches I would recite the poems I had written, and I also began to prepare simple sermons and preach them. Since churches were strictly forbidden to hold any young people's meetings or Bible studies on weekdays, we used to meet secretly in small groups in the homes of certain families to do this. This was how the first year of my childhood in Christ passed, and how I became established in my faith.

A Soldier Spy

At the beginning of October 1966, I received notice from Timişoara Army Board for my military service. I joined hundreds of young men, in a packed courtyard, to hear our names called out for various units. But my name and those of nine other young men – three of whom had been my classmates at night school – were not read out, and as darkness was descending, we were still in the courtyard. At last we were summoned to a room where a young lieutenant from the Buzău paratroop unit, the only such unit in Romania at the time, introduced himself.

"Lads, you've been selected for a special unit. You're going to be paratroopers. What d'you say to that?"

All the others exclaimed: "YES!!! Fantastic!"

I myself was shaking with fear. Though fearful, I knew I was a child of God and I said to myself: "If these people who don't know God are not afraid of making parachute jumps, how can I say that I'm scared? Some of them know me. It would be too shameful." So I agreed as well.

After being issued food for the journey and travel warrants for the train, we set off for Buzău accompanied by our officer. The journey took 24 hours. On arrival, we learned that we would be trained as scouts to perform sabotage activities deep behind enemy lines. We shared a base with the other battalions making up the paratroop regiment, but our mission was quite different. We had a separate parade ground and came under the direct control of the Bucharest central military command. We were to carry out special Warsaw Pact exercises.

I wondered whether the people who had sent me there knew that I was a repenter, belonging to a religious denomination that was considered to be sectarian and American – an evangelical group. In my daily life I tried to bear witness by example, just as Pastor Pitt was always telling us. He used to say that if you were a real disciple of Jesus Christ, then those around you ought to be able to see it.

An aeronautical panel from Bucharest came and subjected us to a second medical checkup, despite the first one at the commissariat in Timişoara. We were examined from head to toe, as it was vital that we should be a hundred percent fit. Two of the ten failed this medical examination. I passed, though I would have preferred to fail. I was absolutely petrified at the very thought of having to make parachute jumps.

We started drilling on the parade square and doing basic field training – which was very demanding. My comrades would buy bottles of wine which they then passed round at mealtimes and during breaks in our instruction. The fact that I didn't join in made them whisper about me. About three weeks passed in this way but no one had yet asked me why I didn't drink wine, or why I didn't swear and join in when they were telling dirty jokes. I used to pray secretly under my blanket at night, after lights out; I prayed in the lavatory; I prayed when I was on guard duty with my gun strapped to my back. I prayed that God would help me to be like salt and light, a living witness for him.

One day, two corporals came up to me: "Dugulescu, tell us the truth, are you a repenter or aren't you?" the first one asked, the leader of my group.

"Yes, I'm a repenter," I said.

"Great!" he said triumphantly to his mate, "I've won the bet. I guessed he was a repenter!"

I felt a great joy in my heart that people saw that I was a repenter, that I was a child of God, and I began to pray for them even more than before. I had a booklet by Brother Pitt Popovici called "Daily Power" that contained scriptural verses for different situations that I memorized. It was my little Bible, my daily spiritual nourishment, my consolation in difficulties. We were not allowed to have a Bible or any other religious books with you while you were doing your military service.

Our training was unique, because of our mission as saboteurs. It was in the army that I acquired the rudiments of English, because we needed to know the languages of the NATO forces. If war were to come, we would have to be deployed deep behind the enemy lines. There, dressed as civilians, we would have to eavesdrop on the general public and on the military, understand what people were saying and react accordingly. We learned to set demolition charges to destroy the reservoirs, bridges, main roads and other vital infrastructure of the countries we were in. There were also special classes in which we learned about the how the American and British armies were structured and organized, and about their weaponry.

We also learned how to keep ourselves alive in extreme conditions: how to live off wild plants, cook rats and mice, filter water to make it drinkable, and survive in extreme cold, and more. We trained hard in the gym – the vaulting horse, the fixed and parallel bars – then came ground instruction for parachute jumping, to teach us how to land. We jumped from a 25-meter (80 foot) training platform to which I was attached by straps and came to a stop, 2 yards above the ground. It was exhilarating to leap into the void. We also went through a course of tactical ground training in which we were deployed in platoons or companies in the villages around Buzău, which always involved heavy drinking and all my colleagues and even the officers invariably got drunk.

As the first real jump approached, I felt extremely nervous. I seriously asked a sergeant what would happen if my parachute didn't open. "Go to the stores, ask for another one and jump again!" he replied, making light of my worries.

The night before March 23,1967, I barely slept. I dreamed that when I jumped from the plane, the parachute didn't open automatically. I tried to pull the rip cord, but still the parachute didn't open. I was hurtling towards the ground at a dizzying speed. When I hit the ground – in my dream, of course – I suddenly woke up. I opened my eyes and thanked God that it had been just a dream and not the real thing.

The next we boarded the Russian Litonov (L.I.2) aircraft and took off from Buzău airfield. We made our jumps from above the airfield, as its runways were only grass, not concrete. As I reached the edge of the hatch and stood, as instructed, with my left hand on the ripcord and my right hand clutching the straps of my harness, I closed my eyes and leapt into the void, praying: "Lord, I have put my trust in you, I am now casting myself into your arms." I counted: "101, 102, 103, 104." As I looked over my shoulder I saw the parachute unfurling and opening. I reached the ground without problems.

The fact that I had survived my first 1,000-meter parachute jump was a great victory for me and a great experience. I couldn't believe that it was true – that I was capable of doing such a thing. I kept trying to work out why things had turned out the way they had, why God had brought me, of all people, to this paratroop unit. Maybe he had some future plan for me? My naive, childish explanation was that later on God intended to send me as a missionary to a tribe living in some region of an African or Latin American country inaccessible except by parachute. After many, many years I understood more clearly why it was that God had wanted me to do my military service in the paratroop regiment.

I feel now that being a servant of the Gospel in a Communist country like Romania, where the regime was extremely harsh and ruthless in its attitude towards those evangelical groups that dared to live and preach the Gospel, being the pastor of a church in an atheist country is very similar to being a paratrooper. For me, every single day of the fifteen years in which I worked to spread the Gospel under Communism was a leap into the void – a leap into the unknown. Every new day meant taking risks. For fifteen years, I learned how to leap into the void with God, to rely on God, to take the risk and undertake the adventure of relying only on Him. One of our training films was called "The School of Courage." I understood that God had brought me–cowardly, unconfident, shy and scared–to this "school of courage" to be prepared for his work. In a strange way, the communist military prepared me to fight the great spiritual battle that lay before me.

As the first instruction cycle finished, I was nominated for the training to take command of a group. The corporals and my fellow paratroopers knew that I was a repenter and that was why I lived in a different way, but the officers did not. I was worried that I had not lived out my Christian life well enough for my superior officers, the platoon, company and battalion commanders, to realise that I was a Christian. One day, my platoon commander, Lieutenant Major Spânu, asked me to polish his flying boots. I picked them up, applied the polish, gave them a shine and then before leaving I stood at attention and said: "Comrade Lieutenant Major, permission to speak."

"What do you want, Dugulescu?"

"I don't know whether you knew everything about me when you proposed me for the training school."

"I believe I did."

"I don't know if you knew I was a repenter. I'm a Baptist."

"What is the difference between Baptists and Orthodox?"

And I replied: "We have the same Bible, we believe in the same God and in the same Saviour Jesus Christ. But whereas they make no effort to get to know the Bible or to live it out, we want to live by it. That's the difference."

He asked me: "Do you eat pork?" This was because there were some Seventh Day Adventists in certain units who were causing problems by their refusal to eat pork. I said: "Yes I do."

"Do you use firearms?"

"I did so only yesterday on the range."

"Do you carry out parachute jumps?"

"I jumped today," I told him.

"Well then, if you eat pork, use firearms and do parachute jumps I don't have any problem with you."

I saluted and left his office. But he passed the information on. I was called in by the battalion commander and the political instructor and taken to task. I remember one occasion when I was duty sergeant in my company and they subjected me to a barrage of questions: "Dugulescu, why are you a repenter? Why are you involved with those fanatics, those ignoramuses? You're an intelligent young man! You'll be sorry one day if you don't live your life to the full."

And I said: "I assure you that I'll never be sorry. *You* are going to be sorry that you are not obeying God now. As for me, I'm experiencing real life, life as it should be lived, in obedience to him, and I feel great doing so. But I assure you that one day you are going to regret the fact that you didn't turn to God."

"Enough of that nonsense! We'll wait and see what happens in the end."

I was the only repenter, not only in my battalion but in the whole of that Airborne. In the evenings, I would stroll around the base whistling church hymns. I thought I might hear someone take up the melody and that I would find a brother in the Lord. I did not meet a single person.

I became a corporal and took command of a group, but I was warned not to carry out religious propaganda or talk about God with other airmen. Two new trainees that I was instructing asked me to push them if they ended up being too scared to jump, so that they wouldn't be exposed to ridicule. So I put one of them in front of me and the other behind me and told them to watch me and do what I did, so that they wouldn't be afraid. In these ways, others had opportunities to see that I behaved in a different way from other people, even though I was not allowed to give any verbal witness to the Lord Jesus Christ. When we went out as a platoon, for skiing instruction, and the platoon commander took a bottle of brandy and a glass with him and gave all the others a drink, I would keep my group behind me and refuse to drink. At this, he would have a go at me and laugh at me for being a repenter in front of the whole group. But he would then ask me to look after his map case so that he didn't lose his ID or his pistol. When we did jumps, he would jump right after me so that God's hand would be over him as well as over me. He did this whenever we jumped, day or night – so that he could be protected by God too, he said.

At the beginning of November 1967, our battalion, under the control of the central military command, carried out a joint exercise with the Securitate and the militia forces of the Ministry of the Interior. In the war game exercises, we were to act as a sabotage force in a real-life situation behind the front, while the Miliția and Securitate had the task of identifying and capturing us. So we were dropped at night somewhere around Făgăraş on specialised missions. Each of us carried in his sock a sealed envelope that contained his name, rank and mission. If we had our envelopes taken off us it meant that we had been taken prisoner. We were dressed as civilians; I for example was a Romanian Railways workman. My mission was to destroy the bridge over the river Olt at Făgăraş and some places. I had a piece of green chalk with which to mark the objective with a cross to indicate "blown up, destroyed." I had a radio set to relay information to my platoon commander, who, though still scornful of me for being a repenter, had opted to be with me on this operation so that he wouldn't be captured yet again; on all his previous exercises the Securitate had taken him prisoner. Now he wanted me to bring him luck. We kept sending ground reports using small transmitters, since the big transmitters were easily detected by the Securitate's direction-finding apparatus. There was so much radio traffic for our group to handle about the targets we had "destroyed" that I had no sleep at all for about three days and nights. I kept vigil over my commander several times while he slept. Finally, somewhere in the Făgăraş mountains, I fell asleep on observation duty. When I woke up, I was surrounded by militiamen. They arrested me, took my pistol, tied my hands behind my back and handed me over to the Făgăraş mountain area Securitate chief. My commander succeeded in getting through the ranks of the men who had surrounded us by drawing a dagger, threatening them with it and escaping capture. But our team of saboteurs was seized and taken to Făgăraş. We slept one night at the Securitate base; we refused the food they offered us and when they interrogated us and wanted us to reveal our mission, I kept my mouth shut. Then we were taken to the prisoner exchange area at Ghimbav.

The exercise ended badly for me; had I not been captured I would have been promoted and sent on leave. However, I was only reprimanded in front of all the troops for having fallen asleep from my exhaustion.

In February 1968, when I finished my military service, I returned to Timişoara. I was delighted to receive a letter from one of my former subordinates, Airman Sandu from Bucharest, who had become a Christian after observing my actions and hearing that I was a repenter. He felt convicted because he had lived a filthy life and had often been drunk and done a lot of stupid things and now he was seeking my forgiveness. I felt grateful that he became a Christian as a result of my prayers and witness while I was in the army. Later, while I was at the Seminary in Bucharest, we by chance. He was attending Popa Nan's Pentecostal church and was living as a true child of God.

Called to God's Service

By the time I returned to Timişoara, brother Pitt Popovici had left for America in the autumn of 1967. He was born in America and was an American citizen, and now returned because he had suffered such severe persecution in Romania. Within a few months, Brother Liviu Olah was chosen and ordained pastor. I had come back with undiminished zeal and love for the Lord went out to villages every Sunday with my group of young people . Brother Olah tried to moderate our activism and encouraged us to stay at home more to recharge our batteries as we were going on too many missions.

We met on Wednesday evenings for Bible study, at different homes which we communicated secretly to people we trusted, because the Securitate stalked us. Brother Telescu, a saint and man of prayer taught us much during prayer meetings in his home. We also met at the home of the Miheţ family, whose son, Titus, later became a pastor. The Ilie family held students' and young people's fellowship. From time to time informers reported us to the Securitate and the family in whose house we were meeting would suffer unpleasant consequences.

Immediately after my return from military service, I met a girl at a Saturday evening service at the church on Romulus Street where I had recited *It Will be Late*, which I had written in the army while on guard duty. At the end of the service, this girl came and asked me for a copy of the poem. At that time I had not published any books of poetry, as I have since; my verses circulated on loose sheets, either hand- or type-written. I told her that if she wanted me to give it to her she should come to the Second Baptist Church in Traian Square the next day, which she did. She was a student in the Russian-Romanian section of the Modern Languages Faculty and came from Haţeg, and we first became friends, and to my joy, our betrothal ceremony took place on December 29, 1968, and we were married on August 3, 1969 in Haţeg. Coincidentally, that was the date of the first visit to Romania by a U.S. President, Richard Nixon. Later, our first daughter, Ligia, was born on July 4, America's Independence Day!

During this period, Brother Olah would take a young man into the pulpit with him to give a word of encouragement or a short message to the congregation. After that he would send us to churches in the local area: Hodoni, Giroc, Beregsău, to preach in his place. I made many mistakes at the beginning, but over time, I learned to preach the Word of God. Brother Stanca of Second Baptist organised a Homiletics course developed by Brother Alexa Popovici of the Bucharest Seminary for those eager to learn. It was then that I learned how to evaluate sermons according to their preparation, content and delivery as well as how to construct and deliver a sermon effectively. Brother Liviu Olah encouraged me to go to the Seminary. The time for me to fulfil the promise my mother had made so long ago as I lay feverish with pneumonia, had come.

In the autumn of 1969, my wife was still a student in the Modern Languages Faculty. One class of six students had just graduated from the Baptist Theological Seminary in Bucharest and a new class was meant to be starting. Brother Liviu encouraged me to go and enroll but told me not to rely on First Baptist for support, but only on God. But, when I went to Bucharest, the Seminary did not re-open. It was closed that year (1969-70), the only time in our history that the Baptist Theological Seminary has been closed for an entire year.

I returned to Timişoara but had lost the job with Romanian Railways' carriages department where I worked since military service, so I got a job constructing glass hothouses for tomatoes, and later at some pre-fabricated concrete works, where the pay was very good.

Although I had been hoping for a son, I fell in love with my little girl Ligi from the moment she was born in that July of 1970.

Peter Dugulescu

My wife was still a student,but even after I left for the Seminary that autumn, we managed to survive. The Seminary opened in October and was a risky choice, because being a pastor in those times was not a safe occupation. All clergy had a work permit issued to them by the Department for Religious Denominations which could be taken away from you, if you displeased them. And if you lost this state-issued pastor's authorization, you were prohibited from working in any capacity at all in Romania. Brother Pitt Popovici had already had this experience and Brother Liviu Olah was very soon to have it too.

But the call from God was irresistible, a feeling I poured into my poem *When You Called Me*. This poem, requested by Brother Liviu Olah, dealt with Peter's call to service within the metaphor of being a fisher of men.

> *I did not grasp then what it meant. Your call,*
> *But I received it, and obeyed it too*
> *I left behind my boat, the sea, my all*
> *And empty-handed now I followed You*
> *I gave up all I had – 'twas Your desire*
> *And never thought "too great a price to pay"*
> *Stronger than fear or shame, brighter and higher*
> *There burned in me the longing to obey.*

With a burning desire to tell people about God's love, I left behind my wife, a student in final year at the university, our infant daughter, a well-paid job, and all security to study ministry under a state-controlled seminary, together with eleven other disciples. Eight of the students were Romanians, three were ethnic Hungarians from communities in Romania and one was an ethnic German from the city of Sibiu. This Seminary, which was founded at Buteni in 1924 by the American Southern Baptist Convention and moved to Bucharest in 1927, had a large number of students – young men and women training for God's work – in the years before the War. But after Romania became a Communist, atheistic state, this theological school was preserved for purely propaganda reasons, a proof Romania had religious liberty and a Constitution. Internally, the State held this theological school under very strict control, as it did with all the churches and institutions of theological education.

On the evening I departed, brother Liviu Olah advised me : "Pete, if you want to be a pastor, remember to set aside at least one hour of prayer every day and at least one day of fasting every week." I never forgot these words, and during my four years at the Seminary and after, I continued to set aside at least one hour a day for private prayer and fellowship with God, and one day of fasting per week. At the Seminary I arose at 5 and prayed kneeling on empty sacks in the storeroom, or some office. Some of my fellow students also kept this special hour of prayer. When others rose at 6, we prayed again in the dormitory, beginning the day with God together. We had Chapel at ten every day.

In my last two years, I had the privilege of studying under Brother Iosif Ţon recently returned from his studies in Oxford in the summer of 1972. I was like a dry sponge, thirsty for knowledge and he was replete with all that he had gathered, so I tried to spend as much time as I could in his company, filling exercise books full of the notes I took during his lecture courses, sermons and messages in Chapel. I even went out to buy milk for his tea, learning for the first time this English way of drinking tea, so that he could have it at seven every morning, and brought kerosene for the heating stove in the room in the Seminary courtyard.

God used this man as a stimulus and a model for me and for many of my fellow students to broaden the horizons of men who were going to work as pastors in the very particular circumstances of Romania. He epitomized the ideal of Seneca: "Happy is the man who improves those around him, not only when he is among them, but even when they think of him."

Graduating the Seminary in June 1974, I was invited to pastor a church in in Haţeg where we had bought a small fourth-floor apartment. Brother Teodor Cenuşe, the man who had baptized the first lepers at Tichileşti some years earlier, had just retired. The church had a membership of around a hundred at that time, plagued by factions and problems, but by making pastoral visits and through the sermons, I was able to bring the brothers together so that a general reconciliation took place and the wounds of the past were healed.

Listening to God

"But to stop this thing from spreading any further among the people, we must warn these man to speak no longer to anyone in this name." Then they called them in again and commanded them not to speak or teach at all in the name of Jesus. But Peter and John replied: "Judge for yourselves whether it is right in God's sight to obey you rather than God." (Acts of the Apostles 4:17-19)

"If life on earth is a contest between good and evil, between darkness and light, then it is important that we should spread the divine word as speedily as possible." (M. Halter)

On August 4, 1974, I was ordained as pastor of the Haţeg Baptist Church. On the same day, the service of blessing for our son Cristi, the third child God granted our family, took place. Cristi's arrival on May 22, after our two girls, Ligia and Cristina, was an answer to our prayers. Born while I was taking my final examinations at the seminary, it was no coincidence that he receive God's blessing on the day of my ordination: it was my wish that he should be dedicated to God's work from his infancy.

I began my work as a pastor with two powerful desires: to be a servant absolutely dedicated to the work and to give my family a happy life. I little then that in a Communist country, with a atheistic government hostile to those who love God, my two desires were incompatible.

Our difficulties began early. My wife, a University graduate and a qualified teacher of Russian and Romanian, was assigned to a school in the Apuseni Mountains. The children lived with her and she came home twice a month, by bus. The authorities found out that she was a repenter and demanded she would:

- stop going to church;
- implement atheistic education in class;
- and organize meetings to teach the village people that God did not exist

Since she was not able to do these things, the officials at the Alba County Schools Inspectorate compiled a dossier on her with the aim of having her dismissed, which also blocked the transfer we requested to Haţeg. She was forced to give up her job and care for the children full-time. My pastor's salary was very small and the demands were growing all the time. Besides the Haţeg church, I also pastored six other smaller churches in the surrounding villages using a bicycle to carry out pastoral visits and services. The church families there gave us vegetables, eggs and milk, which meant a great deal to us. Our children wore second-hand clothes that we received from friends or in consignments sent from abroad.

With every authority, from the simplest clerk to the national leaders, arrayed against God, it became clear that I had a choice: to obey men and compromise my faith in order to safeguard my family's peace and security, or I was going to obey God and submit our family to diabolical pressure and persecutions that would sometimes rival those recorded in the Acts of the Apostles. Through the grace of God, I chose the second alternative. Over the fifteen years during which I served God under the Communist regime, I learned the methods which they used against the Church of Jesus Christ.

Regimentation

Under Communism, private initiative was forbidden. Officially sanctioned and rigorously controlled groups were the norm. People worked in state enterprises, state farms or collective farms. Children and young people went to state schools and universities, whose structure included politically-controlled children's and youth organizations such as the the Pioneers, or the Communist Youth Organization. The theatre, the opera, sports, the Romanian Academy, the Writers' Union – these were all ideologically and politically controlled, subordinated to the Romanian Communist Party and the Secret Services (the dreaded Securitate). No one could hold any position in these institutions, even the leader of a team of ten, if not a member of the Romanian Communist Party.

Therefore, the communists needed to gain control over religion and use it for propaganda to create a favorable image internationally. The seemingly democratic constitutions in which liberty of conscience and freedom of religion were, in theory, guaranteed were never, in fact, respected.

The biggest irritation to the rulers was the spiritual leaders of hundreds and even thousands of people could not be required to be members of the Party. It infuriated them that the masses of people stubbornly kept on believing in God and going to church every Sunday in spite of the atheistic education that was carried out in schools, universities and state enterprises. To control the churches, clergy were coerced to collaborate with the Securitate by becoming secret informers. Some did so and became undercover agents, and were privileged and protected by the Communist authorities if they signed up. They were nominated for their posts and received the official recognition of the Religious Denominations Department on the basis of the loyalty agreements they signed, which Securitate told us at every opportunity was a true proof of patriotism. Not only church leaders but also elders, deacons, choir directors and even ordinary church members were enlisted. It was their duty to spy on their pastor and to inform the Securitate about his friends, visitors from abroad and about his sermons. They were also to start malicious rumors in order to cause problems for the pastor and the church. While the organs of the Securitate and the local administration behaved in a harsh and merciless way towards those who would not accept these kinds of compromises, those who succumbed were given leadership positions in the official structures of their denominations.

Once, as a young pastor, I suggested one brother become a deacon, seeing in him a godly standard. He requested a private interview, thanked me for the trust I had shown in him but told me that he could not accept; he was the accountant of a state enterprise in the town and because he belonged to a repenter church, the only way he could occupy this position was by signing an agreement with the Securitate. Had he refused, reasons would be fabricated to have him thrown into prison. With tears in his eyes, he confessed: "Brother Pete, I signed that agreement, and I am ashamed. They constantly call me in to give them information about your activities and about everything that goes on at church. I want to know as little as possible, so that I can tell them as little as possible. If I become a deacon, they will put even greater pressure on me."

But other members of the church carried on these activities either secretly or openly, causing pain and suffering to the faithful.

Intimidation

"Fear of man will prove to be a snare, but whoever trusts in the Lord is kept safe." (Proverbs 29:25).

Two of the most effective weapons used by the Communists against the Christians were fear and terror. This is how they were able, despite being neither loved nor respected, to control millions of people for some fifty years. They understood mass psychology and spread this disease of fear all through society. They were not powerful, but they created the impression of being powerful; they did not know everything, yet gave the impression of knowing everything; they did not have anything under control, but created the illusion of controlling all aspects of life.

In every encounter I had with them, whether it was at the Town Hall or in the offices of the Securitate, they tried with all their might to plant fear in me. They did not know that God had set me free from fear; one of my favorite verses, which my beloved teacher, Iosif Ton, had impressed upon me was I John 4:18 – "There is no fear in love. But perfect love drives out fear, because fear has to do with punishment. The one who fears is not made perfect in love."

They knew nothing of the promise of Leviticus 26:13 – "I am the Lord your God, who brought you out of Egypt so that you would no longer be slaves to the Egyptians; I broke the bars of your yoke and enabled you to walk with heads held high."

During my seminary studies Pastor Iosif Ton wrote a book entitled *Whosoever Loses His Life*, which was followed by a petition which was drawn up by the courageous pastor Vasile Talos and signed by fifty Baptist pastors, addressed to Nicolae Ceaușescu, protesting the treatment of the Baptist churches under the Communist regime. Then, Professor Iosif Ton wrote *The Christian Manifesto* or *The Christian's Role within Socialism*, asserting that Communists ought not to hate Christians because society needed people like them. Through the power of the Gospel, the 'New Man' preached by communism became a living reality: "Therefore, if anyone is in Christ, he is a new creation; the old has gone, the new has come!" (2 Corinthians 5:17)

My role was arranging for the manuscript to be typed, and distributed the book throughout the country. A high-ranking officer from Bucharest came to Hațeg and attempted to paint Pastor Ton as a hostile element and a secret agent working for American and British espionage organizations. He indicated that Ton spoke against me and he was not as loyal to me as I was to him. I replied that I did not believe this but that even if Ţon had done these things, it was his business; I respected him and loved him as my teacher and my brother in Jesus Christ.

The investigator asked if I agreed with the content of these works and I replied: "Yes, totally." They warned that if I believed these ideas my pastor's authorization would be withdrawn and I could even end up in prison. But, they said, concered for my wife and children, they "wanted to help me." Respectfully but firmly, I told them that I did not need their help; if they had sufficient proof that I had broken the laws of the land, they should send me before a court to face judgment.

Repeatedly, they said that my life and the life of my family were in their hands; they had the power to put me in prison or to ensure us a more prosperous life. I reminded them that Pontius Pilate had said the same thing to Jesus of Nazareth during his trial: "Don't you realize that I have the power to crucify you and the power to set you free?" Jesus replied: "You would have no power at all over me if it had not been given to you from above." Keen to display his biblical knowledge, he said: "Yes, it says that in Romans 13." I corrected him: "No, Major, it's from John 19: 10-11."

Just as the devil quoted Scripture to tempt the Lord Jesus Christ in the desert, the Communists quoted certain Scripture at the conferences they held for the clergy of the Christian denominations in Romania; most dear to them was Romans 13, which says: "Be subject to the governing authorities."

The harassment was not limited to myself. While I was away from home, at the smaller villages for services, my wife would often receive threatening or obscene telephone calls. Once, when she was pregnant with our fourth child, some garbage collectors and gravediggers from the cemetery arrived to throw her, the children and our furniture out of the apartment, claiming we had no written authorization to live there. While they were hammering on the door and shouting curses, my wife reached me in Bucharest where I was preaching at Pastor Taloş' church. I got into a train and returned to Haţeg that very evening.

On Palm Sunday 1977, I was returning from the village of Nălaţi, a village near Haţeg, on the way to the evening service in the Haţeg church. The Haţeg Securitate chief and lieutenant stopped me and ordered me into their car to go and search my home. I said that 300 people were awaiting me at service, and I was expected to preach. It was no concern of theirs who was waiting for me at church, they replied; they needed to search my home because they were informed that I was in possession of dollars and Bibles. (In that period a Romanian citizen was not permitted to have even one dollar in his home or in his wallet, since dollars were the symbol of the power of the corrupt capitalist system.) As for the Bible, it was considered the most serious threat to the materialistic and atheistic state ideology. In the time of Ceauşescu, thousands of Bibles were confiscated from foreign tourists at the border; they were either soaked in petrol and burned in the yards of the police headquarters on the spot or re-cycled into toilet paper. When I arrived, three officers were already there ransacking our home. My wife and the children were huddled in a corner of the living room, forbidden to move; they were weeping in terror. Our extremely small three-roomed apartment was cramped; the kitchen was so narrow that two people could not pass each other in it, the roof leaked all the time and there was often no running water in the bathroom, so visitors had to use a bucket to pour bath water in to flush the toilet. The officers searched every drawer, cupboard, and the pockets of clothes hanging in the wardrobes. Naturally, they found no dollars and no other foreign currency. Miraculously, they completely missed the place where the Bibles were stored, a sofa storage box filled with dozens of Bibles and a variety of Christian literature. It was clearly the hand of God, and I understood the part of John Bunyan's *Pilgrim's Progress* in which the lions that frightened the traveller were very fierce, but when thy came towards him he saw that they were chained up and that they could not come any nearer to him than their chains allowed.

The three hours of terror for my family and the church member who came to find out why I wasn't at service, ended with an interrogation at Securitate headquarters. My wife and children were left behind, weeping and terrified, and I told my wife as I left that if I did not come back she must take care of the children and pray for me. As the five Securitate officers herded me outside, our neighbors, who had gathered in front of the block, were shouting and asking them: "What have you got against that man? He's a good man and he hasn't done anything wrong. Why don't you concentrate on thieves and criminals?"

At the headquarters, they again wanted a statement against Pastor Ton and Aurel Popescu and Pavel Niculescu, two influential Baptists in Bucharest who had organised a support group for the imprisoned Orthodox priest Calciu Dumitreasa and had connected to the Geneva Committee for the Defense of Religious Liberties and Freedom of Conscience. Pastor Niculescu had been savagely beaten up at the Securitate headquarters in Bucharest, and others of the committee had been imprisoned. Eventually, all these men had been forced to leave the country and had settled in the U.S. I then knew that the Securitate were afraid of the unity that existed among evangelical Christians and were making efforts to set us against one another.

My interrogators were very curious about Pastor Guy Davidson of Arizona who had heard from pastor Iosif Ton that I was serving seven churches for three years using a bicycle to travel among them. In February 1977, an hour after my prayer time, a sister in the Hațeg church who worked for the Post Office telephoned me and told me that a letter had arrived for me from America and that she wanted personally deliver it, to ensure that it reached me. Great was my astonishment when I opened the envelope and read the letter, which said:

"Dear Peter,

We have heard about you and the way God is using you to pastor seven churches in Romania. We, your brothers in Arizona, feel it would be a great honor for us to provide you with means of transport to these churches. We have therefore sent you the sum of $2,668 via Comturist in Bucharest, so that you can buy yourself a Dacia station wagon."

As this was one of the most beautiful experiences I had ever had in connection with answered prayer, I would never have believed this could be seen negatively. My interrogators wanted to know who Guy Davidson was and what interests he had in Romania. They also wanted to know what obligations I had taken on towards him and towards the Americans in return for the money I had received. Then I looked at my interrogators and felt pity for them. I saw that in the world they lived, relationships of this kind did not exist. Living in a world without God, they were incapable of understanding what I described – love, fraternal links, fellowship, altruism. In their eyes, Pastor Guy Davidson was an American imperialist with suspicious secret interests in Romania and I was a fraud, a traitor to my country, a tool of the Americans.

Again, they told me again that they could put me in prison but were holding back because I had a wife and three children.   I looked them straight in the eyes and replied firmly: "Gentlemen, I am not afraid of prison. Please do not break the laws of the land in order to protect my family and me."

I put my hands together and held them out, ready to be handcuffed, adding: "Arrest me right now if you want to. I would like to be like Peter and John or Paul and Silas in the Bible and praise God in prison. Please give me the opportunity to do so."

They looked at one another in bewilderment. Then, they told me, "You're a lunatic, a fanatic, and we are not going to give you that satisfaction. Do you want to become a martyr? Do you want your brother Jimmy Carter and the American Baptists to pray for you? Are you trying to get us into trouble with the Americans? We are not going to make a hero of you, don't worry. We have other methods of dealing with you."

Then I understood; this modern form of persecution was even more subtle and more diabolical than that in the Acts of the Apostles. Not once did the Communists admit that they had killed or imprisoned people on religious grounds. It was always on political or criminal charges that they were found guilty. The Communists even robbed them of the joy of suffering for the Lord.

Secularization

Communism is a secular religion – an imitation, inspired by the evil spirit which usurps the throne of God. In all Communist countries, the excesses of this pseudo-religion bloated to unimaginable size and unbelievable grotesqueness.

Ceauşescu, who took over the political leadership after the death of Gheorghe Gheorghiu Dej in 1965, initially proclaimed: "The Party does not need idols," yet as he accumulated power and set himself increasingly higher, he became an idol, an object of worship. At the 1974 Romanian Communist Party Congress he took over the role of President of the Socialist Republic of Romania in addition to his high position as the General Secretary of the Central Committee of the Romanian Communist Party. When he swore the oath, his left hand rested on a copy of the Constitution in which he never really believed, and in his right hand, held a sceptre which historically represented the absolute power wielded by kings and emperors. This man, a former shoemaker, now believed himself the political messiah of the Romanian people. He was intoxicated with power and greatly enjoyed being lauded, hymned, flattered and applauded wherever he went. Inspired by the example of Kim Il Sung in North Korea, he established cultural/political festivals throughout the country. In packed stadiums, thousands of people had to applaud on cue and sing songs dedicated to the country, to the Party and above all to the beloved Leader. Poets frenetically declaimed verses in his honor, and worker's choirs sang hymns of praise:

Eternal Glory to the Party
Eternal Glory to our Beloved Leader, Nicolae Ceaușescu
He is leading us towards the Light
He is leading us to Victory

To these anthems, hundreds of children waving tricolor sashes formed Ceaușescu's name and the initials of the RCP on the stadium turf.

Whenever the head of an institution spoke in the radio or the television, whenever a scientist published a book, it was compulsory for them to preface their talk with the words: "As comrade Nicolae Ceaușescu has taught us…" He took on the title "The Most Beloved Son of the People," and his picture and that of his wife were displayed all over the country.

Among the slogans which were posted everywhere, on factory walls and at street corners, I saw one which captured the essence of this secular religion: "Let us think, let us work, let us live as the Party teaches us, as its General Secretary, comrade Nicolae Ceaușescu teaches us!" The emptiness of the secular faith became clear when this Great Leader and teacher was summarily executed by his former acolytes in 1989, and his star plunged overnight.

To replace Christian holidays was an important priority under Communism. When I was a child in the early 1950s, the school organized a 'Winter Tree' event in the village Cultural Center, and the entire school was told that we would not be celebrating Christmas any more because Jesus Christ had never existed, and Christmas and Easter were just mysticism and superstition. The children were now to sing songs addressed to Winter and to the Party, after which they were given little presents. At the same time, owners of sweetshops and grocery stores were instructed not to bring chocolate Christmas tree candies or other tree decorations out of their store rooms until after Christmas.

As a repenter, I was forced to come to school on Christmas Day for Pioneer activities and atheistic lectures called "Friends of the Truth." This was repeated on Easter Day and on many Sundays. It was only the children of Baptist, Pentecostal, Brethren and Adventist repenters who were made to go to this group to take course in atheism at which the teacher of scientific socialism or the biology teacher would teach the children the 'truth' about evolution, the non-existence of God and religious fanaticism. Nearly every Sunday, patriotic work sessions were organised for firms and schools. Pupils, students and employees of state enterprises were mobilized to harvest corn and dig potatoes and beets at state farms and collectives, or were taken to parks or factories to pick up rubbish, or collect scrap iron. Planting flowers in parks, improving the town environment or sports activities were also mandated. The idea that Sunday was a holy day must be banished from the minds of young people and the general populace, Party activists insisted. "We must involve them in all kinds of activities, keep them busy and get them out of church." I remember how on Christmas and Easter, which were regarded as normal working days, the mayor of Hațeg would hide in the municipal works department yard to record the names of all the people who went into the Baptist church. Then he would send these lists to the people's places of work, where their wages would be docked and they would be harassed in various ways.

The secular society used threat and intimidation to encroach upon the sacred. For instance, in May of 1977, this mayor, who bore a deadly hatred towards the Repenters, summoned me to the Town Hall to an inquisition by the Secretary of the County Council, the Chief of Police, the Inspector of Religious Denominations, the Inspector of Teaching and Education, the Deputy Mayor and the secretary of the Town Council.

"Now then, why do you keep inviting young people to church on Sundays? Why do you brainwash them, eh?" asked the council secretary. We had recently had a believers' baptism with sixteen candidates, most of whom were pupils at Hațeg High School."What business of yours are young people? What right have you got to stuff their heads with these stupid ideas of yours?"

I replied politely: "I am acting, Mr. Secretary, on the basis of Article 30 of the Romanian Constitution, which guarantees religious liberty and liberty of conscience, and on the basis of the Helsinki Final Act, which guarantees the right of parents to give their children an education which conforms to their own convictions."

He continued hectoring: "Education is the job of the school, not the church! Have you got it? You people are brainwashing children."

I again replied politely but firmly: "Mr. Secretary, the Inspector of Education will be able to confirm that our children are always the best behaved and earn the highest marks. The teachings of the Bible do not brainwash people; on the contrary they ennoble them. Those who teach evolution and tell our children that they are just evolved animals are the brainwashers, because when a person believes that he is an animal he will behave like an animal."

He flew into a rage, jumped to his feet and shouted at me: "You'd better come to your senses, or I'll take you by the seat of your pants and throw you out of the window! You're a stupid ox! I'll send you to Hunedoara to work in the blast furnace if you won't do what we say!"

The mayor now took over: "With ideas like yours you're going to be leaving Hațeg fast, do you understand? We'll take away your pastor's license and you will work in the steel furnace in Hunedoara, just like the comrade secretary said. What are you trying to do – convert the whole town?" He pointed his finger at me, turning to the others and said: "This man has filled that church on the edge of town with children and young people. He has even installed loudspeakers so that people standing in the street can listen to him. I tell you once more," he turned to me, "if you won't do what we tell you you're going to be leaving Hațeg fast, do you hear?"

At this, I rose and said: "Gentlemen, I have to tell you that because I have been insulted and humiliated here in the Town Hall, I refuse to take any further part in the discussion. But you, Mr. Mayor, who have threatened me with having my preaching license withdrawn and being thrown out of town, do not be so sure ... These things are for God to decide, not you. Your present status is not set in concrete either, and life is uncertain." I then left.

His zeal against repenters must have been noted with approval from the Party. About two weeks later, this mayor was given a new post as political secretary at the hydroelectric plant that was under construction on the Great River in the Retezat Mountains. There too, he threatened all of the repenters with the loss of their jobs. He was being driven to Deva for a Party meeting when, on the highway between Hațeg and Deva, his car collided with a large truck and ended up crushed underneath. Both he and the driver died instantly. The coronor reported that the mayor's heart was ruptured into four parts. In his briefcase was a list of names of 32 Christians whom he had intended to recommend for dismissal from their jobs. Rumors flew around town: that his heart, filled with hatred, had burst from his anger, or that the repenters had cursed him. Of course, we had prayed at church that the Lord would change his heart or move him to a different position, but we had never cursed him.

In fact, after that incident at the Town Hall, I had prayed for each of those present, and prayed to remove the feelings of fear or anger. Then I asked the Lord to grant me a request which I have made only a few times in my life – that when I opened my Bible and put my finger on a verse, that verse would be his specific word for the situation in which I found myself. My finger landed on Isaiah 49:23, "Kings will be your foster fathers and their queens your nursing mothers. They will bow down before you with their faces to the ground; they will lick the dust at your feet. Then you will know that I am the Lord; those who hope in me will never be disappointed."

This verse seemed tailored as a source of encouragement to me. After that, whenever I had confrontations with the authorities and was feeling discouraged, I would request the church to join in three days of prayer and fasting and hold a prayer meeting at church every evening. There, I would read this verse and assure the brothers that we were not going to be put to shame because God was with us. Many years later, this promise was fulfilled, in an amazing way.

Surveillance and threats

When the previous methods of controlling Christians were unsuccessful, more drastic ones were employed. One method was surveillance, using human agents and electronics.

My phone was tapped constantly. On one occasion I had gone to the home of one of our church families to meet a group of brothers from England. Iosif Țon, the pastor and dissident, was there as well. When my wife tried to call me there, she was amazed when, instead of someone at the other end of the line answering her, she found herself listening to a conversation between myself and a Romanian pastor which had taken place some hours earlier! This presumably happened as a result of technical glitch in the bugging department. Since the telephone exchange could not explain this phenomenon, it was clear this was the work of the 'blue-eyed boys'. I felt that my car was bugged as well, but lacking the necessary equipment I was not able to find the devices.

Former General Mihai Pacepa, Nicolae Ceauşescu's Secret Services chief, describes this routine use of listening devices in his book *Red Horizons*. A Virginia State legislator, who in 1969 was working at the US Embassy in Bucharest at the time Richard Nixon visited Romania, described an awkward moment after the Secret Service guards discovered a large number of tiny microphones in Nixon's hotel suite. They were concealed in flower vases and similar places. Nixon assembled them all on a table and summoned Ceauşescu to the hotel. When asked what these 'insects' in his room were for, Ceauşescu replied: "You know, Mr. President, it's a method employed by Secret Services the world over. You Americans probably use it too."

Despite the secrecy of surveillance, the security methods were rather obvious. Once, Pastor Guy Davidson from Arizona called me from the Haţeg hotel and mentioned visiting the hard currency shop at Deva at 9 the next morning, to make purchases for my family. Surprisingly, the only person, apart from the assistant, in the shop turned out to be a local pastor suspected of working for the Securitate. He had absolutely no business, and couldn't make purchases in hard currency since he was a Romanian citizen, but happened to be there, as if by chance. He asked me to introduce him to the American pastor and his wife and to translate so that he could ask them why they were in Romania and other questions. A few days later, when I was summoned to my routine questioning, the lads from the Securitate already knew a wealth of details about my visit to Deva and the various purchases made at the shop!

Shortly after the Revolution my wife and I were visiting our first church in Hateg, and were in the town centre when a man I know only by sight came up to me. He introduced himself and revealed that he was an electronics expert and that he felt guilty every time he saw me because he and other Securitate officers had been responsible for installing listening devices in the ceiling of the apartment below ours. He explained to me how Securitate men used to sit in their car in the parking lot beside my block and listen to and record conversations taking place in my apartment. I told him I forgave him and that I appreciated his honesty and the courage it had taken to make such a confession.

That same General Mihai Pacepa, who was head of the secret services in Ceaușescu's time, subsequently defected to America. There, he testified that if someone became *persona non grata* in the eyes of Ceaușescu and the Securitate, and all efforts to control them by means of regimentation and intimidation had failed, the final solution – physical elimination – would be applied.

Although the pressure against me kept increasing, I could not bring myself to believe that a peaceful Baptist pastor in the Hațeg valley would become a target for assassination. Why would anyone fear a man who only prayed, taught the Gospel, and lived according to Jesus's commands? But to those who sought to stamp out God, such a person was indeed an enemy of the state, and a target for execution.

Controlling Contact

As a Christian, it was natural to have brothers from the USA, England or Germany visit my home or my church. However, this was a serious infringement of the law or even an act of treason by the 'blue-eyed boys', as the Securitate agents were called. There was a law that forbade Romanian citizens to have foreigners stay in their homes, ensuring that they could get the hard currency from their hotel stay and making it easier to keep track of them. Another legal restriction by the Religious Denominations Department was that pastors must not allow foreigners to speak in their churches. I obeyed the first ruling – with some exceptions – but I never obeyed the second.

"Pastor Dugulescu, who were the foreigners who were in your church yesterday? Why did you let them preach?" I was asked by the official.

My reply was always: "Colonel, I didn't have any foreigners in my church. Foreigners cannot preach in my church."

He would fly into a rage and shout: "Are you trying to lie to us? Didn't you have that group of Americans/English people in your church yesterday? If you like I'll tell you what they said, too."

I would reply: "They are Americans but they aren't foreigners. They are brothers and sisters in Christ. We are all part of the same family – the family of God. I couldn't let *you* preach because you are an atheist and a foreigner in God's house."

I cannot express how furious these words made him. The next question was always: "How many Bibles did they bring you? What kind of Christian literature did they leave you? Please tell us what other friends they have in Romania and what secret networks for illegal Bible distribution they have set up here. You are a repenter and a pastor. You are not allowed to lie. You must tell us the truth."

I knew that I could not lie, but I could not tell the truth either. That would have meant betraying my brothers and becoming a Judas betraying Jesus into the hands of his enemies. The only response I could make was: "I refuse to answer your questions. If you consider me guilty on the basis of the laws you say I have broken, I request that you bring charges against me and send me for trial. The court will be able to establish my guilt or innocence."

"You will indeed end up on trial, but not because of Bibles or because of your connections with Christians in America. It will be on other charges. We've got you by the short and curlies!" Then, a very important question, one they never forgot to ask: "How do these foreigners view our country? What do they say about our government, and especially about Comrade Nicolae Ceauşescu?"

My decision was to act in my capacity of a pastor defending his flock and as an honest Romanian citizen. I listed the names of the foreign guests who had visited the church – names that they could have obtained anyway from the border officials, from the hotel or from the informers within the church. I never gave any information that would have put their lives in danger or compromised their reputations or the work they were doing for the Lord in Romania. I would always give the texts they had preached from and some points from their sermons – this because I wanted my interrogators to hear the Gospel. I would tell them that my guests had been in raptures over the beautiful places they had seen in Romanian and the hospitality of the Romanian people. I would also tell them that my guests loved the traditional Romanian breakfast and chicken noodle soup and stuffed cabbage leaves.

After a while they tired of my dutiful reports, and said they wanted to get something different from me. They wanted me to inform them about the secret political interests of these foreign tourists who had come to Romania. As a good patriotic Romanian I should collaborate with them as an informer. They said that many pastors and priests were doing just that and that it was not a sin. I assured my interrogators that I loved my country and tried to demonstrate my loyalty to the Romanian people through my deeds, but that I could not accept their proposal.

The Underground Church

In one sense, the government was correct to suspect me. I was involved in a secret scheme, and it was revolutionary in nature, although not the way they suspected.

Starting in summer of 1979 I was one of ten Baptist pastors secretly trained as leaders for Romanian churches. This was run by the Biblical Education by Extension program and Campus Crusade for Christ. American teachers living in Vienna used to enter the country under false names as tourists, stay one or two weeks to deliver lecture courses or administer examinations scheduled for that time. The high academic and theological level the programs offered was very important. We began at the Baptist church at 22 Popa Rusu Street, in Bucharest, pastured by Iosif Sărac. The first generation of leaders trained in the BEE school program consisted of pastors Iosif Sărac, Vasile Talpoş, Vasile Brânzei, Pascu Geabău, Iosif Ştefănuţ, Alexandru Bodor, Teodor Vereş, Titus Miheţ, Buni Cocar and myself. We were privileged to learn from Jody Dellow, Bud Hinkson, Bill Temple and Tom Lewis, dedicated men of God and well-known teachers.

Knowing that we were being watched by the Securitate, we tried to avoid going out onto the street; entering the church building on Monday and not leaving until Saturday. We slept in the church offices and the women of the church prepared our meals. Over time, we formed a group for the second generation, with Pastor David Nicola, and later still another group at Haţeg and Timişoara for the third generation.

When I look back today I do so with thankfulness to God for his good hand of protection over us and for those American teachers who took the risk of coming to Romania. By teaching us how to become more effective in the Kingdom of God they enabled us to enter a new dimension in our church work. I also praise God for all those who were trained through those three generations of leadership programs and who are all now deacons, elders, pastors and evangelists in different parts of the country

Not surprisingly, the repeated visits of these American 'tourists' and our meetings came to the attention of the Securitate, and the Minister of the Interior also alerted the leadership of the Baptist Union. I remember driving back from one of those meetings late one evening with Mihai Sârbu – who was then a deacon in the church in Haţeg. It was 11 o'clock and we were stopped by the traffic police. Such harassment was common for me. When the traffic policeman pulled me over, I would see behind him the 'blue-eyed boys.' I knew that the militiaman was only an instrument in their hands. When I asked him what I had done wrong, he replied that I had not dipped my headlights as I should have done. He asked me if I had been drinking and I said no, which was proved by the breathalyzer bag he made me blow into; naturally it didn't turn green. The militiaman then escorted our care to the Militia headquarters, where the head of the Securitate and his deputy were waiting for us. They gave orders for the doors and seats to be removed from my car so that it could be searched for Bibles and Christian literature. When they found nothing, they seized our briefcases and took them apart, reading every scrap of paper with great attention.

Just as I suspected at the time and was able to confirm later, microphones had been planted in the walls of our little apartment to monitor our conversations at home. When my wife and I needed to speak about visitors we were expecting from abroad or about Bibles they had brought or the money they had left with us for the church or for our family, we would speak in whispers or in sign language. Even in the room where we slept we could not speak freely. More than once, I was shocked while being interrogated by the Securitate concerning people on matters that we had carelessly mentioned in normal conversational tones.

Temptation

Again, the devil took him to a very high mountain and showed him all the kingdoms of the world, and their splendor. "All this I will give you," he said, "if you will bow down and worship me." (Matthew 4:8-9)

In his dealings with ordinary church members, the devil was satisfied if they agreed to work as secret informers for the security apparatus. However, this was not enough when it came to church leaders. From them he required outright worship. Many were recruited to work as trained informers, and were given secret instruction courses, ranks, undercover work as informers, a code name and clandestine meetings. Of course, all this was rewarded with a suitable secret salary.

I do not say this in supposition. Once, I was summoned to a certain address in Deva, to meet the Securitate chief. It was a private address, an apartment and I realised that it must be a Securitate 'safe house'. I pondered what I should do. I repeat that a perfect Baptist pastor would not have responded to such an invitation. But as I was not perfect, and always tried to be as flexible as I could – without compromise - and to convince those who were the eyes and ears of the political power in Romania that Baptists loved their country and sought her good in every way, I went to the address I had been given.

There the Securitate chief was indeed waiting for me. He stood up, greeted me and thanked me for making the effort to come all the way to Deva. Then he took out an envelope full of money, a pretty fat one, held it out to me and told me that it was my travelling expenses and represented only an advance payment. I was shocked by this gesture and, in that instant in my mind's eye, I saw Judas reaching out and taking the bag containing the thirty pieces of silver from the hand of the High Priest.

I said, "Colonel, I feel offended by your gesture. I made this effort for my country, not for money." He insisted on my taking the envelope and tried had to push it into my pocket. I resisted this with determination, aware now that I had reached the critical threshold in my discussions with the Securitate. If I crossed this threshold, I would have sold myself to the devil and there would be no going back.

At that moment Judas flashed through my mind again – Judas who wanted to put right the wrong he had done but found it was too late. When he brought the bag of silver back and wanted to return it to Jesus' enemies, they laughed in his face in scorn, saying "What do we care? That's your problem!"

I shuddered at the ease with which I could have become a Judas to my brothers and to the Lord Jesus, whom I had vowed to serve at the cost of my life, and I asked the colonel not to keep putting pressure on me as I had no intention of accepting the envelope.

He then took from his briefcase a pistol, much smaller and more elegant than the one I had been issued with when I was a saboteur paratrooper, and asked me if I'd like a 'toy' like that. He said I could have it straight away if I wanted, and wrote me out a gun license. I replied that I was a pastor and that it would hardly be appropriate for me to put a pistol in my bag beside my Bible. Also, I said, God was my protector and so there was no need for me to defend myself. He asked me with a bitter smile: "So you're not interested in this either?"

"No!" I replied curtly.

Then I asked him a direct question: "Colonel, what did you invite me here for?"

"Well ... yes ..." he began, "I wanted to ask you what Mr. Iosif Ton is up to these days. Has he written any more anti-Romanian books? Has he been to see you in Hațeg again? – because I know he likes this part of the country."

Calmly but firmly I replied: "Colonel, Dr. Iosif Ton has never written any anti-Romanian or unpatriotic books. He is a great Romanian and a true patriot. That is the reason why he came back here from England after finishing his studies. He was my teacher at the Seminary and I know him personally. His most recent work, the one I think you are referring to, *The Christian Manifesto,* is not anti-Romanian but anti-atheistic. In it, he is at pains to demonstrate that Socialism and Christianity are not incompatible and that the ideal of the 'New Man' so beloved by Communist ideologues, must forever unreachable if you exclude the Gospel of Jesus Christ, which makes the New Man a reality. Dr. Ton demonstrates in this book that the leaders of the country ought to give Romania's evangelical Christians the same status and recognition as all other citizens and that they should no longer be labeled as 'sectarian', 'reactionary' and pariahs of society.

"As for Dr. Ton's fondness for this part of the country, it is true that he loves it. He often comes to Clopotiva on holiday as he loves the Retezat Mountains and the Hațeg region with all their rich historical associations. He hasn't been to see me for a long time but he is always welcome. Please do not take offense at what I am about to say, but for me to ring you to tell you that Mr. Ton had arrived would be a betrayal of my teacher."

He looked at me as if disappointed: "You haven't understood a thing. We aren't asking you to betray anyone. We are only asking you to keep us informed and to be loyal to your country. This country needs people like you."

The fatal flaw of the Communist leadership was that they were not capable of separating the concept of atheism from that of patriotism. The state religion declared there was no God. For them, a practicing Christian was automatically an enemy of the country and of the Socialist state.

Beyond the Borders

At the start of the 1970s the World Baptist Alliance, in collaboration with the European Federation, organised a theological studies program for pastors from the countries of Eastern Europe. This took place for the whole month of June every year at the International Theological Seminary at Rushlikon in Switzerland. The Baptist Union in each Communist country would send between three and seven pastors who had some knowledge of English.

My standing with the leaders of the Romanian Baptist Union and the Department for Religious Denominations in Bucharest did not encourage me to hope I would ever be one of those invited to attend. In the summer of 1974, after I graduated from the Seminary in Bucharest, I had been awarded a scholarship to attend this seminary in Switzerland as a full-time student but had not been approved by the Bucharest Department for Religious Denominations.

The following year, Professor Iosif Țon had helped me to obtain another scholarship, this time to Spurgeon's College in England, but once again this never went beyond the stage of a beautiful dream.

But a thaw took place as a result of Pastor Iosif Țon's open letter to Nicolae Ceaușescu, the Romanian government and the Baptist churches of Romania and the subsequent petition initiated by Pastor Vasile Taloș and signed by fifty pastors.

At that time, we were granted more freedom to hold services, baptisms and evangelistic meetings and to open some churches that had been closed in Stalin's time as part of his notorious 'church rationalization program.' It is a fact that, during Jimmy Carter's presidency, Ceaușescu was confronted with the issue of human rights and religious liberty to a greater extent than ever before. A slight but perceptible relaxation also took place in the regime's readiness to issue passports and visas, especially for representatives of religious denominations to travel to international conferences. Ceaușescu set great store by his image and that of communist Romania in the eyes of the rest of the world, especially America. For this purpose, he successfully made use of leaders various religious groups in Romania, including the Jews, for a period of time.

In these circumstances in the summer of 1980, I was informed by the Baptist Union that I should come to Bucharest to collect my invitation from the International Seminary of Evangelical

Theology and their official recommendation that I be issued a passport. In those days, no one had a right to keep a personal passport; it was something issued only for particular occasions. After you returned from your trip, you were required to hand it in within twenty-four hours.

I was told that the summer school course began on June 1 and that my three colleagues and I should arrive there the day before. I couldn't believe it was true. It was indeed a miracle.

Since my seminary studies, I had continued studying English with enthusiasm. I had a self-study book entitled *Learn English Without a Teacher* and for two years I devoted two hours a day to English. Pastor Iosif Ţon had given me and old cassette player, a treasure, and a cassette tape containing two sermons by a pastor in England. One side had a sermon on 'Depression' from Psalm 23 and the other had a talk on 'Fear' from Revelations 1: 17-18. I listened to both sides of this tape dozens of times. At the beginning I understood almost nothing, but gradually grew in comprehension.

I was jumping for joy at the thought that I would soon be in Switzerland, to attend lectures given in English by great teachers, that I would be spending hours in the huge library of this international seminary and that I would be able to get to know fellow pastors from all over the world.

I was extremely disappointed when I went to Deva with my official papers from the Baptist Union and the Department for Religious Denominations to collect my passport only to be put through a series of delays and bureaucratic obstacles. I finally began my journey two weeks late. As I was being handed my passport, the passport officer suggested that it might be just as well if I gave up the idea of going, as there were only two weeks of the course left now. I told him that I did not want to miss this opportunity, and before catching the train in Bucharest I went to the American Embassy and obtained a 45-day American visa as well.

I set out by train from Bucharest on Saturday evening. At four the next morning, my wife and a church member were in the station at Simeria to wish me *bon voyage* and bring me a packet of food for the journey. I cannot forget how I felt as we crossed the border between Hungary and Austria. I keep moving from one window to the other so that I could see everything and not miss a thing. I felt that the train was piercing the Iron Curtain – that it was passing from one world to another. When I got off the train in the station in Vienna, I was absolutely fascinated. Every kiosk with its souvenirs or magazines, every little restaurant with its display of snacks was something that I had never encountered before. My train to Zurich was leaving at later that evening, so I stored my luggage so that I could at least see a few streets in the area of the station. I had brought 100 lei as spending money,which I changed at the station for 46 Schillings of which 16 Schillings paid for the storage leaving me with just 30. After I had bought myself a one-liter bottle of Coca Cola, I had 11 Schillings left in my pocket.

I took my plastic bag of food from home and my bottle of Coca Cola, sat down on a bench in the park next to the station and ate – just like the peasants who came to market in Haţeg would sit and eat in the little park there.

Then I walked through the streets stopping to gaze in wonder at their window displays. They were so full of goods, so beautifully decorated and illuminated. It was a powerful sensation of having crossed from a world of poverty, darkness and oppression into one of prosperity, civilization and freedom. I was astonished and delighted with everything, like a child.

That evening, at around ten o'clock, I collected my luggage and boarded the Zurich train. My fellow passengers in the compartment were two Mexican students, Monica and Patricia, who were on their way to a Catholic university in Lausanne. Some time later a Canadian student named Peter joined us on his way to meet up with his father somewhere in the Swiss Alps.

My modest knowledge of English helped me converse with the other passengers. The train had scarcely left the station when a young man pushing a cart paused at the door of our compartment. It was loaded with all kinds of good things: chocolate, chewing gum, Coca Cola and all kinds of fruit juice and other soft drinks, coffee, tea, beer etc. Another capitalist miracle! I had never seen anything like this on Romanian trains. I had finished my precious bottle of Coca Cola long since and thrown it into a rubbish bin in the station. I was thirsty again. Knowing that I had some Austrian money (the 11 Schillings) in my pocket, I asked confidently in English how much a can of Coca Cola cost. The vendor told me that it cost 17 Schillings. Then I asked what a Seven-Up cost. "The same!" was the reply. "And a bar of chocolate?" "15 Schillings!" Then I took my courage in both hands and said to him: "I am from Romania and I've only got 11 Schillings in my pocket. What can I buy with that?"

"Nothing!" the Austrian replied heartlessly.

Then Patricia said to the vendor: "Give the gentleman everything he wants; I'll pay for him. Give him some Coca Cola and a bar of chocolate and a coffee and a packet of chewing gum."

I tried to protest but Patricia was very insistent. Once the Austrian had got the money he put the things she had asked for into my hands and went on with his 'miracle' trolley. I was left with all these things in my hands and a lump in my throat. I tried to tell my benefactor that I wished to give her my 11 Schillings as a contribution, but she would not listen. It was one of the most humiliating moments of my life. And I was a man too!

I felt compelled to explain that in Romania, people were not allowed to possess foreign currency, that it was my first trip outside the country and that I was going to a summer course. The European Baptist Federation had given me a scholarship to attend and was paying all my expenses. I would be given 50 Swiss francs as pocket money. The young ladies assured me that I didn't have to feel embarrassed: they, too, believed in Jesus Christ and were students at a Catholic university in their own country. They were in Europe to attend a summer course about charity work. They told me that although they were devout Catholics, they were moved that I had chosen the career of a Baptist pastor serving God in a Communist country where Christians were persecuted. I thanked them for their unexpected gesture and for their words of appreciation and encouragement and promised to pray for them and their work with orphans in Mexico.

After a while, we put out the light and all dozed off in our seats. The next morning, as I was returning from the washroom, I found the three students planning something in whispers. When I stood up to take my luggage at the station, Monica held out an envelope to me and told me that it was a small gift to cover my needs until I received the 50 Swiss francs. She asked me to accept it as a token of the love that united us in Jesus Christ. I took the envelope and thanked them with tears in my eyes. I hugged each of them in turn and got off the train, deeply moved. Later, I found they had given me 120 Austrian Schillings (100 from Patricia and 20 from Monica) and $20 in U.S. currency from Peter. Seen through the prism of my human vanity, this was a humbling experience but, from a spiritual perspective, it was one of the most beautiful experiences with God I have ever had.

Like the disciples who brought no money, only faith, I had set out into the unknown, and he had confirmed he was with always. He reminded me that he is a living God who does not forget me and did not leave me even for a moment. He proved his resources can be available to his children in whatever circumstance and often through those least expected.

Meeting Western Christianity

"Crede ut intelligas." (Malebranche)

Switzerland, with its many cantons, is a wonder of God's natural creation; a country full of mountains and lakes, a civilized country where cleanliness and tidiness are the order of the day even in the most crowded cities. The seminary was located on Lake Zurich, a picturesque setting for the course.

I introduced myself to the Director of the Summer School, who was also the European representative of the Baptist World Alliance. He welcomed me and gave me a schedule of courses for the next two weeks and recommended that I choose the course in Systematic Theology which was to be taught by the best-known teacher on campus. I plucked up the courage to register an objection: "I have heard that Dr. L. takes a very liberal line in his theology. If possible, I would like to sign up for the course in New Testament taught by a Polish professor who is known as very evangelical." The Summer School Director cut me off short. "You are here to learn, not to criticize me!" I said no more and signed up for the course he had recommended.

(This brother was one of the American Baptists who were wined and dined by Romania's Baptist Union and were manipulated by the Department of Religious Denominations. When warned about the compromised pastors, and informed about their collaboration against godly pastors who were sincerely struggling to do the will of God, he answered us brusquely: "You Romanians are too suspicious of one another and run each other down too much! Also you need to know that it is the policy of the Baptist World Alliance to cooperate with the official leadership of the Baptist Unions in Communist countries. We would have no access to these countries if we did not." My colleagues and I tried hard to understand this philosophy and did not protest it again.)

Peter Dugulescu

That first evening, I attended Professor L's Systematic Theology lecture. I sat next to a white pastor from South Africa. We were the same age and both of us had become Christians fifteen years previously. After sharing about our respective paths, I asked: "Excuse me, brother, maybe my English is too poor for me to have understood properly, but this professor seems extremely liberal. He is casting doubts on the Resurrection and divinity of the Lord Jesus and the infallibility of Scripture."

"Brother Peter," he replied "In 15 years, I have never doubted the truth of the Scriptures. I have been here for two weeks and already I am experiencing doubts."

The next day, I was even more dismayed: "We do not know whether the Resurrection took place as a physical resurrection or happened more in the disciples' minds; we cannot know for sure whether Jesus was married or not," and similar comments.

At one point, a pastor from Egypt stood up and protested: "Professor, He is divine, He is our Lord, how can you say such things about him?"

The professor replied quite calmly: "I was not making assertions, I was only saying that we cannot know for sure."

It reminded me of Genesis 3, where the serpent began his work of tempting the first man and woman in Eden with the words: "Did God really say…?" When he came to the Son of God in the wilderness to tempt him, using the same technique – speculating and interpreting the Scriptures – Jesus said right at the outset: "It is written!" I realised then, with fear if the Bible is not any longer the infallible Word of the Living God, it becomes only a literary work or a mere religious book like many others.

That's when I thanked God that the Communist authorities in Bucharest had not allowed me to come to this liberal seminary in

1974. I might have returned to Romania with a degree in Theology, yes, but without a living faith.

Despite my disappointment with the course material, I was comforted by meeting Jean Pierre Pont, one of God's 'smugglers' to Romania. Only one year earlier, in June 1979, he and his wife had knocked at our door at 12 o'clock one Sunday night. Speaking in French and English, they told me that they came from Operation Mobilisation and had brought me Bibles, Christian literature and medicine. It was quite an adventure. So when I phoned Jean Pierre to tell him I was in Switzerland, he couldn't believe it. He invited me to his home, reimbursed my train fare, and met me at the station at Bieen. Meeting his family and the Free Evangelical Church was a special blessing for me.

Another pleasant surprise was unexpectedly meeting Tică Faur, a Romanian Pentecostal friend who had fled the country at the risk of his life ten years before and had settled in Switzerland. He had a job at the Zurich University hospital making artificial limbs and surgical boots. The next weekend, I accompanied him and his wife Anuța to an evangelistic tent meeting organised by the Salvation Army. This was a new experience for me and I learned much from the spirit of sacrifice that these men of God possessed. Every evening, the choir led the thousand attendees in a special song that I really loved. I translated it into Romanian when I returned, keeping as close as possible to the original, and it was sung for the first time at the church in Hațeg at New Year 1981. After that it spread all over the country.

> *"Alleluia, let us sing*
> *Grateful hearts to him let's raise*
> *Glory and honor to Christ the King*
> *For he deserves our thanks and praise."*

On July 1, I returned to Vienna, where my American BEE friend, Jody Dillow, met me at the station. We shared a special dinner at Bud Hikson's home and then I went to Corky's for the night. Here was a different face of Western Christianity. Far from sowing doubts in our minds about the Word of God, the secret courses they had held in Romania had strengthened our conviction in Scripture and made it relevant to our situation. As Jody took me to the airport for my flight to America the next day, he tried to prepare me for the huge shock that was in store for me when I reached the American continent. Even before the plane touched the ground, the Statue of Liberty and the skyscrapers of New York seemed to trumpet what I would experience in America.

Faith and Decadence

From that first moment in the summer of 1980, I felt America was huge nation pulled in two opposing directions. On one side are the people who love God. I saw huge crowds parking their cars early Sunday morning in the enormous parking lots of the mega-churches rushing with their entire families to church services, Bibles in hand. They fill those huge buildings with their seating capacity of thousands, yet there is not enough room for everyone, so that there have to be two or three services every Sunday morning. These are the most beautiful people in the world, the light and hope of an America, the true America. I have known both pastors and ordinary church members who are godly people, dedicated to prayer, people who lead such a good Christian life that it commands respect and admiration. Unfortunately, however, these people are a minority

The great mass of Americans and new immigrants are heading in a direction diametrically opposed to that demonstrated in the lives and writings of the Founding Fathers. Drug users, drunks, homosexuals, pornographers fill America's streets--but also bright faced Christians giving out tracts and caring for those who have "fallen among thieves" like the Good Samaritan. In Communist countries, the totalitarian power of the state exerted a coercive pressure that compelled us to be either atheists or believers. In

America, people had freedom, so they could go wherever they pleased.

I will never forget one scene that captured my impressions in a single frame: an old missionary in the asphalt jungle of New York. It was on one of the most notorious streets filled with the dregs of a society that turned its back on God. He wore two large sandwich boards. The one in front said "Jesus Saves" while the back one said "Jesus Died For Your Sins." He walked wearily, silently, but in his face was anguish for those around him. He paced, silent and grave, through that teeming anthill of people seeking joy through alcohol, drugs, sex shops and homosexual clubs. His thin, shrivelled body bore the two huge sandwich boards, a mute and moving Gospel, the silent, serious, grave-faced man, going against the stream. Behind him, at a distance, rose the twin towers of the World Trade Center.

First Impressions

I was in America at the invitation of my good friends Nelu and Lena Lazăr from Hațeg, who had founded the Pentecostal church there and had emigrated legally to America two years earlier. My brand-new Chinese bag, specially purchased in Bucharest for this journey, had split open during transit, and I was struggling to close it and to tie it shut with the belt of my trousers when a young woman working at one of the airline ticket counters saw my dilemma and came to help me. I was touched by her action, so I thanked her and asked if there was a place where such things could be repaired. She smiled and said: "No, sir, here such things are thrown away." Because I had missed my connection for Chicago and did not know how to book myself onto another flight this young woman phoned the airline company and booked me on another flight. Then called the Lazăr family on her phone so I could tell them about the delay. Perhaps this young woman was a Christian, but it gave me the impression that all Americans were friendly and kind.

Exhausted by the long journey, I fell asleep on the plane, and woke up at landing. When I looked out of the window and saw the city of Chicago reaching into the distance like a sea of lights, the regular grid pattern of the streets made this fairy-like nocturnal vista even more striking. I thought of Romania and its gloomy cities, covered in darkness, with all their closely-crowded concrete apartment blocks, monuments of the impact of socialism in town and village alike – blocks where even a few hours of hot water, heating and electric lighting a day were treated as the height of privilege.

"Where's Ceaușescu?" I asked myself. "The Americans surely need him to teach them how to husband their resources more carefully because they are living too wastefully in this land of blessing." Costel and Mia Oglice, close friends of mine since my seminary years in Bucharest, from the church in Mihai Bravu, came to meet me at the airport.

We all went to the Lazăr family home for a Romanian meal augmented by a wide range of American foods and drinks. As visitors from Romania were rare at that time, Romanians settled in the 'Promised Land' missed no opportunity to show off the fruits of 'Canaan' to their relations or friends coming from the 'Egypt' of communist slavery.

We talked late into the night. When I woke up, I was alone as my hosts had gone to work. They had left me a note on the table telling me to help myself to anything in the fridge or the pantry. As well as some of the bananas and oranges that beckoned to me from the huge fruit bowl I decided to try a new dish: cereal with milk. Because I cannot drink milk unless it has been boiled, I wanted to light the gas stove but had nothing with which to do so. I could find no match or lighter, so I stood there at a loss, asking myself: "What on earth do these people light their gas stove with? Could the Americans by any chance be so clever that they have invented a gas stove that lights itself? That would be too much, but let's try." Very skeptically, I turned the knob; to my great astonishment. the burner lit! When I recounted this story back home, they were all amazed too. Such a trivial thing showed the total difference between our lives.

Romanian Transplants

The next day happened to be July 4, Independence Day, and friends from the Second Romanian Baptist Church, Chicago invited me on a picnic. Cars containing Romanian families whom I knew most of them from home arrived, and everyone spread blankets, lit fires and started grilling their meat and *mititei* just like in Romania. But they also brought the whole range of fruit juices and American soft drinks in coolers they took out of the trunks of their cars. They kept reminding me: "Pete, this is America!" and even asked me, point blank: "Pete, haven't you thought of staying in America? Aren't you fed up with Romania with its queues and problems?"

A good friend from Reşiţa said, "Pete we risked our lives when we swam across the Danube at night. Other people slipped across the border, dodging the bullets of the border guards, or managed to stow away in night trains – all for the love of liberty. You are here on American soil. Are you still thinking of going back? I don't think, in the end, you'll be able to resist the temptation to stay."

I did not want to offend them but my reply disappointed them. "I have only been on American soil for two days but I can say that I feel for you."

"You feel for us? Why?" they asked in amazement.

"Because you can no longer enjoy life as you did in Romania. Here you no longer experience those small pleasures that give life its sparkle. When I travel around the country to evangelistic meetings, to Oraştie, Alba Iulia or Sibiu for example, I sometimes find a frozen state farm chicken, some butter, some oranges or some bananas in a grocery store. When I reach home, my children leap on me, asking eagerly: "What have you brought us, Daddy?" When I show them what I've brought, they jump for joy. My wife is happy too. That frozen chicken, packet of butter or kilogram of bananas is something for us to be happy about. Here you live with full fridges, full car trunks and full stomachs all the time so you can't enjoy these small things that make life in Romania beautiful and interesting.

"Also, if I were to come and pastor in this free American climate I would fall asleep. I have a tendency to be lazy and I need an occasional jolt to keep me awake. I need the 'blue-eyed boys' and the Department for Religious Denominations summoning me to interrogations every Monday and asking me: "Why did you preach against evolution? Why did you preach about the principle of private property in agriculture? Why did you refer to the cult of personality?" My style of preaching would not fit here. I would have to change it completely.

"Most importantly, I do not believe that it is God's will for me to settle in America. For some of you, it is God's will that you should be here, and some others wish to have a better life and to escape from persecution. That's their business; I'm not called to judge them. But I know that God wants to use me on the Romanian battlefield. If I stayed here, my own conscience would condemn me as a deserter. God would say to me: "You have left the path of my will and I cannot listen to you. Go back to your own place from which you ran away!" "

Sunday, I visited two Romanian churches where I preached: Lake View Romanian Church where Brother Cocean was pastor, and later, at First Romanian Baptist Church where Brother Alexa Popovici – a former head of the Baptist Theological Seminary in Bucharest – was pastor. On the surface, I was well received, but here and there, I found that many doubted what I said was sincere and from my heart. They thought that I had sold out to the Communists and had been sent on a special mission to spy on the Romanian communities in America. This suspicious attitude hurt me very much, but could be found in the many immigrant Romanian churches. Internal suspicion and gossip had become a ruthless cancer, unsettling and dividing these churches throughout America.

The congress of the World Baptist Alliance was due to open in a few days' time in Toronto, Canada. I was fortunate to obtain a visa, and took a bus since my budget was tight. The 23 Baptist pastors from Romania who had received permission to attend the Congress included my friend Titus Miheţ, who was pastor at Zalău but had grown up in First Baptist in Timişoara where I had been. Due to a mixup, no one met me at the bus station, so I spent the night on the streets of Toronto.

Very early the next morning, I entered Toronto Sports Complex where the Congress was being held and met brother Ieremia Hodoroabă from Paris, who helped me register. I received $70 Canadian to cover my meals. The conference was impressive: a 20,000-seat auditorium full of people from 115 countries, people of different ethnic groups, languages and cultures, all singing the same hymns of praise and worshipping the same Savior, Jesus Christ. You would have needed a pair of binoculars to see who was who on the opposite side of the auditorium. The mornings were taken up with workshops, report presentations and small groups; in the evenings there were evangelistic services with choirs and well-known preachers. One day, Romanian pastors were asked to form a choir and sing two songs. Although I had always known I was tone deaf, I too joined this choir, and when opera soloist, Petru Luluşa, sang a solo, it was greeted with wild applause. Later, an African woman congratulated me on the solo I had sung. Of course, I directed her to the talented Romanian singer who indeed resembled me in size but not in vocal ability!

Nicolae Ceaușescu's efforts to promote his image with a pretense of religious liberty certainly succeeded. One of the leaders of the World Baptist Alliance, noted that the Romanian delegation was one of the largest ones from Europe and spoke favourably about the freedom that the Baptists of Romania enjoyed under the presidency of Ceaușescu!

After the congress, I accompanied Titus to Kitchener, where I visited the Romanian Baptist Church, which was at that time without a pastor. The deacon at whose home I stayed tried very hard to persuade me to accept the position. He promised that the church would provide me with housing, a suitable salary and would arrange for my family to be brought over from Romania as soon as possible. He urged me to think about it until the next day, when I had to leave.

I thanked him for the offer and said that I was honored by the invitation but that I did not need any time to think it over, because I had taken the decision many years before. The deacon was somewhat disappointed and said that he could not understand me.

Returning Home

Although I was to depart on August 13, there was a mechanical problem with the plane, so we stayed an extra day at TAROM's expense. Several passengers said that it was a sign from God that we should stay in America. We left the next day – August 14 – and arrived at Bucharest Otopeni on the 15th, where my wife met me with Gheorghe and Veta Simedronis, who were a great comfort and support during our time in Hațeg.

Having spent only two months away from Romania, I never expected such a great shock on my return home. When one Romanian passenger with an American passport, wearing a cowboy hat, was lagging slightly behind the group, an armed militiamen escorting our group began to shout at him. At this, the

American Romanian, accustomed to democracy, replied: "Is this all the welcome I get when I come back to Romania after fifteen years? You're escorting us as if we were convicts!" I realized that this man didn't know what he was doing and that there was a good chance that he wouldn't be allowed through customs but would have to catch the next plane back to America.

After seeing the big airports of America, the Otopeni International Airport terminal looked like some wretched whistle-stop at the end of the world. The ubiquitous militiamen and armed soldiers were were depressing to me. We had to wait on lines for passport control and again, for the customs check, and both the police and the airport staff there spoke to us sharply and rudely and all had sour, scowling faces. Comparing them to the kind young woman who had helped me when I arrived at the airport in New York, I found myself thinking "What have I come back to?"

This icy bath was just the beginning. Of course, the customs officials helped themselves to various contents of my suitcases, in accordance with the unwritten rules of socialist ethics and equity. Climbing into my Dacia station wagon, I thought: "Is this really my car? I thought it was bigger." After six weeks of being driven around in Oldsmobiles, Cadillacs and other large, comfortable, air-conditioned American cars, it seemed to have shrunk. The streets seemed so narrow that I constantly had the impression that the oncoming traffic was going to hit us. Everything struck me as small now, in stark contrast to the scale of everything in America.

My wife and children were dumbfounded when I told them: "In America, the buildings are enormous, like ten of our blocks piled one on top of the other, the roads have four or five lines of traffic in each direction, the fridges are almost as big as wardrobes, a sandwich is as big as one of our Romanian loaves but is filled with lots of meat, lettuce and mayonnaise, and ice-cream is eaten by the tub." When I told them that in America oranges and bananas might sit on a table for days without anyone touching them, they could hardly believe it.

I will never forget the joy with which my children ran to meet me. Ligia was ten, Cristina eight and Cristi, six, and they hurled themselves at my luggage.. They were pleased with the clothes, the school equipment and the school bags I had brought them, but what made them happiest was the many packs of chewing gum. They and other children always shouted "Gum, gum!" whenever they saw a foreign car, so their greatest delight and special thing to share with other children was a special kind of chewing gum sent from a friend in Chicago. These American goodies and novelties didn't last long, because they shared them freely with friends, and Cristi even began to give his friends personal things off my desk until I caught him.

In two short months, the Romanian economy, which had been sick for some time, had gone into a coma. When my wife and I went to the largest grocery store in the center of Haţeg to do our shopping, there was nothing in the window but bottled cherries and jars of beets. In the 1970s, the grocery store had been full of all kinds of Chinese foods, but now the climate had changed. Very soon, basic foodstuffs – flour, sugar, butter, oil and eggs – would be rationed. "Lord, what have I returned to?" I thought again. Now, in the shop, my wife said to me in a reproachful tone: "Do you see what you've come back to? I hope you don't regret it." My wife and children would have been glad if I had stayed in America and sent for them to join me. My children said to me again and again: "Daddy, let's go to America! Daddy, we don't want to lose you. Don't you see how many people are leaving Romania? Let's go too!"

When I went to the county militia headquarters in Deva to turn in my passport the next day as required by law, the officer who took it asked me if anything unusual had happened during the two-month period. I said "No." He told me that his commanding officer wanted to speak to me and that I should come back in two hours' time, so I did and I was taken to the office of the county Securitate chief.

After he had shaken hands with me, he said "So you are back, Pastor. I, for one, didn't believe you would ever return."

I replied: "Yes, I came back, Colonel, as I promised you I would. I am a Romanian and I love my country. I am sorry you don't believe that Baptists can be good patriots."

"Patriotism is demonstrated by deeds, and so far you haven't given us all that much proof of it. Speaking of that, tell me honestly, did the lads from the American Secret Services make contact with you?"

I replied categorically: "No, Colonel; I am, and wish to remain, a man of God, not a man belonging to any secret service." These people were convinced I was a CIA agent. He told me I must detail in my report what the Romanians traitors who fled their country were saying about Romania and Ceauşescu, and especially how the Americans viewed Romania.

I said in my report that I had not become aware of any plots being hatched by the Romanians in America against our country or against President Ceauşescu. I cited the comments of the leaders of the World Baptist Alliance who had congratulated Romania and Ceauşescu on the large delegation of Romanian pastors who had attended the Toronto conference. I also said that this was something very positive and that if greater steps were taken to reduce restrictions on evangelical groups this would be to Romania's advantage. I referred to Pastor Iosif Ţon's idea of Baptists, and of evangelical denominations in general, becoming a bridge between Romania and America. I pointed out that evangelical Christians were, in fact, the only point of affinity that could help us form links with America.

I pointed out that the Hungarians were successfully building bridges between nations by using the close links that their Reformed church had with the Presbyterian churches of America.

Of course, I realized that this was a waste of ink, since these things were beyond the colonel's powers of comprehension – and decision-making.

Peter the Atheist

One of the saddest things about communism is how it forced intelligent, gifted people to live a double life, where their official words and beliefs were usually very different than what they really wanted and felt.

In my childhood, our close neighbors and friends included the Berar family, who were also repenters. We used to wear the clothes and shoes they had grown out of, and when our food was low, my mother would borrow something from them, repaying them by helping with their farm work. When the Chelmac 'New Times' Collective Farm was established, Mr. Berar was sent to Russia for six months to attend a special course on organizing vegetable growers on collective farms, which also included a political component. He returned from Moscow to run one of the most productive vegetable farms in the Banat, including an excellent irrigation system using water from the Mureş, and was nominated as village secretary of the Romanian Workers' Party. He broke off fellowship and his children didn't attend the repenters' meetings either.

Petru, their eldest, was twelve years older than me, and attended High School in Lipova and the Philosophy Faculty in Bucharest. He became editor of the main Romanian Communist Party propaganda organ – 'The Class Struggle' – later called 'The Socialist Era.' He held many prestigious posts: professor at the Ştefan Ghiorghiu Academy of Political Science in Bucharest; head of the Department of the Philosophy of Religion; and Senior Instructor of the Atheistic Propaganda brigades of the Central Committee of the Romanian Communist Party.

During the 70s, he wrote several well-known books *Cultural Revolution: Marx, Engels, On Religion, Youth and Religion* etc. Most people thought he was a true Communist, but in fact, he served the system and hated it at the same time, and he was not the only one.

During my first year at the Seminary, I happened to meet him on a trip to my home village of Chelmac. There we were: Peter the Repenter and Peter the Atheist. He was warm and friendly, and invited me for a meal. I told Seminary colleagues to pray for me as I was going speak with one of the top ideologues of the Party,and I wanted to use the opportunity to bear witness to the Lord Jesus.

I asked permission to pray before the meal, and he and his wife stood hand in hand with me as I blessed the food. During the meal we chatted about childhood memories and the people of our village. He presented me with copies of his books, inscribed a special dedication "To Brother Peter Dugulescu, with all the love that a free-thinker is capable of."

I, in turn, had gifts for him: *And Yet the Bible is True* and *Are You Sure?* by Pitt Popovici and *Fill the Void* by Richard Wurmbrand. I warned him that these were books were regarded as illicit by the ideological department that he headed and that the Securitate were on the lookout for such books. He said he would read them carefully in private, without anyone's knowledge. Before I left he said: "Peter, can I ask you something?" "Of course," I replied. "Can you let me have a Bible? ... You know, it's not for me, it's for Monica, my wife. She's a psychiatrist and she wants to read the Bible".

I brought him a Bible, when we met a few weeks later, inscribed: "To Brother Petru Berar,with the sincere wish that as he reads this book he will encounter the One who said: "I am the Way, the Truth and the Life!" I said: "Pete, I'm giving you this book along with my advice as a friend: don't use it to fight it, but rather, to get to know it".

"Fine, fine" he said in some confusion, "I told you it was for Monica".

When we met again, he said he had read the books I gave him with great interest and observed: "Pitt Popovici's books are written in a spirit of love and compassion towards us atheists, whom you regard as lost sheep, but when you read Richard Wurmbrand you are aware of a sharp critical edge in his attitude towards us. That could be a consequence of the fact that he was tortured and endured many years of suffering in prison" he concluded.

"Brother Richard bears no hatred towards Communists as people," I responded. "In all his books, one can discern a profound spirit of love and understanding towards his guards, interrogators and torturers. The sharpness that can be felt is directed at the brutal and absurd system of atheistic Communism, which he demolishes with arguments spiced with characteristically Jewish humor."

In discussing Pitt Popovici's book *Are You Sure?* I said to him: "Pete, you are one of the top RCP ideologues and your responsibility under that system is to deny the existence of God and to root out belief in God from in Romanian minds. Your goal is the formation of the 'New Man,' but I believe that this will be impossible without God. Jesus Christ created the New Man two thousand years ago, and he is still creating new people today. The job you are doing is very dangerous because it compels you to fight against God!"

"Yes," he said "but I only fight with philosophical arguments, at the level of ideas. I don't agree with the use of coercion against evangelicals. The people who persecute you in your schools, universities and workplaces are idiots. I've told them so, to their faces, during the Central Committee meetings. I've also told them that after studying the sociology of religion in Romania, the only people who don't steal from collective farms and factories are the repenters. The repenters also have large families, which the Party encourages, and their ethical principles and family life are exemplary. Marx and Lenin said that coercion cannot break the hold of religion on human minds, only persuasion. That is why I only fight on the level of ideas. I know very well who the repenters are, and I don't attack them in my books – as you have seen – but concentrate more on the Catholics and the Orthodox."

"But, Pete, that still doesn't absolve you from having combated God by saying that he doesn't exist. But what if he does? Have you ever asked yourself that question?" Just at that moment, he received a phone call from Radio Bucharest, booking him onto a program on the subject of Atheism and Religious Mysticism.

"Comrade," he replied, "you still haven't paid me for the last program I did. I blasphemed the name of God for nothing. Until you give me the money I'm not going to do any more broadcasts!" Overhearing this, I strongly felt that God had brought me to this man's house for a purpose, to bear witness to him, and I was more and more convinced of God's deep love for him.

I took my courage in both hands and said: "Pete, you are an atheist philosopher and you earn your living by writing and speaking against the existence of God. But have you ever thought of what you're losing if he does exist? I'd like to encourage you to carry out an experiment. Do it on your own in your study after I've left, or before you go to bed. Kneel down and say these words to God: "God, I don't believe in you, I tell people you don't exist, but if you do actually exist, don't leave me to wander in ignorance. Reveal yourself to me and help me to come to know you so that I don't lose my soul for eternity!""

"No, I can't do that; that's going too far. But come and see me again, and we'll talk some more."

I decided to bring my teacher from the Seminary, Iosif Țon, who had recently finished his studies at Regent's Park College in Oxford on my next visit. Over the meal, generously provided by our atheist host, the two professors, faced each other in the arena of ideas. While for the teacher of Protestant theology the words he spoke were a creed and a *raison d'être*, for the professor of Marxist philosophy, the words were the slogans of a lifeless ideology.

Professor Ton asked Peter a question: "What is the basic moral code of atheism?"

"The principles of socialist ethics and equity are that you should be honest, altruistic, committed to your native land and to those around you and ready to sacrifice yourself for the good of others."

"But how can you be like that if you don't have a moral basis that is firmly anchored in eternity?" reasoned Professor Ton. "If eternal rewards and punishments have no reality, why should I be honest and altruistic, why should I sacrifice myself for others, when by lying, stealing, deception and evading the laws of the land I can look out for my own interests much more effectively in the here and now? If this life is all there is, and there is not going to be another life after death, there is no longer any point in my thinking about the morality or immorality of what I do. If I have come from an animal and am going to die like an animal what does it matter how I live?

"Professor Berar, you are one of the top ideologues of the RCP. You should know that this ideology is an ideology of despair and that it will never produce the 'New Man.' By contrast, the Gospel of Jesus Christ which we preach tells us who we are, where we have come from, where we are going to go after we die and how to live a good life here that is patterned on the unique life of the Man, Jesus Christ, so that one day we may be like him and with him in glory."

The last time I saw Peter as after I returned from a trip in September 1980. As usual, he drank a lot of wine with his meal, and become very talkative and extremely open. When Nicolae Ceauşescu appeared on the TV news, he turned it off with a curse, and started criticizing the personality cult of the dictator and his wife and saying: "That shoemaker and his 'high-powered intellectual' wife have brought Romania to the brink of ruin." Everything he said about the presidential couple was accompanied by a string of full-blooded Romanian oaths.

Then he looked at me and said: "Peter, put in a word for me with the American brothers. Get them to find me a job as a pastor in America and get them to put those two away. I want to move from the 'socialist heaven' to the 'capitalist hell' and never come back." He was serving a political and ideological system that he hated in his inner heart.

In the Fall of 1983, Petru Berar went to Chelmac for a brief holiday, and met two friends, the Orthodox priest and Ion Piţl (Iovescu), who was a forest ranger. Ion Piţl was from a repenter family too, though he himself had chosen to be Orthodox. The three old friends visited my father, who was crippled with arthritis and after, Petru Berar said to my mother, who had accompanied them to the gate: "Irina, where do you think we will meet? In heaven or in hell?" My mother replied: "I have no wish to meet you in the other world, because you have chosen hell, you are opposing God!"

"Well, who knows?" he said, laughing "we'll see what happens by then. Tell Peter to come and see me again".

From there, they visited the cemetery at Şarlău where his father had recently been buried. At the end of his life, Mr. Berar had struggled hard to regain the faith he had renounced as a young man. He used to call the brothers in the village to come and pray for him. They came with the love of Christ, prayed, sang and encouraged him. This helped him to make his peace with God.

There in the cemetery, Petru Berar stood at his father's grave. The other two stood off, and could hear him saying something, but the words were not discernible at that range.. With his left arm circling the cross on the gravestone, he raised his eyes to heaven and said aloud: "Oh, I've been seeking you for such a long time, and I don't know where to find you! I want to call you by name, but I don't know what to call you. Eternity – that is your real name, Eternity, I want to find you!"

Time passed, but he couldn't tear himself away from the cross. Finally, the priest said to him: "Come on, Pete, don't keep grieving. After all, you're not a woman. Let's go home, because my wife's got a meal waiting for us!"

At dinner, before starting to eat, Petru Berar said to the priest: "Father, if you have grace to release people from their sins, release me now while you are asking a blessing on the food. Say: "I release the servant of God, Petru Berar, from his sins on the basis of the grace given to me by Jesus Christ."

This request took the priest by surprise and he didn't know what to do, but his friend persisted: "Pray for me and say that I should be released!"

Finally, the priest prayed as he was bidden. The next day, Petru Berar returned to Bucharest. Only two days later, his brother's family in Chelmac received the news that he was dead. Due to his love for his birthplace, his body was brought to Chelmac to be buried. Many of his friends from the Ştefan Ghiorghiu Academy came for the funeral, and talked among themselves about the mystery of their colleague's death.

It was said that he had gone to an official reception for the leaders of the RCP Central Committee and that, after a few glasses of wine, his tongue had run away with him. He had described Elena Ceauşescu as "that stupid idiot" and "uneducated." One of the secret informers – they were everywhere – had written it all down and sent a report to the Securitate, who had passed it on to Ceauşescu. He immediately ordered that the 'heretic' Petru Berar be eliminated.

One day, when his wife was on duty at the hospital, a 'friend' came to visit him. After some hours, during which they drank coffee and a few glasses of wine, the friend left. When his wife returned from the hospital, she found him dead in his armchair with his hand reaching out for the telephone.

The false god that he had served repaid him with death, but standing on his father's grave, he cried out to his eternal Father, and asked the priest to forgive his sins in the name of Jesus Christ. Peter Berar was 'Peter the Atheist' no more.

Cry from the Mountains

In August of 1982, the ten pastors that were the original nucleus of the BEE program in Romania and who were part of the 50 who closed ranks around Pastor Iosif Ţon in 1973 after the publication of his book, *Who Will Lose His Life,* by signing the petition to Ceauşescu, began a new initiative. The churches were facing serious problems caused either by local authority abuses of power or by the global strategy applied to religious groups by the atheist regime in Bucharest. Thousands of Bibles were being seized at the borders and turned into lavatory paper; Christians caught transporting Bibles had been arrested and thrown into jail; in many places, including Bocşa, Bistriţa, Tigăneşti, Comăneşti, Bucureşti Giuleşti, church buildings had been demolished. Whenever the time came for elections to the regional Baptist associations or to the Baptist Union Congress, and the representatives from the churches wished to propose leaders in whom they had confidence, the representatives of the Department for Religious Denominations would say to us scornfully: "You can elect them, but we won't recognise them. We are the body appointed by the State to give or deny official recognition to religious leaders. The only people we are going to recognise are those who know how to cooperate with us."

At one of the secret BEE courses in Bucharest, in June 1982, I suggested to my colleagues that we should climb up to the Pietrele chalet in the Retezat Mountains for two days of relaxation, prayer and consultation. Vasile Brânzei, Geabou Pascu and Iosif Ştefănuţ came. Vasile Taloş had planned to come but was rushed to hospital in Bucharest a few days before with suspected cancer, so we prayed fervently for him. There, in the heart of the mountains, at an altitude of almost 2,000 meters, we decided after prayer and consultation to address a new petition to Ceauşescu and the Romanian government. The rights reluctantly granted in 1973 (more freedom to hold baptisms and church services) were important – but they did not go far enough. We composed a petition of seven points outlining most serious issues that pastors and churches all over the country were facing. These were:

- Official recognition of leaders chosen by the general meetings of churches, regional associations and the Baptist Union Congress.
- The granting of permission to repair church buildings and to construct new ones where the local church considers this necessary.
- The opening of new churches and daughter churches wherever statutory conditions are fulfilled, without the need for an authorisation to function from the Department for Religious Denominations.
- Freedom to use church finances without state control.
- Freedom to print Bibles and Christian literature.
- Freedom for local churches to train their own church workers within the framework of programs they themselves organise.
- Freedom to educate our children in accordance with our own convictions, and ending discrimination against them in schools and universities.

The order of signing this petition was important. The two veterans, Brânzei and Geabou, were of the opinion that we should allow the younger generation to step to the fore. Thus, the honor of signing first fell to me, and Iosif Ştefănuţ signed second.

We came down from the mountain that day, and we began to collect signatures. Vasile Taloş signed the petition in hospital. Each of us took responsibility for collecting signatures in one particular part of the country. We succeeded in gathering 66 signatures. We posted the petition to Ceauşescu by recorded delivery from a post office in Bucharest, but not before leaving a copy at the U.S. Embassy for the American Congress. At the same time, we posted copies to American friends in Vienna and New York to send to the Voice of America, Radio Free Europe and BBC radio stations. If a document of this kind was not made known to the American government and the international mass media, it would remain only a cry in the wilderness, and we ourselves would very likely disappear without a trace.

We were not without hope that the Americans would hear us. Only a few months earlier, Republican Congressman Frank Wolf had visited Romania, and requested Pastor Vasile Taloş and I be invited to the reception for him at the American Embassy. He was there to investigate human rights and religious liberty in Romania.

Shortly after, Congressman Tony Hall, a Democrat from Ohio, visited our country. Congressman Hall has always been a spokesman for the oppressed, the poor and the defenseless, and they both wrote letters to Ceauşescu calling for an end to the persecution of Christians and comparing the Romanian Constitution, and his own comments on official visits in the U.S. to what was actually happening in Romania. Both of them mentioned my name in their letters.

To this day, we are grateful to these two distinguished and Godly members of the U.S. Congress for their courage. They called the dictator to account, on our behalf, for his arrogant abuse of power, at a time when we were still groaning under his iron rule and were unable to do so for ourselves.

Our petition was also mentioned by David Freudenburk, former American Ambassador to Romania, in his book: *An American Ambassador between the State Department and the Romanian Communist Dictatorship, 1981-1985.*

After sending off the petition copies to their destinations by the most reliable means, we felt rather like a company of gunners who, having put their rounds into the mortars and fired them at the objective, have to wait for the inevitable recoil. We did not have long to wait. Pastors who had signed the petition were quickly under investigation by the Securitate and called before the regional inspectors of the Department for Religious Denominations.

Each one was subjected to pressure and threats designed to make him remove his signature. A few them did so. I will never forget a phone call from a young pastor in Transylvania, a close personal friend. After leaving the Securitate building he went to his church office to think. He rang me from there. In a voice choked with tears he said to me: "Pete, they've broken me, they've broken me. I feel wretched. Pete, they've broken me. Please forgive me for betraying you. Please pray for me."

I replied: "My dear friend, I understand. I, too, have been subjected to these pressures for years and years and I know how hard it is to resist. Thank you for calling to tell me the truth. I want you to know that I understand you, and love you just as much as before, and that we are still friends. I won't tell anyone; you won't be discredited. I don't condemn you and I promise to pray for you. I'm convinced that the one who forgave Peter sees your wounded heart and your bitter tears and will forgive you!"

That same day, I was summoned to the Securitate. I was questioned by three officers in turn. When one got tired, he left the room, another would take his place. They wanted me to declare on paper that, as the first signatory of the Petition, I regretted my action and took back what it said. The first officer was angry and hard, the "bad cop" but the second was friendly and pleasant, the "good cop," saying reasonably: "Now, Pete, you know this would be the best thing to do. We have other people asking us to do this and we have no alternative. Let's just do what it takes to make things okay for us and for you, too. Come on, just write a coupld of sentences here, and sign them. After all, God knows what's in your heart."

I explained that I couldn't do as he suggested. First, I would be lying, and second place, it would show disrespect to the President of Romania, Nicolae Ceauşescu. After 66 pastors from different regions of the country had addressed the Head of State and had dutifully presented the serious concerns of the several thousand believers whom we represented, I could not abuse his intelligence by just sending a note saying: "Sorry, Mr. President, I lied to you; we are not really experiencing these hardships and problems."

The next officer, "Bad Cop II" came in and started shouting violently at me: "Who do you think you are, eh? Making a petition, collecting signatures, stirring people up against us? Do you think you're the center of the universe? Come on, answer! Put it down in black and white who encouraged you to put together that petition. Whose idea was it? I don't doubt that hostile elements from outside the country were involved--maybe from America – what do you think? Come on, speak up! Are you deaf?"

In that office I felt like Jesus before Pilate in the Praetorium and I decided to remain silent as he had done and let him defend me. Because I would not speak, my interrogator kept up a monologue, smoking cigarette after cigarette: "Why are you poking your nose into this business? You're only a wretched little Baptist pastor in the Haţeg valley. These are matters for your leaders in the Baptist Union to discuss with the Department for Religious Denominations in Bucharest. It is they who represent your denomination to the state – not you and this list of nobodies who signed the petition!"

At this I broke my silence to say politely: "Colonel, unfortunately they represent you to us rather than us to you."

"Do you mean that they are compromised because they cooperate with us? That you do not trust them? You should know that the true patriots in all the fourteen religious denominations in Romania cooperate with us."

He wanted to know how the petition had reached the U.S. Embassy, the American Congress and the Voice of America. I truthfully told him I did not know, as I had no idea how the papers were passed to the final recipients. Suddenly, there were screams nearby, as if someone was being beaten: "Arrgh! – stop hitting me, stop hitting me ... arrgh! they're killing me!!" I do not know whether it was a recording or whether someone was being tortured, but the intent was clear. My interrogator looked at me through his cigarette smoke and said: "That's what's in store for you, understand?" I silently prayed that if I was beaten, he would give me the power not to succumb and to be faithful to him to the end.

The cries from the neighboring room eventually stopped. My interrogator left me alone staring at that pad of blank paper. The "good cop" came back in. Seeing the paper still untouched, he said: "Pete, is it really so hard to write two lines? Come on, just write them so we can all go home, because I know you must be hungry, too."

This man was a colonel, and also a general in the Ministry of the Interior in Bucharest. Within the State Securitate, he dealt with the Department of Evangelical Religious Groups. He did not smoke, did not raise his voice and used politer language. He told me that he had dealt personally with Pastor Iosif Ţon and had been his shadow and that from now on he would be dealing with me as well. He seemed an intelligent man, so I tried to convey that we who signed the petition were not spoiling the image of Romania and her President, but rather, those who deceived President Ceauşescu by not reporting the truth. I told him that the seven unresolved points would be a continuing source of injustice within the country as well as a source of criticism from the American leadership and the Western media. I explained that my respect and loyalty to my colleagues would forbid any change on my part. As one of the writers and the first signer, any retraction on my part would have been like spitting in the face of every one of the 66 pastors who had signed after me. I would have to stand in front of a mirror, spit on myself and slap my own face, too.

After that interrogation, it was as described in Luke 4:13: "After the devil had tempted him in every way, he left him for a season."

Dissident Preaching

In Romania under communism, even my sermons made me into an enemy of the state. Several of my lessons were enough to constitute major offenses to the government, as indicated by the charges made against me in the thick file held by the Securitate, which I only later learned of.

The Miracle of History (Acts 4:32-7)

One theme which seriously disturbed the Communist authorities was about the early Christian church. According to Acts 4:32, "All who believed were one in heart and mind." For the first time in human history, a great mass of people, made up of several thousand extremely diverse individuals, became one in heart through a Person and a creed. They became not an organization as much as an organism. For the first time in history, a huge number of people were thinking, feeling, acting and speaking in harmony. After being cut to the heart by the Word of God, repenting and being baptized, they became members in the body of Christ – not members of an organization. In this living body, whose head is the eternally alive Christ, the members serve one another in love. None of them held his possessions as his own; everything was held in common (Acts 4:32). And not one of them was in want. Those who owned lands or houses sold them, and brought the money and laid it at the apostles' feet. Then the money was shared out according to each person's need (Acts 4:34-35).

The apostles did not institute agrarian reform or nationalise the houses of the rich and then start an ideological campaign to create the 'New Man'. Confiscation is never going transform his heart. But when the Holy Spirit changes a man's heart, he himself will freely give his house, his farm and all his material possessions on God's altar, to distribute them to those in need.

From then until the present day, this miracle of history has been repeated unceasingly throughout the world. Jesus Christ is the contemporary of every generation, the radical progressive of history and the 'most beloved leader' of nations, because millions of followers have given their lives for him or are ready to do so.

I do confess to having proclaimed from the pulpit that the idea of 'communism' is something stolen from the New Testament, and that the father of lies is essentially a counterfeiter, never giving us anything new, original or authentic but tricking people with cheap imitations of the real jewels. I was also unwise in saying that the concept of the 'New Man' was plagiarized from the Gospel of Jesus Christ, the only person who has ever shown – and is always showing – that a human being can be regenerated . "If someone is in Christ, he is a new creation." The new man in Christ is not just a new patch on an old garment, or a result of force, propaganda campaigns or re-education. Rather, he becomes a new creation by being born again (in Greek creation is κτίσις, ctisis).

One of the fundamental principles of Communist ethics and equity is the emergence of humanity so law-abiding and altruistic that "each will work according to his capacity and receive according to his needs" But how can this happen when, human beings do not change from an egotistical, greedy, dissatisfied and dishonest fallen nature?

Against the background of the cult of the personality of the dictator Nicolae Ceauşescu and the hosannas that 23 million Romanians were supposed to offer to 'the most beloved son of the people' on all occasions in the years 1974-1989, these were radical ideas indeed. For the Securitate officers charged with the surveillance of religious groups who listened to the tape of this sermon, their report to their superiors can be easily imagined.

God's Farmer (Matthew 13:24-30)

The farmer in the Lord Jesus Christ's parable has three things: his own land, good seed and a cunning enemy. In this case, my treason was in noting that the farmer owned his own land. The land belonged to the farmer, not to a collective farm or an Agro-Industrial complex. In Genesis, we are told that God gave the Garden of Eden to Man to work and take care of (Genesis 2:15). After the people of Israel crossed the Jordan and occupied Canaan, God gave each tribe and family its own allocation of land, as described in the Law of Moses, not a *kolkhoz* or even a *kibbutz*. In Luke 12:16, Jesus Christ begins another parable, "The land of a certain rich man produced a good harvest." It is only when land belongs to a man who has a direct interest in it that it will be farmed in such a way as to produce a really good harvest. I recounted my experience of the pioneering 'New Times' collective farm in Chelmac, my native village. After people's land was taken away and they were obliged to work collectively, the land became everyone's--and no one's. The result? Everyone tried to work as little as possible and to get (or steal) as much as possible.

The Rock of Ages (Isaiah 51:1; 26:4)

The Bible describes this in four key ways: The rock that you must look to in order to regain your lost identity – the rock from which you were hewn (Numbers 28:8). What aroused the wrath of the self-declared atheist (i.e. without God) authorities was that if you want to know your origin, to rediscover your lost identity, you must look to the Rock from which you were hewn, to the One who created you after his own image and likeness. "Those who look to him are radiant; their faces are never covered with shame" (Psalm 34:5).

The second point about the nature of the rock is that it is the rock you can speak to, the rock of inexhaustible resources, the rock that endures through the millennia (1 Corinthians 10:4). This is related to the third point, that this is the rock you can strike (Numbers 20:10-11). The two apparently similar experiences that Moses had in Exodus and Numbers teach us that after the Rock had been struck once by the rod of the Divine Law (Exodus 17:16) it does not need to be struck again; now all you need to do is to speak to it (Numbers 20:8).

Finally, this is the rock on which you can build (Matthew 7:24). That is the bedrock of our life, characterized by a pure life, a strong character, an eternal destiny (1 Corinthians 3:11).

This concept of a humanity which is carved from a divine origin, and which seeks to return to that origin through repentence and reform according to the divine word, is fundamentally at odds with the materialistic contention. The ape, that Darwin says was a distant ancestor of ours, does not instill us with a sense of our dignity and honor at all. But when you open the Bible and study the character of the unseen God, the Creator of the universe and your Creator too, you feel honored and a person of worth. Jesus said: "Anyone who has seen me has seen the Father." (John 14:9)

In confrontations with the exponents of materialist atheist ideology, I was accused of brainwashing young people, through my sermons. I answered my accusers that Gospel teaching does not devalue people as animals but rather ennobles them by giving them back a sense of their birthright as the most important beings in all of creation and children of the Lord of the Universe. What destroys human dignity is the falsehood that we are evolved animals, and if we believe that we are animals, we may end up behaving like them. This philosophy of despair makes life wretched and death dreadful. That is what makes youth behave in wild and hopeless ways. The distinction between human and animal is that an animal is driven by instinct, but a human being seeks an ideal.

The stirring song,"God Exists!" would be sung after one of these sermons. These magnificent verses were written by Ioanid Costache, a true poet of the ages for Romanian evangelicals.

We are no dream, no random atoms fleeing
No specks of dust tossed in eternal war
An all-creating Mind gave us our being
Boundless and vast, all knowing and all seeing
Our God is real, He lives for evermore!

We are no soulless, spark-less beasts of burden
By goads of instinct driven on before
We have a spirit, and we live in freedom
He's given us a heart that beats for heaven
Our God is real, He lives for evermore!

I can still see before me the shining faces of the people, young and old, who squeezed onto the benches of that church building on the edge of the town, or stood for lack of space. Their eyes are full of tears and light from partaking in the resurrection of Jesus Christ. Jubilantly, they sing the final verse:

We are not lost – what joy it is to prove
The greatest truth revealed to you and me
Jesus in us – the Light of Life and Love
Even in death we'll take our flight above
Our God is real and evermore will be!

This song was the true revolutionary song, especially for young people in a period when the steamroller of atheist propaganda was 'leveling' people's consciousness into required uniformity of thought. Such inspirational words created problems for those responsible for educating the younger generation: the Department for Religious Denominations and the activists of the Romanian Communist Party.

Windows in Heaven (2 Kings 7:1-20)

This was one of the sermons that increased the hostility of the Communist authorities in Timişoara against me. In this talk, I described a window. A window gives a view of what lies beyond it. If a house had no windows, those inside would be living in darkness and would have no perspective. The vastness of the heavens and the light of all the heavenly bodies and billions of stars tell us that the universe is not an empty house. The lights are on. "Someone is at home!" (Psalm 19:1).

In the time of King Joram, God turned his face away from the ten tribes of Israel. The nation no longer had 'windows'. Before the people of Israel entered Canaan, God said to them, in the final book of the Law: "The heavens will be like brass above your head and the earth will be lead." A nation that turns away from God and lives in immorality, idolatry and wrongdoing is a nation without vision. Without the viewpoint of heaven, everything becomes gloomy and dark.

The expression "the officer on whose arm the king was leaning" is a figure of speech for the commander of the King of Israel's bodyguard. We know that "the mouth of the sinner speaks truth," and so now, this head of the king's secret services recognized that the country was in crisis. But even in this situation he defied God by saying: "Even if God were to make windows in heaven ..." Elisha, the man of God, had announced some good news: "About this time tomorrow a seah of flour will sell for a shekel and two seahs of barley for a shekel at the gate of Samaria" (2 Kings 7:1). The only food that could still be bought at the food stores of Samaria was donkey's heads and pigeon droppings. "In a nation in which the Living God is despised, the head of a jackass becomes highly valued," I said, referring obliquely to the Nicolae Ceauşescu, head of Romania, "The food on sale in the markets of

Samaria then could be the equivalent of the scarcity in the stores of Romania today. This is what a nation looks like when it is being punished by God." In Scripture, the well-being and prosperity of a nation are always linked to the attitude of that people towards God.

Several brothers came in fear and said: "Brother Pete, I was afraid they'd come and arrest you during your sermon." "Brother Pete, stop being so direct and hard-hitting in your sermons," said another. I told the brothers then, and I still say now, that I am called by God to proclaim the message of the Gospel. I must apply it to the needs and aspirations of my generation and relate it to the social and cultural context in which we live. I refuse to preach a gospel that is archaic and out of date and relates only to the Middle Ages. I believe that the Gospel of Jesus Christ has the same power today as it has always had, but that it needs to be understood in terms of the culture and mentality of the times in which we are living in order for it to be relevant.

International Friendships

Another of my transgressions concerned relationships with non-Romanians. Relations with foreigners – especially people from the U.S. and Western Europe – were one of the major nightmares of all the Communist regimes in Eastern Europe. Ceaușescu and the Bucharest government were no exception. They passed all kinds of laws and government decrees and issued Ministry of Interior directives with the aim of laying down regulations and imposing drastic penalties to isolate people from those of other nations.

In principle, Romanian citizens were not allowed to associate with foreigners. If such contacts were unavoidable in the factory or institution where you worked because of the nature of your job, they were constantly monitored by the Securitate agent responsible for that enterprise. If you wanted to have a meeting with a foreigner, you had to speak to the Securitate officer beforehand to

obtain his approval and, afterwards, you had to give him a
'protocol note' (an account of the meeting).

Foreign citizens were not allowed to stay as guests in the
homes of Romanians unless they were blood relatives (parents,
brothers or sisters). They were required to stay at hotels. There
were at least two reasons for this ruling: the need for the hard
currency possessed by those capitalists and to make the
surveillance easier. It was easier to listen to conversations that took
place in hotel rooms and on hotel phones, and when the guests left
the hotel one or two human shadows would follow them
everywhere they went.

Things became more complicated where religious groups were
concerned. The official contacts made by the state-approved
leaders of these denominations were closely monitored by the
Department for Religious Denominations and by the branch of the
Ministry of the Interior that carried out surveillance of religious
groups. The hardest people to monitor were strangers who made
unannounced visits to pastors or members of local churches. Such
visits were usually made to believers in the evangelical Protestant
churches – Baptists, Pentecostals, Brethren – or to some Roman
Catholic priests or priests in the Lord's Army evangelical
movement within the Orthodox church.

These 'foreign tourists' were more accurately 'God's
smugglers' who came as tourists to bring Bibles and Christian
literature to Romania – those brave missionaries from Open Doors,
the Light in the East organization, Eastern Europe Bible Mission
and Operation Mobilisation – avoided staying in hotels. They
generally came to Romania officially on vacations with their
family or friends, towing large camping trailers. They had to stay
at an authorized campsite, but it was easier to disappear from there
than from a hotel, to make contact with the person whose name
and address they had been given by their host organization.

These were very special vehicles equipped with partitions special hiding places that could hold thousands of Bible and Christian books. For those in America who can freely buy a Bible in any bookstore, this secrecy may seem extreme. However, the one question that a foreign person was asked upon entering Romania was: "Do you have any arms, drugs, pornographic materials or Bibles?" If carrying Bibles, the carriers were arrested or expelled and the Bibles were pulped and turned into toilet paper.

For us, receiving such a consignment was a dangerous ooperation that would take place at night, out in the open country or in a brother's yard. I was amazed when I saw how ingeniously and neatly these special vehicles had been adapted, and was struck by the love and spirit of sacrifice of these tremendous people of God. As a result of their sacrificial service, I was able to provide Bibles and Christian works to the people of my church, and, in particular, to new converts, including members of the Communist Party who had repented and received Jesus Christ into their lives. The visitors helped me to replenish both the smaller stash in the storage box of my sofa and the larger supply secretly kept in a church member's cellar.

Possession of such contraband would have condemned the citizen to years of imprisonment. But one incident in particular demonstrated both the danger and the comic side of the eventful history of those years.

One Sunday in June of 1979, my former classmate, Iosif Ştefănuţ, and his wife and children had arrived to spend a week's holiday with us in Haţeg. That Sunday, we had preached together at three churches, as well as conducting a wedding service. Despite our busy day, at midnight we had not yet gone to bed, laughing over recollections of our days at college together.

A soft knock at the door surprised us. I opened it to a tall, spare, bearded man of about 50 and a long haired woman who were dressed as tourists. In French, they asked if this was where

Pastor Peter Dugulescu lived. I said that it was and invited them in and asked them in. They intoduced themselves, Mr. and Mrs. Jean Pierre Pont, and told me that they were voluntary workers with Operation Mobilisation and had were spending their vacation bringing Bibles to Romania. They were from the French-speaking part of Switzerland and had been given my address by the organizers in Vienna, who stressed that it must not be discovered if searched by the border guards. Their camping trailer and their children were back at their campsite in Simeria but under cover of darkness, they had transferred a large number of Bibles, New Testaments, Romanian language Christian books and medical supplies to the trunk and back seat of their car. They had parked their car in the main parking lot in the center of Hațeg which was patroled by the militia. They wanted us to figure out how to retrieve the car and materials.

After feeding them, we decided they would return to their car, and Ștefi and I would then drive past the parking lot and they would drive out and follow me. I described the color and tag number of my car. When they got back to the parking lot, the militiaman and the night watchman were still there. They asked some questions in Romanian, but the Swiss couple replied in French and drove away. We were afraid that the militiaman would go and tell his commanding officer, and we would be trailed. The Ponts caught up with us and followed us. We drove up and down the hills around Hațeg and only when we were a good distance from the town, I turned onto an unpaved county road and switched off my lights. They did the same. After about 3 kilometers of driving in the dark, we stopped, and without even a flashlight, we began transferring the contraband books into my Dacia station wagon.

They then drove back, with no lights on until after they reached the main road. After setting them off towards Simeria, we left too, but not before praying. The car was chock-full and so were our hearts – full of fear and apprehension. We switched our lights back on when we came to the main road and headed back to Hațeg.

We knew we couldn't bring all this to my apartment, so we decided, "We'll go to Brother George's. He's got a big house with a cellar and yard." George was a close friend and we could wake him up, however late it was.

We rang the bell, but no one answered. It was now 2 a.m. Ştefi wouldn't give up: "Perhaps they're asleep – let's ring again!"

We rang again, but in vain. "Bang on the window!"

We knocked, but with no result; they were all away.

The town was wrapped in deep darkness and not a person or vehicle moved in the streets. We knew that any car that appeared on that isolated street at that late hour, we knew that it would be the Securitate looking for us. Every second that we stood at that locked door seemed to last a lifetime. Suddenly I remembered something; somewhere in the fence, beside the door, there was a hole that George's family used to hide the gate key. I was overjoyed when I located the hole, and found the key. But this joy was to be short-lived. Less than two minutes after we had opened the gate, driven into the yard, and turned off the engine, locking the gate, a car drove up and parked directly outside the house. Our hearts missed a beat. We tiptoed to the gate. I peered out through a hole in the fence and froze. The care was a white Dacia with a three-digit registration number like those belonging to Party members and the Securitate. I knew that number. It was the one that pursued me in my sleep in nightmares. It was the car of the Securitate chief.

Ominously, the car was parked with its lights on but the engine turned off. There were two men in the front. They must have followed us and wanted to pounce on us with the evidence in the yard – the car and its contents. We took turns looking through the hole in the fence but the two did not move. We could see them talking to each other and they appeared to be using some kind of transceiver.

Peter Dugulescu

We tiptoed behind the house to decide what was best to do. The key didn't fit the house locks, so we couldn't go inside. I whispered: "We must have been followed right from the beginning. They know we are stuck here with the car and the packages and they're just biding their time, waiting for us to make a move. It looks as if there's no way out. We're already in their hands."

"What are we going to do?" asked Ştefi.

"I'm going to go and give myself up," I said.

"What, are you crazy? Let's wait a bit longer."

"I can't bear this tension. Don't you see? There's no other explanation! It's perfectly clear they're letting us stew in our own juice. I can't believe that my interrogator for years has caught me with a car loaded with Bibles." I expected the Securitate chief to stroll up to my car any minute, greeting us sarcastically: "Good evening, Pete, what brings you here at this late hour? And who is your companion? Whatever could that be in your car? May I see? Very good, thanks. And now, we'll just escort you to the militia headquarters!" I saw myself in one room and my companion in another answering questions, while our wives waited unknowing back at home.

It may have been ten or twelve minutes that the two men kept their vigil in front of the house, but it seemed like eternity to me. I said, "I'm going to give myself up... I'll say: "Commandant, I am Pastor Dugulescu and this is Pastor Ştefănuţ. Yes, sir, we have Bibles in our car and we are fully responsible, put us in prison!" I was still saying this, when I suddenly heard the car door open. "It's obvious that their patience has run out too and that they have finally decided to come and get us," I said, steeling myself for the inevitable.

The passenger got out and said to the driver, who had just started the engine: "Okay then, all the best, call me tomorrow!" He then began walking down the street, and I suddenly realized that he was drunk. He stopped beside the gate where we were hiding, and we heard him urinating. He then went to the house next door, muttering something to himself, and let himself in.

Only the next day, did I find out from George that a young woman lived there, to whom this character sometimes paid nocturnal visits.

Stefi and I waited silently in the yard for another half hour, so as to be sure that the visitor was going to be staying for a while. We left the car in George's yard and tiptoed home. It was 3 a.m. by the time we returned, and our wives were frightened, unable to sleep. When we came in, my wife said fearfully: "They caught you, didn't they?"

"It was a close call," I said "we almost caught them!" Suddenly, we dissolved in laughter. The nightmare became a comedy, in retrospect. "What would have happened if went out to give yourself up? I bet they would have gotten scared and run away. They were there on different business" said Ştefi. The hypothetical scenarios we constructed relieved the nervous tension we experienced earlier. There was no time to sleep because we had to unload the car at daybreak before the workers arrived to start their jobs in George's workshop. We found the key, opened up the cellar, and hid everything there. When George's family came home, I told them our adventures, which they thought extremely funny. Brother George's cellar became our secret storehouse for Bibles and Christian literature from then on.

However, not long after this event, Constantin Sfatcu, an engineer who was a member of the Baptist Church in Iaşi, was arrested transporting Bibles in his car, and was beaten and subjected to abuse so great at his trial in Bucharest, I did not recognize him. When Costică, handcuffed and dressed in prison

Peter Dugulescu

clothes, was brought into the dock, he had lost weight and aged greatly in the few months since his arrest.

His lawyer told the judges that the Bible was the fundamental text of Christians, especially evangelicals, that its teaching was beneficial for individuals, families and society, and that if people followed its teachings there would be fewer murders, rapes and divorces and less crime in general. The lawyer acted courageously. He even asked rhetorically why foreigners entering Romania were asked at the border whether they were bringing arms, Bibles, drugs or pornography. "Why was the Bible forbidden and placed on the same level as drugs, arms and pornography?" He queried, exposing the ultimate absurdity of the laws.

But in the reply of the prosecution, the full picture of the state's mindset was tellingly revealed.

"It is a well-known fact that the Bible is a weapon," the state prosecutor said. "Citizen Constantin Sfatcu of Iaşi was stopped with this weapon on him, but without a firearms certificate.

"In conclusion," he asserted, "on the basis of the law, I demand that Citizen Constantin Sfatcu be found guilty!" And, indeed, Brother Constantin was found guilty.

To a country that reviles and denies God, the words that testify to him are a weapon. They correctly see that this weapon is more powerful than bullets and blades. The revolution that it creates in the hearts of mankind is more powerful than all the reigns of terror of all the ages. Brother Constantin was made to suffer for smuggling in the weapons that would liberate imprisoned souls and overturn false dominions.

Entertaining Strangers

It was also well known that no church in the whole of Hunedoara County was so frequently visited by foreigners as the tiny church on the edge of Haţeg. Pastor Guy Davidson from Arizona preached there, as did the Canadian evangelist Benny Moore. A team led by the Kentucky Senator Gene Huff came in 1984, including a woman on President Ronald Reagan's staff and two well-known Pastors, Don Kayer and Jerry Back. Such visitors were even officially welcomed at the Town Hall by my old friends, the executive secretary of the County Council and the Mayor and Deputy Mayor of Haţeg. The American delegation took the opportunity to speak appreciatively of me and to politely ask the local authorities to stop persecuting me and my family.

At that very moment of the reception at the Town Hall, December 15, 1984, my wife was in labor in the hospital, a very painful and prolonged labor to bring our fourth child, into the world. During service at the church that evening, the distinguished American lady who was an advisor to President Reagan told how she had become a Christian and prayed specifically for my wife and the child who was about to be born. Our daughter, Eunice did not actually arrive until the next morning, Sunday, December 16, 1984.

Since 1981, when Congressman Frank Wolf visited Romania, I was invited every year to the reception that was held on America's Independence Day in the extensive gardens of the U.S. ambassador's residence in Bucharest.

Since the Secret Police read all my correspondence, they always knew of any invitations I received. They would always to their headquarters to persuade me not to attend. I could not comply, I told them. Such an invitation was a great honor for my family, and Ligia, our first child, had been born on July 4. I explained to my 'guardian angels' that there was no finer gift I could give my daughter on her birthday. Not only were we moved by the sight of the American Marine Guards, reverently bearing the Stars and Stripes past the hundreds of guests pledging allegiance to the flag, but best of all to the children were the well-stocked buffet tables laid out in that splendid garden. There they could consume McDonalds, pizza and hot dogs--as they wanted--and drink lots of Coca Cola – all for free. At that time none of these American foods and drinks had yet appeared in Romania.

"Pastor, you've sold yourself to the Americans for a sandwich and a glass of Coca Cola!" one Securitate officer said with irritation.

"Colonel, I want to be honest with you," I replied to this zealous patriot. "I have a great admiration for the American people and their history. That great nation is 'a nation of blessing,' to use a Biblical expression, and it owes its power, prosperity and greatness to its faith in God. You yourself know that their dollars – which we so much need – bear the inscription: 'In God We Trust'."

"Come off it, be serious, are the Americans really that religious?" he scoffed. "But what about their drug addicts, the murders in America – come on, tell me, are those people Christians too?"

"Colonel, that's the other side of the coin, and the other side of America that has alienated itself from the Bible and from God. But the Founding Fathers of America established it as a God-fearing nation that they called 'a nation under God's authority'."

Changing the subject, he demanded, "Tell me what information the Americans want from you as the price tag for being invited to these receptions. If you are a real repenter, who never lies, tell me what information Ambassador David Freudenburk asked you for."

"Ambassador Freudenburk has never asked me for any information, Colonel. And, what strategic information could a poor Baptist pastor in the Hațeg Valley have that the Americans would want? I don't even know how many cows died this year on the Hațeg collective farm from lack of fodder."

"You're playing innocent, pastor. Cows are not the only things that there are in this area. There are also several rocket bases in the forests near Hațeg" he said, referring to the bases relocated after General Mihai Pacepa, Ceaușescu's right-hand man defected to America in 1978. "Everyone knows this, and I think you know it as well."

"Colonel, if the Americans are interested in our military bases, their spy satellites can detect them," I said. "They don't need information from me – and I have none to given them."

Ambassador David Freudenburk and his wife, Betty, were godly people, who lived by the Bible and prayed for Romania. In their home state of North Carolina, they belonged to the Southern Baptist Convention. They were very concerned for my family's safety, and every so often, they would send a few Embassy staff members to visit our home and see if everything was okay. He even presented me with an English Bible inscribed with a personal dedication.

In the 1980s, those invited guests were normally drawn from the upper echelons of the Communist Party. You can imagine how they felt about seeing me and other persecuted pastors at such an event! The ambassador must have been aware of their thoughts. At one Christmas reception at the Ambassador's residence, he was circulating among the guests, shaking hands. As he gripped mine, he looked into my eyes and leaned forward to whisper in my ear: "Peter, I admire your courage and I am praying for you. God bless you!" His words encouraged and comforted me.

The ambassador's faith did not escape the notice of the securitate: "This Ambassador who pokes his nose into everything and wants to know about everything that happens in Romania – is he a repenter like you?"

"Yes, he is a Baptist repenter like me," I replied.

"Then why does he keep lying in his reports to his chiefs in the State Department, casting Romania in a negative light and causing us problems? Why is he such a liar, if he is a repenter?"

"Colonel, I have not read a single one of the reports the Ambassador has sent to Washington; you must realise that I have no access to them. But I can assure you that a man of David Freudenburk's character is incapable of lying."

In his book written years later, David Freudenburk described his warnings to President Ronald Reagan and others that Nicolae Ceauşescu's foreign policy was only a pretense, a ploy. While proclaiming independence of the Russians, he was, in fact, very close to them. He was ruling his own people as an unscrupulous dictator.

Later, in the summer of 1986, when a plot was hatched to discredit me on trumped up charges of fraud, a U.S. Embassy Diplomatic car would be parked in front of the courthouse in Hunedoara for every session. That two members of the U.S. ambassador's staff traveled almost 500 kilometers to observe the trial did not escape the Romanian forces. I understood then how God can make use of politicians and men of high rank for the good of his people.

Turning Stones into Bread

One Monday morning in February, 1985, the telephone rang. It was Major P. I., the Hațeg Securitate chief who ordered me to the Securitate headquarters immediately. Three other people were there when I arrived: Colonel Z.A., a colonel from Deva, and Captain S. from the agency responsible for religious denominations. They offered me coffee and a glass of mineral water, then one of them asked me how my Mercedes was running.

About six months earlier, Pastor Guy Davidson had sent me $7,500 so that I could buy an ARO (a Romanian jeep). I bought the jeep, but then sold it to a sheep farmer near Hațeg replaced it with a 20 year old diesel Mercedes in Bucharest. A Romanian diplomat just returned from a posting in Berne, Switzerland sold me the car, which, though fairly old, had been recently overhauled. It was quieter, stronger and more comfortable than an ARO and far more economical to run. I never imagined that this car would provoke so much envy and hatred against me from total strangers, and most importantly, from my 'guardian angels.'

My first clue should have been these questions. In sarcastic tone, Captain S. asked me: "Mr. Dugulescu, if I repent and become a Baptist pastor, will you arrange for the Americans to send me a Mercedes too?"

Replying that I had not repented for cars, but in order to do the will of God, I told him that when we seek first the Heavenly Father and his Kingdom, all these things are given to us in addition. I concluded by matching his humorous supposition by saying: "Repent, begin serving the Gospel and then come to me and we'll talk some more; I will put you in touch with the Americans."

Colonel Z.A. from Bucharest, who held the post of General and was the State Securitate overseer for all the religious denominations in Romania, changed the tone of the meeting at this point: "Let's stop joking! We have something more serious to discuss. Reverend Dugulescu, the country needs you and your services."

"I love my country and I try to serve her as well as I can."

"Up to now you have not given much proof of it." He said, getting down to their real purpose. "We have had enough of words. It is time to move on to deeds. We have called you here today because we want a clear reply from you. We want to use you in connection with Romania's foreign relations and particularly in relations with the USA. We want to send you on a special secret training course. After that we will ensure that you are elected as President or General Secretary of the Romanian Baptists.

"You are young, you speak English, you are one of the best-known Baptist pastors in Romania. No one will guess that you are working for us. We can assure you of our discretion. You will have a diplomatic passport and a secret salary and you will go on secret missions that you will discuss with no one, not even your wife. Do you understand?

"For the image of Romania and of comrade Nicolae Ceauşescu, we need a man like you. For your country, this will be all gain. The same goes for the Baptist Union and your family, and even the church you pastor here in Haţeg. We know that you have been struggling for 10 years to get building authorization for a new building. I can assure you that it will be in your hands next week!"

I have to admit that for a split second, this sounded extremely attractive. I teetered; there were so many reasons to accept the proposal. All these years I had felt worse about the suffering of my wife and children than about my own. It was they who had paid the price for my decision to serve the Gospel. I remembered them frightened and scared on Palm Sunday in 1977 huddled in on corner of the living room, ordered not to move a muscle, watching the five Securitate officers turn our apartment inside out searching for Bibles.

I heard my wife's words: "If they kill you, I'll have to bring up these four children on my own." I heard the children saying: "Daddy, we've had enough, we're afraid for you. Why don't you want us to go to America as so many other people have done?" I remembered my begging them: "Don't break my heart! I know God wants me to serve him here in Romania."

And now I was being offered a chance to work in Romania without any more threat. For a moment I was even tempted to believe that it was God who was opening a special opportunity for me. Flitting through my mind came rationalizations: I could do it for the love of my family; I would secretly be a kind of Joseph in Egypt or a Daniel at King Nebuchadnezzar's court, who sought the good of his people and his brothers. I thought I could infiltrate them, the way they infiltrated the churches.

My lengthy silence apparently gave them hope. "Come on, Pete," said the one from Deva, "What the hell, be a man and don't put yourself through all this heart-searching. Orthodox priests work for us, and so do Pentecostals and even your leaders in Bucharest. It's no sin to serve your country. Doesn't the Bible say in Romans 13 that you should be subject to the authorities?"

Words cannot capture the spiritual battle that was raging in my soul. Again, the image of Judas the traitor appeared before my eyes, trying to repair up for his mistake and give the silver coins back only to have Jesus' enemies laugh in his face, saying: "What do we care? That's your business!"

I remembered one pastor, rumored to have helped the Securitate track down the route for Bibles brought into the country, who later was found dead, under mysterious circumstances, believed to be liquidated. These images and suggestions played through my mind in rapid succession.

All at once, I woke up, as if from a dream and I said to the four men: "I cannot! As a citizen of this country and as a Baptist pastor, I will serve my country and her good in any way I can, but I cannot agree to underground activities and a double identity. I simply cannot. It is against my conscience."

"You cannot?" said the colonel from Deva, enraged. "We'll destroy you!"

"You won't be able to," I stated. "You have no way of doing so."

"You'll see. First we are going to destroy the good reputation you have and then we'll destroy you physically as well. You'll see! How would the public like to know that six months ago you received the sum of $7,500 from the USA to give to the poor and you bought yourself a car to drive around in?"

"If you wish, I'll go home and bring you Pastor Guy Davidson's letter in which he says perfectly clearly that the money sent was to cover the cost of the car I bought!"

"You don't need to bring us any letters. You'll be disgraced as a cheat, a charlatan. We will expose you in the media, and you won't have any voice. And we've got some other surprises lined up for you, too. You better think again before you make up your mind. We'll give you until tomorrow, how about that?"

"I don't need any thinking time. I've thought already. I cannot!"

"Shame on you! You're young and have four children!" said the colonel from Deva. "Your life is in our hands and we are trying to help you."

"My life is in God's hands and he will help me!"

"Very well, Reverend, we'll see what happens."

This discussion had continued for four hours. I stepped outside, into a hard frost, but, instead of going home, I went to the apartment of my friend and brother in the Lord, Mihai Sârbu, who was the head of a meteorological station near Hațeg and was a deacon in the church. I gave him a detailed description of the meeting. Then, we knelt and both prayed, and encouraged ourselves by reading Acts 4:29-30 "Now, Lord, consider their threats and enable your servants to speak your word with great boldness. Stretch out your hand to heal and perform miraculous deeds and wonders through the name of your holy servant Jesus."

Indicted

The agents of darkness kept their word and proceeded with a full-scale assault to destroy my reputation.

In the beginning of June, 1985, I found a letter in my mailbox from the court in Hunedoara. When I opened the envelope, I almost had a heart attack. It was an attorney's letter giving notice of an action being initiated against me by the sheep farmer to whom I had sold my ARO off road vehicle one year and one month earlier. The complaint drawn up against me by the Party Secretary of the Hunedoara County Bar Association alleged that in May 1984, I had collected from him the price of two AROs on the understanding that I would deliver the second one by Christmas 1984. I was quoted in the legal document as saying that the repenters in America had enough money to buy me two cars because they were very rich. Since a year had gone by, and I had not kept my word, I was now summoned to attend court on June 15, 1985 and required to produce either the car (the second ARO) or its value in cash to the sheep farmer I had deceived.

I showed my wife and children this document, and they couldn't believe it. That Friday evening, it was a struggle for me to go into the pulpit and gather my thoughts for the sermon.

Immediately after church I got hold my good Brother Gheorghe Simedroni who stored our secret supply of Bibles and Christian literature in his cellar, and we went together to Tuştea to see the sheep farmer who named as the complainant. He was surprised to see us, and asked us why we had come. I asked him straight out what he had against me. He said he had nothing against me, as the car he had bought from me was going well and he was very pleased with it.

"They why have you taken out an action against me? We've met in town many times. Why didn't you say anything to me then?"

At this, the man looked at me in surprise and said emphatically: "Sir, I haven't taken out an action against you, I don't have any claim against you, but wait a minute, now it's all coming together ... Ah, that was why they summoned me to the Militia station two weeks ago."

"Who did?" I asked.

"The station chief called me there because a gentleman had come from Deva. He was in civilian clothes but he said he was a captain in the Securitate and he asked me to sign a document in connection with you."

"And what did it say in that document?" I asked.

"I don't know, he never let me read it, but he said you were selling Persian carpets and changing dollars on the black market and that you were a dangerous man. At first I refused to sign it, but he told me that if I was obstinate he'd throw me into prison, because they've got a hold on me in connection with some collective farm business. I've been in prison once already because of some wool and cheese that went missing from the stores and I don't want to end up there again. I signed that document out of fear, but I haven't taken out an action against you and I'm not even going to go to court!"

"But you must come and tell the truth. You've signed on for this and you can't pull out now!"

"I've already told you that I'm not going to show up because I don't want to do you any harm. You behaved fairly towards me and I don't have anything against you."

"You've already done me harm by signing that document, and if you don't come and tell the truth you will be doing me even more harm. Look, this document that I've been sent telling me to attend court on June 15 is drawn up by your attorney. Tell me, have you engaged an attorney?"

"I'm not crazy enough to do anything of the kind. I don't even know who this person is who has signed here as my attorney. He's never spoken to me. This is his business, not mine!"

It was in vain that I persisted, telling him that it was now our business and that he had to come and tell the truth. I was unable to persuade him.

The next day, the next assault was launched. The deacons, committee members and a large number of the 300 members of the church I pastored all found anonymous letters in their mailboxes. Some were in verse and others in prose. They read like this:

Green leaf, nothing but trash
Dugulescu is with us
Green leaf, green jasper
He's just swindled a poor sheep farmer

They also alleged that I was an American spy (a CIA agent) receiving a fat dollar paycheck from the American Embassy, and that I stole the brothers' money from the church collection and spent it on debauchery with girls in various hotels.

These letters arrived in my mailbox too. At first my wife did not want to show them to knowing they would make me angry. They had evidently been handwritten in an office in which people had smoked a lot, because they all reeked of cigarette smoke.

Simultaneously, the Securitate informers in the church (there were even some on the church committee) were instructed to spread similar rumors among the church members. Out of respect for the church of Christ to which they belonged, at least nominally, I am not going to give their names. Some of the immature believers and those who were new in the faith were inclined to give credence to these rumors and discuss them with others. In town or at church, I would feel a coldness from some; it hurt me greatly to know that my own brothers been poisoned by doubts and rumors concocted in the laboratories of the State Securitate Disinformation Service.

The next days, weeks and months were terrible for our family. Every day more and more brothers, including pastors and leaders in different regions of the country, contacted me saying they had received these strange letters. I began to lose my peace and to become a nervous wreck. I could not sleep at night. I had begun to experience the first symptoms of high blood pressure and nervous tension. I would wake up suddenly, terrified, with my fingers and toes itching violently. To my wife, to the brothers and to those who did not waver in their attitude of love and trust towards me, I kept saying that I ought to be doing something to defend myself and the Gospel, that I ought to demonstrate the falsity of what was being alleged, but I had no way of doing so.

And yet God did encourage me. Many of the pastors in the country, who knew me well and knew that I was the victim of a Securitate plot, exhorted their churches to pray for me.

Before the first hearing at the court I was visited by the vice-consul and the political counsellor of the U.S. Embassy in Bucharest. They told me that they had been sent by Ambassador David Freudenburk, who sent me a leather-bound English Bible with a personal dedication, and a message: that the Ambassador and his wife Betty were concerned for my safety and that of my family and were praying for me. This cheered and strengthened me.

And so, each Thursday morning that the case of the 'Charlatan Pastor' was heared in the court in Hunedoara, a U.S. Embassy car would park in front of the Courthouse and two members of the embassy staff would attend the hearings and take notes. This absolutely infuriated the Securitate. Usually, courtroom was packed with people from all over Hunedoara County and particularly from the Hațeg area. My case had become famous. From the second week onwards, the Voice of America and Radio Free Europe ran reports on my trial.

God provided me with a lawyer who was equal to the task: Nelu Prodan from Bucharest, whose wife Virginia was also a practising lawyer. The Prodans were about 35 years old and had been baptized only the week before at Golgotha Church in Bucharest! Nelu Prodan affected the moustache, hat and umbrella of a renowned Romanian intellectual and humorous playwright, Caragiale, and echoed this in his style of pleading, which invoked the famous lawyers of the inter-war years. For instance, instead of addressing the judge according to the Communist formula of "Comrade President of the Court," he would say, "Your Honor."

Unfortunately, he was rarely permitted to speak, and then, only very briefly. The lawyer appointed by the Securitate not only could speak for as long as he wanted but he was also allowed to insult me: "Comrade President and honorable members of the court, my client believed that if this man was the repenters' minister, he must be an honorable man, and so he paid him money in advance without anything in writing, but he didn't know that this man was a thief and charlatan of a preacher!"

Silent and humiliated in front of an overflowing courtroom I was unable to defend myself. I attempted to do so on two occasions, but was not permitted. I prayed silently and fought back tears. "Is God blind and deaf?" I wondered. "Why doesn't he do something to put a stop to this grotesque performance with me in the role of a fraudster?" And then the Holy Spirit reminded me of the testimony of Traian Dorz, who had visited me secretly by night some months earlier to ask for some packages of Bibles and Christian literature.

Traian Dorz was one of the most famous Christian poets in Romania and one of the most highly respected leaders of the Lord's Army, the evangelical movement within the Orthodox church. He was 72 years old and dragged a crippled leg behind him, the reminder of the beatings and torture he had experienced in prison.

"I returned home to Livada Beiușului after seventeen years in prison. The Collective had been set up during my absence and had taken everything we had. My wife worked on the Collective and all we had left in our byre was one old nanny-goat. We decided to sell the goat, as we had nothing left to eat. I started taking her to the livestock market in Beiuș every Saturday. I was always the last to leave. I couldn't sell her. She was old and thin and no one was interested."

"Some of the enemies who had handed me over to the Securitate used to walk past me, turn their heads, and laugh among themselves: "Look who's here ... Here he is in the market again with his old nanny-goat!" As they passed, poking fun at me and laughing at me, I would stand there beside the goat tethered to

*the fence and pray: "Humble me Lord, that's what I deserve.
Humble me Lord, may you alone be exalted. Humble me Lord."*

After 17 years of his life in prison for the Lord, being starved, beaten and tortured, his vines and land confiscated by the Collective, only an old nanny-goat that nobody wants, his enemies mocking him cruelly, he could still pray: "Humble me Lord, that's what I deserve. May you alone be exalted!" I marvelled at Brother Traian Dorz as one might look at a saint when he shared this, not believing that I could ever have had that heart.

But now, remembering that moment, the Holy Spirit helped me to pray the same prayer: "Humble me Lord, that is fitting for me. May you alone be exalted. Crush me Lord, humble me Lord."

The trial was prolonged for over two months, right until the end of August. For several days, I immersed myself in prayer and relection at Hotel Scorilo in Poiana Mărului. Fighting against my own feelings of discouragement, I tried to work out what my enemies' next move would be. The words of that colonel from Deva kept ringing in my ears: "We're going to destroy you, do you understand?" I suspected that what would follow was my physical destruction.

At that time I was inspired to write several poems to the glory of God. Two of them, *The Search* and *To My Enemies*, define most accurately my state of mind at that time.

The Search

*I seek for you among the stars -
Galaxies whispering to my mind
That you are higher than them by far
You are the One I want to find*

*I wish that you could weigh my sorrows
Or count them - they're like grains of sand*

I have no power to face tomorrow
I'm drowning, out of sight of land

O Eli, Lama, Sabachthani
I seek for you 'twixt earth and sky
Look, Lord, and see my foes around me
Digging a pit that I may die!

I asked and could not see your face
But heard your answer when it came
"I'll rescue you from this disgrace
For Jesus is my holy name!"

I've conquered by the Resurrection
I've climbed above the Milky Way
But here I live in sad dejection -
Don't seek me from so far away!

I wrote these verses sitting on the balcony of my hotel room, with the vista of the hills, the sky and a beautiful sunrise spread out before me. I poured my heart out to God in verse and when I finished the final stanza, tears washed my cheeks. Then, unmistakeably, I felt God's hand comforting me. Then, I felt a powerful inner conviction that I must address a poem to those who hated me so much and wanted to destroy me. Thus was born the poem *To My Enemies*. The second to the last stanza, I stopped, afraid to write down what the Holy Spirit was saying to me:

"Assassinate me if you do
I'd still have not one curse for you!
Dying, I'd even bless you too
For Someone lives to lead me through...
But you?"

I tried to fight this, afraid of what it meant. I said to myself that it would be better not to accept the thought of something like that being possible, not to even mention anything like that.

But I could not prevail against the insistent voice of the Holy Spirit. I decided to let the inspiration flow through my troubled mind unhindered. Here is the poem that resulted. It differs from all the others in the volume *Enigmatic Journeys*. Every time I re-read it I am unable to believe that it was written in June 1985.

To My Enemies

My enemies, my enemies
Who've hated me without a cause
And brought me suffering down the years -
You foes whose spite leaves me no rest
I say to you: "May you be blessed!"

My enemies, who past years fill
How did I ever do you ill
To make you hate, and hate me still?
I prayed and loved with all my might
And won the fight!

Striking not wisely but too well
You over-reached yourselves and fell!
And where you are now, who can tell?
Somehow you're rather hard to find.
But I don't mind!

My enemies, many and grim
With bitter hatred all aflame
You hoped to see me die in shame
But in the pit you dug for me
It's you I see!

You once despised me--proud and sure;
The wheel has turned, you're on the floor.
Your days of power are no more
The time has come for me to fly

With Christ I soar above the sky!

My foes with whom I have to do--
We are not rivals, it is true
Rather, potential foes are you!
I pray for you now as before,
You are for war ...

Your wrath is understandable -
I know I'm not infallible
But in Jesus I'm invincible!
For in my heart against your hate
Is Romans 8 verse twenty-eight!

On all the times our swords have crossed
In pain and blood I've paid a cost
But not a battle have I lost
For you've not fought with flesh and blood
But with my great Protector, God!

Assassinate me if you do
I'd still have not one curse for you!
Dying, I'd even bless you too
For Someone lives to lead me through ...
But you?

You foes whose spite leaves me no rest
Take my forgiveness, all the best.
I say to you: "May you be blessed."

By mid-August, the staged performance at Hunedoara was approaching its end. Because of the reports going out each week on the Voice of America and Radio Free Europe, the First Secretary of the Hunedoara County Communist Party, ordered his subordinates to find out "what was going on in that circus," according to one of his lieutenants. "It's time to end it!" he was saying. God gave my attorney the wisdom to play a card that took the presiding judge by surprise, and honor Him in a brilliant way.

"Your Honor, gentlemen of the jury, I must draw to your attention the fact that this trial of Pastor Dugulescu has its political side as well, and that you are on the point of committing a political error and compromising the image of socialist Romania and of our honored President Nicolae Ceauşescu in the eyes of the U.S.A."

Sensation in court. The President and the whole jury froze and sat stock still for several moments. They knew better than anyone about the political intrigues that were going on behind the scenes, but officially, political trials no longer existed in Romania at that time. They did not know where Prodan, my fearless attorney, was heading.

He continued: "My client, Pastor Dugulescu, has told me that this sheep farmer told my client that he had absolutely no complaint against him. It was the Securitate who made him sign a piece of paper that contained a complaint that they had invented. Now we know that the Socialist Republic of Romania has a Constitution, article 30 of which guarantees freedom of religion and conscience. We know that the State Securitate Service does not persecute religious denominations that are recognised in Romania. And, Your Honor and honorable members of the jury, I would ask you to take into consideration the fact that Pastor Dugulescu is a member of the Lausanne Committee for World Evangelization and is well-known both in the U.S. and in Europe. It was for this reason that he received money from the Christians in America to buy the car. If you grant victory in this case to this sheep farmer who wants to get rich, the signal that you will be sending to America and to the world will be that in Romania the Securitate is a political police force that persecutes pastors and Christian churches. I ask you, Your Honor, to take all these considerations into account, and I am convinced that you will return the correct verdict."

The hearing was immediately suspended and the jury retired to consider their verdict. The other attorneys present congratulated Prodan on the courage and cleverness he had shown. The representatives of the U.S. Embassy also congratulated Prodan, and we went to lunch together at a restaurant on the shores of Lake Cinciş, followed by the ever-present Securitate agent, who was carrying a briefcase that he kept pointing in our direction, obviously a camouflaged camera. At one point, when he was close behind us, Prodan turned round to face him, twirled his Caragiale moustache in an elegant pose, and told him: "Do send me a copy of the photo!"

After one week we were summoned for the verdict to be pronounced. More than an hour went by, and we were still waiting in the corridor, even though there were no other cases being heard that afternoon. The courtroom was empty. I wondered why we were kept outside. I found out later, when the U.S. Embassy car arrived. The just verdict, exonerating me of the false charges, had to be given in the presence of the representatives of the U.S. Embassy, so they could report that Romanian justice operated fairly, and that this had not been a politically-motivated trial.

Of course, their primary purpose, of slandering me, had already been accomplished. No one was in the courtroom that day to hear that I was declared innocent. From a larger perspective, however, more people had been listening to Radio Free Europe and the Voice of America than had been present in the County Court at the trial. Ironically, my reputation had grown as a result of this frame-up and public humiliation.

In one of those "mysterious ways" that God works so well in, this actually became a path for some to find God. One man who worked as the chief lab assistant at the Hunedoara steelworks had been listening to the Radio Free Europe and Voice of America reports about how I was being persecuted. He called me one day, asking if he could visit me at home, and arrived with his wife and little girl, apologizing for disturbing me.

"Pastor, for several weeks I've been listening to reports about the trial taking place in Hunedoara and about how you are being persecuted. Please tell me the truth. Why are you at the receiving end of this harassment? Are you guilty? Do you want to become a hero? Are you trying to get publicity? I want to hear the facts from your own lips."

I shared my commitment to Christ and the continuing and ever-increasing problems with the 'blue-eyed boys' as a consequence of refusing their proposals.

He replied: "I am a Communist and an Orthodox Christian: you should know that I am never going to leave my ancestral religion."

I told him that these two things were incompatible, that he could not be a true Communist and true Orthodox Christian, at the same time; the ideology of the Romanian Communist Party that he belonged to was atheism. One week later, he visited me again, for more discussion based on the Word of God. Then and there, he and his wife received the Lord Jesus Christ into their hearts in our living room and began a new life.

Bus Stop

It was autumn – starting again
With broken bones that caused me pain
With a new field I had to sow
And tears to make the harvest grow

A transfer refused by those at the top
And a bus that didn't stop
An accident not minor at all
And a stay in hospital

Following the fraud trial, in beginning of September 1985, my fortieth birthday was approaching, and I wrote the autobiographical poem *The Conductor* in which I compared my life with a train journey along the two rails of time and space. I related the events of my life journey in the poem. In autumn 1965, when I was approaching my 20-Year station and my train was passing through Timişoara, a kind man, who bore the figurative name of the Conductor, woke me up and asked for my ticket. He asked me where I had come from and where I was going. Then I realised that I had come from nowhere and was heading nowhere and that if I had to get off the train of life that evening I would be getting off in hell. Then that kind conductor, representing my Brother Pitt Popovici offered me a red ticket with GRACE written on it and with my final destination inscribed: New Jerusalem. It was at the beginning of September 1965 that I had received the Lord Jesus Christ into my heart, in First Baptist Church on Romulus Street.

Now, exactly 20 years later, that same Church invited me to become its pastor. Brother Ioan Trifa was getting ready to retire; he was in poor health. The invitation ws a pleasant surprise, but I was attached to the church in Haţeg and to the surroundings, so rich in history and beauty. I told my wife and children and we all prayed about it together. And as the Securitate had eyes and ears in every church, it swiftly learned of the decision taken by the committee of First Baptist Church, Timişoara to call me to be their pastor.

The first phone call I received was from the President of the Baptist Union who asked me to confirm or deny the story that I was going to be going to the church in Timişoara as senior pastor.

I confirmed it saying I felt honoured by the invitation, and added "I hope you are happy too."

"I am not happy and I am not in agreement with this move! I will not sign your transfer! The leadership of the Baptist Union has decided to transfer pastor D.N. from Lugoj to Timişoara and transfer another pastor to Lugoj. You will remain where you are. Neither the local authorities nor the central ones want you in Timișoara. The Department for Religious Denominations will not approve this transfer!"

"President," I said, "it says in the Acts of the Apostles that after the church in Jerusalem had prayed and fasted, they said: 'It seemed good to the Holy Spirit and to us.' It doesn't say that it seemed good to the Baptist Union and to the State authorities. I find myself wondering what there is left for the Holy Spirit and the church to do if you are the only decision makers. Further, I don't need State approval for a transfer, because I am already a previously recognised pastor. My pastor's licence has not been suspended. All that is necessary is for you to approve is the request of the church in Timișoara."

"I will never give my approval! You are staying in Hațeg. That is our decision."

"I am sorry but I cannot obey you. I have prayed and fasted and God has told me to go and pastor First Baptist Church, Timișoara. Also, I owe them a debt; it was in that church that I met the Lord Jesus Christ and that I was baptized, 20 years ago. I know that God's will is for me to move to Timișoara."

"Brother Dugulescu, if you don't do what I say you will suffer the consequences and you will also be bringing many troubles upon the church."

I was summoned to the office of the County Inspector of Religious Denominations in Deva, where I was told the same thing. I had a meeting with the county Securitate chief in the office of the Secretary to the County Council where I was told that if I did not come to my senses but went to Timișoara in defiance of all these warnings, I should not be surprised if a truck or a bus were to cross my path me one day. Despite my recent experience with the threats and subsequent trial, I did not waver.

On September 29, I was invited to preach at First Baptist Church of Timişoara and to have a discussion afterwards with the committee. My wife and our daughter Cristina, aged thirteen, accompanied me. The church welcomed us very warmly and my message was well received. When I met with the committee, the brothers told me that the church had been doing special days of prayer and fasting for me, and were awaiting my answer. I thanked them for the love they had borne towards me and told them that I felt honored by their invitation and that I would accept it.

The next morning, I went with the retiring Pastor Ioan Trifa, to the Regional Inspector for Religious Denominations so that we could inform him of the transfer.

He looked at me and said: "So you are Pastor Dugulescu! I need to tell you that I'm not the person who will be taking the final decision, but as far as I know, my superiors in Bucharest and the leadership of the Baptist Union are not happy with this transfer. You will not be given permission to preach in Timişoara."

Fighting my impulsive nature, I tried to keep cool and to be polite: "Inspector, I am a Baptist minister; I graduated from the Baptist Theological Seminary in Bucharest in 1974, and the pastor's licence I was given then has not been withdrawn. In the case of licensed pastors, a move from one church to another does not need to be authorized by you; it is an internal matter for each denomination."

"Yes," he said, "but yours is a special case and you need our approval as well."

"Inspector, I'm in the right as far as the laws of the land are concerned, but as for authority to preach the gospel of Jesus Christ, that is something I am not going to request from any human being. I received this directly from Jesus Christ when he gave his disciples the Great Commission, two thousand years ago."

He smiled and said dryly, "Very well, Mr. Dugulescu; we'll see what happens."

Tribulations

About three hours after that conversation, Sept. 30, 1985, I was driving with my wife and daughter back to Hațeg. It was 2:20 p.m. and I was driving very slowly along Mărășești, a one-way street behind the Opera House. I reached the first intersection, at Gheorghe Lazăr Street, driving through as I had the right of way.

Suddenly my wife screamed: "Watch out! It's not going to stop!" A bus, empty except for a driver, was hurtling towards us from the left, aiming straight at my door. Despite the stop sign, it didn't even slow down at the intersection, rather, it accelerated. The speeding bus hit our car full force, shattering every window and caving in the heavy steel door. The stanchion between the front and rear doors buckled and struck me on the head. Both bones of my right forearm were snapped from the colossal impact to the steering wheel. Although I had been wearing a seatbelt, my wife was not, and was thrown against the dashboard, seriously damaging her ribcage and breaking her right thumb. Cristina suffered a blow to the head. The bus was traveling so fast that it picked up our car and kept going. Oddly, a Dacia parked at the sidewalk to the right of the intersection on Gheorghe Lazăr Street, with the best view of the entire collision, suddenly sped away from the scene of the accident.

The people in the street had opened the front passenger door and helped my wife out. But when I slid over to get, I found that my right arm would not bear my weight. I realised that it was completely broken above the wrist and was dangling down, held only by the skin. "My arm is smashed up," I told my wife and daughter, who began to cry in shock. A crowd had gathered, discussing on what they saw. The bus driver just stood beside his vehicle with his arms folded. He was impassive. Some of the men present told me: "Look, mister, he didn't brake at all. It's obvious that that criminal was intending to kill you. Look at him standing there like a swine, not even bothering to help you! Go over there and hit him in the face, mister! If you can't manage it with your right fist, use your left!" In shock and pain, I couldn't believe that what this was real. Surely, it was a nightmare that I would wake up from? But this nightmare was not ending, I wondered: "Lord, why have you allowed this? I wanted to obey you. That's why I came to Timişoara."

Someone led me to the nearby Military Hospital where I received a painkilling injection so my broken forearm was straightened and stabilized with two splints. During this procedure, I was asking myself why this had happened, and felt the Holy Spirit speak to me. "What did you preach about yesterday morning at the wedding service?" I remembered I talked on 1 Thessalonians 5:18: "Give thanks to God the Father in all circumstances, for this is God's will for you."

"And what did you say in your sermon?" the Spirit reminded me.

"I said "Give thanks to God for health, for sickness, for plenty, for poverty, for a car accident, if God lets one happen.""

"And what are you, a pastor and teacher, doing now?"

Then I pulled myself together and said: "Lord, I don't understand a thing about this nightmare. Lord, it hurts, but I thank you, I thank you. You know why you let this accident happen."

In that moment, I felt a sense of detachment, as if I was watching everything from the outside in peace and calmness. This whole conversation with the Holy Spirit lasted no longer than the trip to the Military Hospital. I returned to the car where my wife and daughter were waiting with the traffic police who had now arrived at the scene.

Lieutenant E.C. had two traffic policemen there who took measurements and wrote a report. As I was unable to use my right hand, the lieutenant took my wallet out of my back pocket.

I was wearing the same white suit I had worn for the wedding I presided over. When he extracted my driving licensce and ID card from my wallet, he also saw my pastor's card and said: "Reverend, you are not to blame, because the street you were on had the right of way. You did not disobey any traffic regulations. But he" – pointing to the bus driver – "failed to stop at the stop sign. He is to blame for the accident, and for that reason I am going to confiscate his driving license." He returned my license.

"You will now be taken to the Orthopedic Hospital. I will see you there tomorrow, so that we can fill in the insurance and vehicle repair forms."

Until this moment, I still thought this was an accident.

In the meantime a Dacia arrived bearing the same initials on its side door as the bus (Timişoara Local Transport Administration) and a radio set. There was a civilian sitting in the passenger seat. We were told to ride in the back and they would take us to the Orthopaedic Hospital.

The civilian in the passenger seat started asking me questions and taking down my answers: where I was from, where I worked and so on. I told him that I was from Haţeg and that I was a Baptist pastor – a member of the same faith as the evangelist Billy Graham, who had preached at Timişoara Orthodox Cathedral two weeks earlier.

"Billy Graham?" he said. "Oh, he caused us a lot of problems, too!" On that occasion so many thousands of people had gathered that they could not all be accommodated in the Cathedral. At the request of Billy Graham's team, loudspeakers were installed in the street outside, but as soon as Billy Graham began to preach, Securitate men cut the loudspeaker wires. At first the crowd raised an outcry, but then they began to sing "Glory, glory, Halleluia" and other evangelical hymns. Opera Square and the whole city resounded with the praises of the children of God. You can imagine the feelings of the dark angels of the Securitate who had been ordered to control the situation and minimize the impact of Billy Graham's visit.

The anonymous civilian in the car, whose presence was unexplained, handed me over to the duty doctor, who injected me with anaesthetic and put a temporary plaster cast on my arm. Since all the eight beds in the ward were full, he told me to rest on consultation couch in the corner.

After the formalities of admission had been completed, my wife and daughter left. My good friend, Viorel Oprea, and Doru Gherga, an excellent motor mechanic, who were both in the Navigators discipleship group, took charge of my damaged car and got Mărioara and Cristina back to Hațeg that evening.

Trying to rest on that hard couch, too short for my frame, I tried to collect my thoughts. As I pieced things together, a chilling certainty swept through me: This was not an accident. The words of the colonel from Deva echoed in my ears: "We are going to destroy you!" Even more telling, those of the County Securitate chief: "If you defy our orders and go to Timişoara, don't be surprised if a bus or a truck crosses your path one day! Do you understand?!"

Lying there, I understood. This was an attempt on my life, a physical liquidation. How could a professional bus driver have failed to stop at a stop sign? Or, having hit me broadside and seen our injuries, just stood there beside his bus with his arms folded? It would be normal to apologize and offer to drive us to the hospital--

but he had done nothing of the kind. The Militia officer and the onlookers all concluded that the driver was at fault. Otherwise, they would not have returned my license and confiscated his.

Where had that car with the radio set had appeared from, the one carrying that civilian 'volunteer' who transported us to the Orthopaedic Hospital and asked me all kinds of suspicious questions?

I lay there on my back on that hard couch, trying to make order of my confused thoughts. I couldn't believe that just as I accepted the calling to Timişoara, I landed in the Orthopaedic hospital with a totally shattered right arm, and no bed.

Around me, accident victims
Recently brought in or post-operative
Carried their destiny with them
Muttered and sighed

And time, as if weary
Of groaning and snores
Halted in its eternal progress
In the orthopedic hell.

The next morning, I was examined by Professor Şora, the head of the Orthopaedic Clinic, and Dr. Horia Vermeşan who not only headed the ward where I was treated, but also served as Secretary of the Romanian Communist Party organization in Timişoara Orthopedic Clinic. They scheduled me for an operation the following day, and, that evening, moved me from my hard couch to a bed that had just been vacated.

The next day, I was taken to the operating theatre. I was less afraid of the surgery than of the sinister presence of the 'blue eyed boys' whom I could feel lurking nearby. Of course, they were everywhere, controlling the entire country, and that they were capable of anything. But I also knew that they could do no more than my Heavenly Father permitted. I prayed, and told the doctors that they could put me to sleep. My wife and children were in Haţeg, but my sister Cornelia was waiting outside and Professor Stoian, the anaesthetist, went out from time to time to reassure her that everything was going well and my heart was standing up well to the operation.

I woke up around lunchtime to find my arm in a cast. The ward nurse told me that they had put a plate on one of my broken bones – it was held on with four screws – and joined the other with a metal pin.

I was barely awake when the brothers and sisters of First Baptist Church, who had heard what had happened to me, arrived bringing food, drinks and, above all, encouragement. During the first two days after my operation, my three sisters who lived in Timişoara, Cornelia, Mili and Tania, and my brothers-in-law, Nelu and Ovidiu, took turns staying with me, day and night. When the anaesthetic wore off, I was in great pain. I remember that one night, when I was twisting and turning in my bed, I said to my brother-in-law, Ovidiu: "It would be better if they'd finished the job and killed me. I feel I can't bear any more." Later, when I found out that there are painkillers for post-operative pain, I wondered why I was allowed to suffer like that.

The militia lieutenant who had taken the accident report was supposed to come to the hospital with the bus driver the day after the accident. This would complete the written report and the other documents connected with insurance. Despite his promise, and the law, he did not come. Then, the day after the operation, a senior militia officer came into the ward and introduced himself as Major D., the commander of the Timişoara County traffic militia. He asked which of us was Pastor Dugulescu. I replied from my bed that I was.

"Have you got your driving license with you?"

Knowing it was in the briefcase under my bed, I momentarily thought of lying. But, since his junior officer at the scene of the accident had pronounced me innocent, I told him that I did have it. Assuming he needed it for some paperwork, I asked my brother-in-law to get my bag out from under the bed. As I held my driver license out, he took it, announcing to the other patients in the ward: "This is what happens when people drive carelessly and disobey traffic regulations!"

"What do you mean?" I said. "I obeyed all the regulations. The bus driver didn't stop at the stop sign. And what kind of man can that driver be, Major? I've been here four days already, and he still hasn't even come to see if I'm still alive or to say sorry."

With great arrogance, the major made a big show of pocketing my license, and leaving. The other patients were dumbfounded. "The head of the traffic police for the whole county coming to this hospital to suspend a driving license? Why didn't he send someone else? Reverend, you shouldn't have given it to him, because you're not going to see it again."

"Impossible," I said, "I was pronounced innocent at the scene of the accident. If the traffic policeman who investigated the scene did not confiscate my license, how can another officer do so four days later, in a hospital? He didn't find me driving my bed and colliding with one of you!"

"You'll see, Reverend. I doubt if he would go to all the trouble of coming here for nothing."

Some four hours after Major D.'s departure, the bus driver finally came. Expecting him to be feeling guilty and wanting to say sorry, I thought he would try to bring me a pot of jam or some fruit, as I had seen happening with some of my fellow patients who had been injured in accidents. Far from it. He took a sheet of paper out of his briefcase and asked me to put my signature on it alongside his. I read it and was astounded; It was a joint statement in which we accepted equal responsibility for the accident!

At exactly that moment, a group of brothers entered the ward to visit me.

I asked him: "Who sent you to me with this document? I thought you would have come to see me on the very first day to apologise and to see if we could resolve this. You wait four days and present me with a piece of paper typed for you by goodness-knows-who, and you ask me to sign it and take responsibility for that accident? Do you take me for a fool? Mr. C., you intended to kill me, didn't you?"

As I posed the question I looked into his eyes. He hung his head.

"How many children do you have?" I asked.

"Five" was the reply.

"I think you ought to feel obliged to give me a considerable sum of money to pay for this operation, which was painful and cost an enormous amount, as well as the money for the second equally painful and expensive operation, that will be needed when they take out the metal pins. And I also need to have my car repaired."

The man looked at me, frightened.

"But I don't believe that those who asked you to kill me have any plans to give you a single penny for your family. I am a repenter, Mr. C., a pastor, and my conscience will not allow me to take the food from your children's mouths. I forgive you in the name of the Lord Jesus Christ. As he was dying on the cross for me and for you, he prayed for those who were driving the nails through his hands and feet. "Forgive them", he said, "for they do not know what they are doing!" I believe that you, too, were ignorant of what you were doing, because other people were using you as their instrument."

The man stood stonily before me, silent.

In the end, I signed a document in front of a notary, stating that I had no claims against the driver. I also gave him a Bible, which I had inscribed.

Not long after, my friend Viorel Oprea came to the hospital to see me. He had been to the Militia to find out what had happened to my file and my driving license.

"Which file do you mean?" the secretary had asked.

"The 'C' file" said Viorel. At this one of the officers murmured to the other: "C, our client."

This made me curious to discover what kind of client of the Militia he was, so I contacted Dan Crişan. Dan had been a major in charge of radio transmissions at Timişoara Airport until he was discharged from the army for becoming a Christian. He used to go around the country with me on my evangelistic tours, acting as my driver and giving his testimony in churches. I asked him to go to the bus driver's home and do some investigation while I was still in hospital. Dan often used to say: "Better a driver for Dugulescu than an officer for Ceauşescu!" I requested him to ask the bus driver where he had been coming from, where he was heading and why he had not stopped at the stop sign. Then he was to put a final question to him and watch his eyes and expression closely.

The man said that he had just taken a party of schoolchildren to help with the maize harvest and that he was heading for the bus garage in Buziaş Avenue (even though the street he was driving along was not one where buses were permitted) and that the reason he hadn't stopped at the stop sign was that he hadn't thought anyone was coming. Then my friend Dan put the final question to him. When I had asked him to carry out this little interrogation he hadn't believed that we could be dealing with anything more than a normal accident, but now he became convinced that we were.

"Tell me, Mr. C, was it just an accident or had you been instructed to liquidate Pastor Dugulescu?" The man went pale and began trying to defend himself, but what he said was totally disconnected: "What do you mean ... I don't understand ... I didn't intend ... "

"OK, but tell me what kind of 'client' of the Militia you are, because they say you're a client of theirs."

"Yes. Some years ago I hit a little girl with my car. It was a serious case, and possibly it's as a result of that that they regard me as their client."

But I understood that it was then that he had either been recruited or had fallen into their net. He had been obliged to collaborate with them in return for not having criminal charges brought against him which would have meant a spell in prison.

I stayed in hospital for a week after the operation. I thought about what would have happened if my wife and daughter and I were driving the ARO that I sold to the farmer, rather than the solidly-built Mercedes. We would have been killed instantly. My friend, Pastor Guy Davidson, had been upset when he heard that I had sold the car he had sent me the money for, and had bought the Mercedes instead, which, from a human point of view, was justified. However, after I told him the story of how God had used the solid bodywork of the old Mercedes to save our lives, he told me: "Peter, God even uses our mistakes in the working-out of his plans." And it was he who then helped me to replace that damaged Mercedes with a newer model, from Germany.

After leaving the hospital, I stayed at my sister Tania's for several days to convalesce. The brothers from the church came to see me there. Before returning to my family in Hațeg, I went to see Colonel D. at the county militia headquarters to recover my driving license. My right arm was in plaster and in a sling. He was surprised to see me: "Are you out of the hospital?" I don't know what was in his mind or what he was expecting, but I responded to his question with another question: "Did you think I wouldn't be coming out?"

"No, no, but ... ".

"Major, I've come to pick up the driving license that you took from me while I was in hospital. I gather you needed it for some paperwork. Now I need it."

"Look ... " he began, trying to justify himself, "our colleagues in Deva asked us for it and we sent it there. Go and ask them for it, because there are still some issues that need to be discussed."

This made me very indignant. "Major", I said, "the accident report is here in Timişoara and it would have been natural for my driving license to have been here too. I cannot understand why my license should be in Deva."

"Ask the people there and they'll tell you the reason."

This was maddening. My nightmare was not over yet.

A friend of mine from Sânpetru-Hațeg, Samson Hajdățan, had offered to act as my driver until I was able to drive again. Now he came with his ARO and took me to Deva, where I spoke to the sergeant there. He asked for my ID, looked in a file and said: "Yes, we have your driving license, but I have instructions to tell you that you cannot have it back until you have had some thorough medical checks and passed a written examination and a road test."

"Exactly like a learner driver who has never had a license?"

"Yes, something like that. These are the instructions I received from my superior officers. I'm just carrying them out."

Since that moment in Timişoara when Major D. told me that the people in Deva had asked for my driving license, I had had a hunch about what was going on. I could see the scene now: Captain S.I., the person in Hunedoara County who dealt with Religious Denominations Department business, waiting for me to come knocking at his door asking for help. I could almost see him smiling in satisfaction and blowing a long plume of smoke from his cigarette as he looked at me and said: "Well, Pete, I'm glad that you've finally come to ask for my help. You know we've always wanted to help you, but you didn't want it. Look, if you accept the proposal we made to you in Haţeg and sign this piece of paper I can promise you that you'll have your driving licence back by the end of the day!"

I shook myself like a man waking from a bad dream and said to the sergeant at the window:
"I'll take my ID; you people can keep my driving license as long as you wish. This is a farce. I would like you to pass this message on to your superior officers: they took away my driving licence and are holding on to it illegally. I will be making a complaint to the Minister of the Interior and to the Head of State and requesting an investigation."

My friend Samson drove me from Deva to Haţeg. I was happy to be back with my loved ones again after two weeks. Eunice was still under a year old, and when we had set off on our visit to Timişoara we had left her with the Hajdăţan family in Sânpetru and Sister Ana had taken care of her as if she was her own. Cristi was 11 and had just started the sixth grade. Ina was in the eighth grade and Ligia was in the second year of the nursing high school in Hunedoara.

That evening a brother in Haţeg rang me and told me to turn on my radio straight away and tune in to the BBC. I couldn't believe my ears: it was a report on the accident in Timişoara in which it was described as an assassination attempt carried out by the Communist authorities against the Baptist pastor Peter Dugulescu, who had been forbidden to move to Timişoara by the Department for Religious Denominations. The commentator said that the pastor had been in the car with his wife and son. When Cristi heard himself being referred to on the BBC he said to his sister Ina: "Listen to that! It wasn't you in the car, it was me!" And he ran all over the house shouting for joy.

The next evening the Voice of America and Radio Free Europe carried the same news item. It was what the Securitate and the Communist regime feared most: a situation in which the brutal human rights abuses and violations of religious liberty that were taking place in Romania became known to the Western mass media and were reported by them.

When the brothers heard that I had come home, they came and prayed for our family with great love. On the Sunday after my return, I went to the little church on the edge of town and preached with my right arm encased in plaster. I used my left hand to turn the pages of my Bible and when I wanted to emphasise a point I thumped the pulpit with the plaster cast. The faces I saw when I looked out at the congregation moved me deeply. People were weeping profusely and looking at me with great affection. Their tears and their faces said, without a word being spoken: "Brother Peter, we love you. We do not believe the filthy rumors that have been spread about you. We love you and we are with you and your family. Don't be afraid!"

I heard more prayers for us than I could count. I have to admit that there was sadness in their faces too. They knew that I had accepted the call from First Baptist Church Timişoara and that I would soon be leaving them. I, too, was saddened. I had fallen deeply in love with this region and with our little church on the edge of town, as we affectionately called it. It was my first flock, my first love.

Years earlier, when my former teacher Iosif Ţon had invited me to come and take his place in Oradea, I had told him that it would be hard for me to give up the traditional lifestyle of this town among the mountains, this most beautiful land, 'Haţeg Land.' At that time my teacher had replied: "Peter, you have not been called to live in traditional spots. You've been called to live where the big battles are being fought." Now, the time had come for this prophecy to be fulfilled.

I spent a lot of time with Marius Sârbu, the deacon. He was a godly and extremely talented young man. He was originally from Cărbunari in the hills near the Danube and had come to Haţeg when he married Ani, a pharmacist who belonged to our church. They had met while both were students in Cluj. Mihai was a geography graduate and was the head of the meteorological station near Haţeg. His parents were believers, but it was while hospitalised in Charkov in the USSR that was he had been born again, during his university studies.

When brother Iosif Ţon and I had ordained him a deacon, we had reported that this ordination would also qualify Mihai to serve as a pastor when the time came for him to take my place. Mihai belonged to the second generation of BEE students and used to teach the Homiletics course when the usual teacher was unavailable. I discussed sermon plans with him explaining how I received a message from the Lord, from the initial inspiration right down to the final part. He knew that part of my evangelist's spirit had affected him, but I felt that he had his own calling and gift as an evangelist. I tried to prepare him by reporting my various confrontations with the people from the Securitate and with the local and Bucharest Department for Religious Denominations officials.

On December 8, 1985, the First Baptist Church of Timişoara held a general meeting and confirmed me as their senior pastor. There was only one vote against. I spent Christmas with my new congregation. My driver was Brother Aron Moldovan, who had been a prominent Communist less than a year earlier. He had been moved to contact me through Radio Free Europe and the Voice of America. He and his wife had given their lives to God in our living room. Now he was working as my driver, since Brother Samson Hajdățan had also had his license taken away because he had been driving me. The 'blue-eyed boys' wished me to be desperate to get my own driving license back.

With the assistance of my attorney, I wrote an appeal directly to the Minister of the Interior and the Head of the legal system and to President Nicolae Ceauşescu. Trusting in the truth that makes us free, I set down on paper the entire truth about the slanderous trial in Hunedoara, the harassment and searches that I and my family had been subjected to, and the accident in Timişoara on September 30, 1985, which had been followed by the confiscation of my driving licence in an arbitrary and illegal way. I named the Securitate officers who had threatened me, what they said and how it took place. I requested a special inquiry into my case and a halt to all these abuses which were doing grave damage to the image of Romania and of Nicolae Ceauşescu.

I pointed out that the Polish Catholic priest, Jerzy Popieluszko, had been killed only one year earlier in Poland by being drowned in a lake, and that a similar fate was clearly in store for me. I also made it clear that my allegations against the State Securitate agents could be proved true in a court of law. I even said that if I failed to establish the truth of my accusations, I stood ready to pay the penalty for breaking the article in our Penal Code which made "slandering the Socialist order" a crime.

Within 60 days at the most, I should have received a written response. Instead, less than two weeks later, I was called to the Hațeg traffic police to be given my driving license back, with no explanation. If my allegations were untrue, my letter would have brought me the severest punishment, not a sudden release of my license.

The first Monday after my return home, I was summoned to Deva, to the regional Inspector for Religious Denominations. He asked me to write a letter denying the news report that had gone out on the Voice of America, Radio Free Europe and the BBC. I was to address it personally to each of these 'imperialist' radio stations.

"And what am I to put in the letter?" I asked.

"That the accident in Timişoara was caused by your careless driving and that the Securitate was not involved! If you do not write this letter, a copy of which we will keep, you will have problems and your transfer to Timişoara will not be approved!"

A few days later, I requested an appointment with the Secretary of the Hunedoara County Council to lodge a complaint about the pressure that was being put on me. The President of the Baptist Union had also insisted that I deny what happened to the radio stations. The Secretary of the County Council was a lawyer and seemed to be a good man. He had tried to help me obtain building authorization for the new church building in Haţeg. But now he was scared, so he had requested that the Securitate director be present at the meeting. There, I openly voiced my conviction that the accident was a Securitate assassination attempt. "Colonel, the words you spoke right here in this office: "Don't be surprised if a truck or a bus crosses your path!" became a reality."

"I said nothing of the kind. Don't try to implicate me in this story of yours. I deny having spoken those words."

His next words were couched in Socialist rhetoric. "It is my responsibility, as a man of the law, to see that in this Socialist country every citizen should have equal access to sun and rain, should breathe the air of liberty that our party generously guarantees to all. No distinction is made here between Communists and non-Communists, workers, peasants, intellectuals, Orthodox,

Roman Catholics, Baptists, etc. If you persist in making allegations that the Communists are persecuting you and causing you to have 'accidents,' this must mean that you have a psychiatric illness and are suffering from persecution mania. We will have to have you admitted to a psychiatric hospital for treatment!"

Here was a new threat. I could be silenced and subjected to the more subtle and sophisticated incarceration of the mental hospital. I returned to Hațeg, wrapped up in my own thoughts. At times, I was fearful, not so much for myself as for my family. All four of my children were still minors and needed me, and my wife had no job. When I told her what he said, she worried: "If they kill you, or give you drugs that destroy your sanity, how am I going to manage all by myself with four children?"

My only anchor was that God was capable of guarding us and that he would not desert us.

I spent New Year with the Hateg church that I was soon to leave. In January, I travelled around the country, preaching at revivals. In February, my doctor advised me to undertake a mud bath treatment at Eforie Nord on the Black Sea coast because my broken arm was still giving me serious pain. During the three weeks I spent at the seaside, a new set of attempts were made to render me useless.

Snares

It was February, and the weather on the coast was exceptionally cold and frosty. Occasionally, you might see one or two people wandering along the seafront. The majority of the patients in the few hotels that had winter treatment facilities were country people who had been given reduced price tickets through their collective farms, and workers who had come on trade union tickets. There where few who had bought their tickets from tourist agencies, as I had.

I was assigned Room 121 in the Dolphin Hotel. A chambermaid whispered to me that the rooms on the first floor were official rooms normally given to foreigners in the summer, and that almost all of them were bugged. This did not bother me, as I had no one to talk to anyway. On the first evening, a man sat down at my table. He said he was an engineer in Bucharest. I was surprised by his negative comments about Communists and Ceauşescu. The Holy Spirit warned me that this was an attempt to entrap me. When he found out that I was a Baptist pastor, he said: "I've heard on Radio Free Europe and the Voice of America how those evil Communists persecute the Baptists and Pentecostals, but we know that the Americans are on your side and act in your defense, isn't that so? They've got liberty and democracy there, unlike us, don't you agree?"

"I feel free even in Romania. I'm a pastor. I preach the Gospel and the Bible teaches me to pray for those in authority."

"What? You mean to say that you pray for Nicolae Ceauşescu and for those who persecute you?"

"Yes, I pray in all sincerity that they and their families may come to know God and have their sins forgiven."

He tried the same tactics again, on the second evening. After that I didn't see him again, although he had said he was there for and 18-day stay through his union.

The next day at lunchtime, a very attractive young blonde sat at the table next to mine and kept looking over at me as I lunched with two other men.

Suddenly, she rose, came to our table and addressed me: "Excuse me, might I join you?"

"Yes, yes; have a seat," I replied.

She sat down and lit up a cigarette. "Which room are you in?" she asked.

"In 121," I said.

"Well, what a coincidence, they've put me in the one directly above yours," she said, meaningfully: "I'm in room 221."

The Holy Spirit once again warned me. I awaited her next move.

"I've got a terrible virus. You haven't, by any chance, got any imported flu medicine, have you? These Romanian ones are totally ineffective!"

I realised that someone had searched my room, because I had two packets of American flu treatment on my bedside table. She obviously knew this and was banking on my response.

"Yes," I replied, "I've got some American flu medication and you can have it."

"Oh, great, I'll come to your room after lunch and you can give me something. I'm ever so grateful to you."

"There's no need for you to put yourself to the trouble of coming to my room. I'll go up right now and get it for you."

I went immediately and got her the medicine. I sensed that I had spoiled her plan.

At the evening meal, she told me that the American medicine had made her much better but that the food provided for the patients at the spa was of very poor quality. She suggested that the two of us go to a nearby restaurant where the grills were excellent.

I replied that I was glad the food was scanty and not all that good as I wanted to lose a few kilos.

I disappointed her again. If I had accepted the invitation, a number of things could have happened. Walking along the shore in the dark, she could have taken my arm and a photographer could have taken a picture of us for the newspaper. Or even worse, a couple of 'drunks' might have shown up to stage a fight and leave my body floating in the sea. Witnesses would have told the coroner investigating the case that "the pastor left here with a blonde to spend the evening at a different restaurant."

In my room, I was translating some young people's Bible studies from English to Romanian. I was preparing to start a weekly Bible study in Timişoara for the youth. I could hear my upstairs neighbor running a bath, splashing the water about, singing and dropping things. She did all she could to remind me that she was there, naked, available at any time. The next morning she didn't come down to breakfast, probably hoping for me to come and see if she was feeling ill. At lunchtime, however, she did come down. She told me she was bored and asked me if I had any good books. Of course, she already knew that in my roome were several classics of world literature.

"Yes, I've just finished reading *The Defamation of Paganini*," I said.

"I can come to your room to get it."

"There's no need for you to bother. I'll bring it to dinner this evening."

Had I given her an opportunity to come into my room, even for two minutes, I have no doubt that a "jealous fiancé" or "husband" would suddenly appear, to violently assault me, killing me in the process. My family and church would be told that I was killed by a husband in a jealous rage when he found me in a hotel room with his wife.

The next day, she returned the book and said it was very boring and had put her to sleep. She didn't appear that evening, having suddenly left, despite her tickets for a 12-day stay.

When I spoke to Mihai Sârbu on the telephone I found out that Major P., the Haţeg Securitate chief, was in Constanţa as a member of a delegation. Very interesting!

On the last Sunday in February, I gave my farewell service after 12 years in the church in Haţeg. Many tears were shed and fervent prayers were uttered for the unknown future that lay before us – both for me and for the Haţeg congregation.

I had earnestly longed to see the day when the church would have a building in which God's children could worship in decent conditions, but this dream was not fulfilled during my pastorship. I told Mihai in my farewell sermon: "You will be the one to take the people across the Jordan and lead them into the Promised Land!" It was a prophetic word, because God used him to fulfill that long-cherished vision, held since the time of Pastor Teodor Cenuşe in the 1950s. Even while I served in Timişoara, I quietly maintained links to some people in 'Caesar's household' who finally, in 1987, helped obtain the long awaited authorization to build.

A New Beginning

On Friday, February 28, 1986, I began my work as pastor of First Baptist Church, Timişoara.

On that day, the table in my little office held two letters from the Baptist Union, one addressed to the church and the other to me. Mine advised me not to start work as a pastor in that church or I would have to bear the consequences. The church committee was advised not to accept me.

The church held an evening service on Fridays, so I preached that same evening. My induction as pastor had been scheduled for the following Sunday, but as no one from the local Baptist association or from the Baptist Union would acknowledge me, the church committee decided not to hold a special service. Nevertheless, many new people came that Sunday to see the new pastor. I felt that the listeners were receiving my message with joy.

At this time, members of Bethany Church, which several brothers from our church had planted in another part of town but was not authorized by the state, asked me to pastor them as well. This aggravated my position even more, because this church, which was officially illegal, was under great persecution. The church windows were being smashed by nocturnal stone-throwing and for some time the leaders of the church had forced to pay fines every single day. Here, I began a series of Thursday evening Bible studies and presided at the Lord's Supper, at baptisms and at weddings.

My sister Mili and her husband Nelu let me have a room in their small apartment. I stayed with them for six months. I travelled to Haţeg to see my family every Wednesday morning and came back Friday at lunchtime.

I began a Tuesday evening youth Bible study on the theme of 'Man – Unique and Irreplaceable Being: Origin, Functions, Responsibilities and Destiny'. Then we studied 'The Antinomies of the Bible'. At the beginning, about 30 young people came, but within two months, the number grew to 300. They came from all the evangelical churches in the city and most of them were university students.

Operation

At the end of March, I was admitted to the Orthopedic Unit again to have the plate with its four screws and the metal pin extracted from my arm. It was almost six months since the first operation. God kept speaking to me in dreams and through the inner voice of the Holy Spirit. I had begun to discern this secret voice and to experience what the Apostle Paul speaks about in Acts 20:23: "I only know that in every city the Holy Spirit warns me that prison and hardships are facing me".

One day before the operation I had a discussion with my surgeon, Dr. Horia Vermeşan:

"Doctor, it is possible that the 'blue-eyed boys' may come and give you some 'special instructions' in connection with tomorrow's operation?"

"Reverend, you're overly suspicious." he said. "I know you have grounds for fear, because I, too, listen to certain radio stations to keep myself informed, but I want to assure you that I have the conscience of a doctor".

"I have entrusted my life into God's hands." I told him. "I only wished to draw your attention to the possibility of a 'visit'."

I asked Sister Florica Tîlvan, one of our church members who was a nurse in that hospital, to stay with me in the operating theatre the next day and to tell me afterwards about everything that had happened. I had a presentiment of evil.

That night I slept little and prayed a lot.

The next morning, at nine o'clock, they took me into the operating theatre. Mine was the first operation that Wednesday morning. Everything was prepared and the surgical team was ready to start work.

As I lay on the operating table I prayed and recited Psalm 23. When I came to the verse: "Even though I walk through the valley of the shadow of death," I began to weep. It was a premonition.

Peter Dugulescu

Then they put the anaesthetic mask over my nose and I was unconscious. I woke up at 2:30 p.m. in my bed in the ward with a rubber tube down my throat to prevent me swallowing my tongue. When I showed signs of coming round, my seven fellow patients began to say to each other: "Finally, he's waking up!" I tried many times to open my eyes but kept dropping off again, until finally I woke up and looked around. They all had their eyes fixed on me and I realised that something unusual had happened. One of them, the spokesman, broke the silence by saying: "Reverend, excuse my saying so, but when they brought you back from the resuscitation unit you looked like a dead man. You look better now."

"What happened?" I asked.

"I don't know. They said that your heart almost stopped and that they had had problems with the oxygen equipment."

I asked the nurse to call Florica Tîlvan, our church sister, who was on duty just then. Florica was an elderly woman, Godly and with a steadiness of character that inspired complete confidence.

"Sister Florica, how did the operation go?"

"Oh, Brother Peter, praise God that we can speak. I've been praying for you a lot. What can I tell you? I don't even know how to begin, I thought you had gone to Heaven. Everything went well until they opened up your hip."

"Why did they open up my hip as well?"

"Because although they took out the metal attachments, your bones had not fused well because of some dead bone tissue and they had to use an instrument to take a graft from your hip bone. While they were doing that, your heart showed signs of stress and they needed to give you oxygen. But when Professor Stoian, the anesthetist, tried to turn on the oxygen, he found that there was no pressure at all in the apparatus. Then, Brother Pete, the doctors panicked. That's the right word for it: panic! Professor Stoian sent a nurse to tell the technician to change the oxygen cylinder for a full one. He told her that in the entire hospital there was not a single spare cylinder available! Then Professor Stoian ran himself to phone Bega Hospital to ask them to send over an oxygen cylinder urgently."

My sister, Cornelia, was again waiting in the corridor, but this time the anaesthetist had no time to speak to her. She could hear him shouting down the telephone at the end of the corridor: "Bega Hospital, send us an oxygen cylinder *fast*, and I mean fast! My patient is dying on the operating table!"

"Your face changed color as a result of the lack of oxygen; you went blue." Sister Florica told me. "Lord, what you went through! But praise the Lord, our prayers were answered!"

She went on to say: "The doctors had a sharp dispute, because they couldn't account for the lack of oxygen in the apparatus during the very first operation of the day, which was yours."

When the surgeon who had operated on me came to see me that evening, I asked him: "How was it, Doctor? Didn't I tell you that the 'blue-eyed boys' would be on duty?"

"Oh, Reverend, I told you that you're a suspicious man. Oxygen isn't a *sine qua non* during operations. We can also operate without it – as witnessed by the fact that your operation was a success." His political role within the clinic may have stopped him from acknowledging the truth, but in other respects he was a fine professional and a man with a heart of gold. He is one of the Timişoara professionals with whom I share a deep mutual respect.

The next morning I met Professor Stoian, the anaesthetist, in the lobby:

"How did the operation go, Professor?"

"Oh, Reverend, Reverend, my coronaries!" he said, referring to his own heart condition. "I thought I was going to die before you, Reverend!"

"Why?" I asked.

"I don't understand anything anymore. When I arrived in the morning I checked the instruments and the oxygen apparatus. Everything was perfect. There was enough oxygen in the cylinder for many operations. Yours was the first. How the oxygen in the cylinder could have evaporated between the time I checked it and the time your operation started I cannot understand. Since we changed our technician, we have had nothing but problems of this kind."

"But when did you change technicians?" I asked.

"About three days ago."

Fifteen years later, the identity of that technician was unveiled. It was the 'Angel of Death,' Beniamin Jianu. It also explained another mysterious incident which took place several days after the botched operation.

On that morning, when the nurses were bringing breakfast to the ward they didn't bring me any. I asked the girl who was giving out the plates: "Aren't you bringing me any breakfast?"

"I've been told that you are on a special diet because you have diabetes. I'll bring you your plate in a moment."

"Who told you that I was a diabetic? I have been eating the same food as the other people in the ward. Who concocted this story?"

"Well, you see ... I think the doctor has put you on the diabetic list."

"Call the doctor to the ward!" I shouted.

The doctor came and confirmed, with surprise, that he had not put me on the diabetic list.

Then another nurse came and said: "Sorry, it was a mistake. We confused you with someone in the next ward".

Once more the Holy Spirit had warned me. I realised that the so-called "special diet plate" was contaminated with something meant to kill me, so to prevent a mix up and someone else being poisoned, my plate had to be brought separately. From that moment onwards I did not eat any more of the food the hospital served.

Only my family knew of his incident because it seemed minor in comparison with the others. However, 15 years later, the government agent commissioned to kill me testified that first he, and later, a female agent posing as a nurse were ordered to poison my hospital food. So with the help and under the protection of God's good hand I came safely through this valley of the shadow of death as well.

I saw how God had faithfully fulfilled one of the special verses that he had encouraged me with at the beginning of my ministry: "No weapon formed against you will stand" (Isaiah 54:17).

The attempts to eliminate me did not end there. A few months later, in July 1986, I was still commuting to Hațeg every week. One Tuesday evening, after the youth meeting we set out for Hațeg at around 11 p.m., including my wife and two visitors, Mia and Costel Oglice from America. My dear friends ever since my seminary years in Bucharest, they were now living in the U.S. and working for Precept Ministries. They used to come to Romania every summer as 'tourists' to run secret Bible study groups in churches and homes, and teach Bible study techniques. Over the years, they had witnessed many of the troubles we had experienced, and each time they left, they would tell me: "Pete, we love you and we are praying for you. But if you can't bear the pressure any more, tell us when you decide to leave."

The four of us were traveling together in my repaired Mercedes, and again, I was at the wheel. Costel was next to me and Mia and Mărioara were in the back. Around 1 a.m. near the border of Timiş and Caraş counties there was a parking place on the left of the road. Here we saw a car parked with its headlights on full beam, pointing in the direction we were coming from. This made me slow down. When I got closer, I saw a man standing in the middle of the road. He was waving his arms desperately to try to make me stop. I stopped on the right of the road and opened my window. The man shouted in very bad English: "Please help me, please help me!! Somebody stoled my car!" Another man was sitting at the wheel of the car in the parking place. The driver's door was open and the man looked drunk. My attention was caught by what the man in the middle of the road was shouting and I wanted to get out of the car to help him, but at that instant Costel seized my arm and said:

"Don't get out, Pete, keep out of this. There's something suspicious here. Didn't you notice what awful English that man was speaking? How does he know that we understand English? Please don't go over. There's some dirty work going on here."

I closed my half-open window, stepped on the gas and detoured around the man in the middle of the road who went on shouting: "Please, help me!!"

But after we passed, I looked in the rearview mirror and saw the man who had been in the middle of the road saunter over to the parked car. There, he lit a cigarette and had a very casual conversation with the man at the wheel. I drove very slowly, watching behind me to see what would happen. Within a few minutes, I saw the car drive off in the direction of Lugoj.

Later, we realized this had been an attempt to abduct me. Someone had known what time we left Timişoara, our route and that the people in the car understood English. Even more insidious, that person knew that I was a compassionate person that would readily respond to someone was shouting for help. If I had gotten out to help, the supposed victim would have pushed me inside. The two of them would have disappeared with me into the night. Interestingly, the car was a Volvo with a black license number beginning with 12B, like the ones foreign students and diplomats used to have in Romania at that time. The investigator would therefore have concluded that, "some foreigners he associated with must have killed him or taken him out of the country."

We arrived home in Haţeg after 2 a.m. and thanked God for protecting us from this trap too.

Bribery

When they could not succeed in killing my body, they tried to kill my soul. In mid-August it was announced that the President of the Baptist Union would be coming to the church in Timişoara. He told me on the telephone that he would be preaching at the morning service and that afterwards he would talk with all the church members in a general meeting.

I knew why he was coming to Timişoara. After the service I asked all the members of the church to stay for the discussion. Over three hundred members stayed. I greeted the President, whose name I have decided not to mention in this book, and invited him to speak. He began his address as follows:

"I find myself in a very delicate position, because I have to give you two pieces of news, a good one and a bad one. God has heard the prayers that you have been lifting up to him for many years for a new church building. He wants to answer those prayers."

The church already knew that Romulus Street and the whole of the Odobescu district in which our building was located lay within an area designated for demolition. We had been told this officially by the Town Hall systematization department. Both our building and that of the Pentecostal Church were going to be demolished, but we were going to be given permission to buy some other properties in the same area that we could remodel for use as church buildings. The price the state was going to pay for the expropriated buildings was a pittance, but for us this was a unique opportunity. Even when I had turned to the Lord in September 1965 the church had already been praying for a new building. When I was appointed pastor 20 years later, I found the church still praying for the same thing; the older brothers told me that they had been having times of prayer and fasting for this specific request for over 30 years.

But the answer to prayer had come at the most critical moment. The President of the Baptist denomination continued his speech as follows:

"I have been instructed to tell you that you will shortly receive authorization to buy and remodel another building. It will be just like you have been wanting for many years."

Despite the seemingly great news, the 'Amen' that greeted his words was very reserved and anemic, because the brothers knew what was coming next:

"But I also have to tell you the some bad news: you will not be given this approval if Brother Dugulescu is your pastor. He is not well regarded by the authorities. I mean that you have made a wrong choice. If you give him up, we, the leadership of the Baptist Union will send you another pastor. Please trust us. Because I love you, I must tell you the truth: you cannot have both a church building and Brother Dugulescu! That's why I am here today: to help you to make a decision."

A brother in the balcony, Dan Laurenţiu, spoke up: "President, I would like you to answer a question for me: who was it that sent you to Timişoara today, God or Satan? Who is paying you, the Communists or the Baptists?" The President placed his hand on his heart in a very dramatic manner and expressed his regret that his good intentions were not being appreciated or taken seriously.

Another brother, Doru Racovicean, spoke from the floor: "President, Brother Peter is building a living church here out of living stones. If God has mercy on us and gives us a church of bricks and mortar, we will be grateful to him. But we are not going to sacrifice a living church for a dead one!"

A sister who was an English teacher, Natasha, spoke up: "President, while I was a student I attended the church that you pastor and I know that you valued intellectuals and helped them. Pastor Dugulescu is an intellectual and our church, which has such a large number of intellectuals and students, needs him. Please help us. I am convinced that you will understand us."

But despite all the efforts of the church members who spoke, the President would not relent. On the contrary, he seemed irritated by Sister Natasha's praise of me and gave a reply which lacked both respect and good: "If you wish to have this 'intellectual'," he said, pointing at me, "you've got nothing ... but that's your business. I wanted to help you. You cannot have both this 'intellectual' and a church at the same time!"

My spirit was grieved and could not believe that the man beside me, the President of the Baptist Union of Romania, was my brother in Christ. I thought of the words of the Lord Jesus in Matthew 24:45-51:

> "Who then is the faithful and wise servant, whom the master has put in charge of the servants in his household to give them their food at the proper time? It will be good for that servant whose master finds him doing so when he returns. I tell you the truth, he will put him in charge of all his possessions. But suppose that servant is wicked and says to himself, "My master is staying away a long time," and he then begins to beat his fellow-servants and to eat and drink with drunkards. The master of that servant will come on a day when he does not expect him and at an hour he is not aware of. He will cut him to pieces and assign him a place with the hypocrites, where there will be weeping and gnashing of teeth."

I was his comrade in ministry but he had struck me in the face in front of the church I served.

The expression 'to eat and drink' has the sense of having fellowship. The saddest thing for the believers and ministers of evangelical churches in Romania in the 45 years of Communism and atheistic dictatorship was that those who were our nominal leaders had much more fellowship with the sons of darkness, with the atheists, than with their brothers. Their obedience to God was conditional, but their obedience to the Communist authorities was unconditional.

I have no wish to put my brothers in a negative light. I would like to be positive and constructive in all that I do. However, as a faithful scribe of the history of the churches in Romania in the period 1970-1990, I have a duty to report the truth. History is not positive or negative, simply objective.

Over three hundred brothers and sisters witnessed this very public and painful attempt to manipulate the entire congregation, in order to uproot me.

"I cannot help Brother Dugulescu because he will not allow himself to be helped. I asked him to sign a brief statement, a few words only, and he will not."

Then I addressed the church and said: "Brothers, have I ever spoken to you about the Securitate in this church?"

"No!" they replied.

"Today I am going to do so, because the President has left me no alternative. He is not willing to tell you what kind of statement he wants from me: a declaration that the road accident that took place on September 30 last year, which I only survived through the hand of God, had not been planned as an assassination attempt. They want me to take the entire responsibility for the accident upon myself."

At this point the President intervened to say: "Yes Brothers, Radio Free Europe, the Voice of America and the BBC were humming with reports. And the Securitate got the blame for weeks on end. This man will not have his transfer here approved unless he signs a statement contradicting these rumors that have damaged Romania's reputation abroad."

I could no longer keep quiet.

"It hurts me a very great deal that the President does not care that I, his brother in the ministry, stands beside him with a broken arm that will be crooked until my dying day. He does not care that people wanted to kill me, but it hurts him a lot that the Securitate got the blame on the radio.

"For me to sign that piece of paper would be to destroy myself twice over, once morally and once physically. In the first place I am being asked to lie, because I have evidence which proves that that accident was no accident but an assassination attempt. I cannot lie to protect the 'honor' of the perpetrators!

"In the second place, if I am once again the victim of an assassination attempt and survive, and if I dare to tell the truth, this will be used as evidence to have me declared mentally sick, that "he said something like this once before and afterwards he was sorry and retracted it." Then they will inject me with drugs to 'treat' me. I have already been threatened that I am suffering from persecution mania. I am not going to sign a statement of this kind, at any price!"

Starting the following Sunday, a group of brave brothers from the church initiated a protest letter, and began to collect signatures supporting me to be sent to President Ceauşescu and the Department for Religious Denominations. As they left the church, the brothers and the sisters went past the table in the entrance hall and signed the protest. I will always be grateful to those people, and will always thank God for their love and their solidarity with me in those times.

One of the elderly deacons, came to me saying: "Brother Pete, I was called in to see the Securitate chief yesterday and he said to me: "Tell that fraud and rogue of a Dugulescu that we are going to destroy him!" But I do not believe they will succeed because we love you and are praying for you!" This strong brother's eyes were full of tears.

That protest and those signatures may not have moved Romania's Communist leadership but it was an opportunity for the flock to show its solidarity with its pastor and demonstrate the love that joins us one to another in the body of Christ.

Harrassment

Unsuccessful in trying to divide the church, the authorities now employed another tactic.

A disabled brother came to me to say: "Brother Pete, I think I can help you obtain a residence permit to live in Timişoara, because I know someone at the census office.

No sooner said than done. I gave brother Voi our documents and a half-kilo packet of real coffee, which was in great demand at that time because it could only be found in the 'shops' that only took dollars. Such under-the-counter deals were run of the mill in Romania. But the poor junior officer at the window did not know that this was not a run of the mill case. He didn't know that Dugulescu was *Dugulescu*, the one causing problems for the Militia and the Securitate. As soon as I received my three-month temporary visa, I brought my family to Timişoara. We lived in the house that the church had bought to convert into a church building. It was a detached house with central heating that did not work so when weather turned cold we lit a feeble fire in a smoky stove. I enrolled my children in school which was to begin on September 15.

One Monday morning I was sweeping up leaves from the sidewalk in front of the house when a tall young man stopped in front of me and asked:

"Is this where Mr. Dugulescu lives?"

"Yes, I'm Mr. Dugulescu," I replied.

"Please leave your broom here, get your ID and come with me to the Miliţia."

"What for?" I asked, "What have I done?"

"You'll find out once we get there!" he replied.

And without another word being spoken on either side we walked together along the bank of the Bega canal to the headquarters of the town Miliţia. There a young officer, whose name I do not recall, left me alone in an antechamber for about 30 minutes. After that he took me into the office of Captain C., who was the head of the Timişoara census office.

The captain said brusquely: "Your ID please!"

I gave him my ID. He opened it and asked me aggressively: "Who gave you this residence permit?"

"You did, that is to say your people at the window did," I said.

Then he picked up a rubber stamp and applied it to my newly-acquired permit. He handed it back to me. When I looked at it to see what the stamp said, I saw the word CANCELLED in capital letters diagonally across it.

In an extremely courteous tone of voice, I said:

"Captain, please help me to obtain a temporary residence permit for me and my family because I have moved here to Timişoara to work."

He rose to his feet and addressed me in a very sharp voice:

"You have no job here in Timişoara. Even your Baptist leaders in Bucharest do not recognise that you have a job here!"

"Captain," I continued in a beseeching tone, "please give me some other forms to fill in, because my children are at school in this town".

"Take your children and your whole family and leave Timişoara. I'm telling you to get out of this town in 24 hours, do you understand! If you won't do so voluntarily we will make you!!"

"Where am I meant to go, Captain?"

"That's no concern of mine. Go to America, go wherever you want!!"

"Captain ..." I tried to go on, but he cut me off short:

"If you don't get out of his office at once I'll arrest you on the spot! Get out!"

I went away discouraged. Just one day before, a restriction had been introduced that applied to all large towns. Food was now rationed. The allowance per person per month was only one kilo of sugar, one kilo of floor and one liter of oil, and this was obtainable only from the store in the part of the town where you lived. The store would have a list with the names of those eligible to buy food these foods there. If you did not have a temporary or permanent residence permit for that town you could not buy these foodstuffs. Neither could you buy salami, meat or butter.

I sat down on a bench beside the canal and looked at the diagonal CANCELLED stamp in my ID. What was I to do? Now, I wouldn't even be able to feed my family.... Where was I to go? Back to Hațeg? Impossible. Then where? Had this country become too small for me? Was there nowhere left that I could move to? Then the colonel's words echoed in my ears: "Go to America, go wherever you want!"

Now, this seemed to be the only course open to me. The U.S. ambassador in Bucharest, David Freudenburk, was a friend. I was certain that I would be given a visa in five minutes, and my status would not be that of an immigrant but that of a political refugee. In America, there were many, many Romanian churches who would be glad to invite me to be their pastor, and many offers of this kind had been made to me.

Everything seemed so simple to me. I could take the overnight train and be at the ambassador's door the next morning. By tomorrow evening I would be back in Timişoara, and we would start packing. We would go to America! But as I paced park, praying, I felt a lack of peace and this made me worried. I knew from previous experience that whenever I was on the point of making a major decision that wasn't God's will I had no peace. Still unsure, I reached home and told my wife and children what had happened to me at the Militia building.

"If we don't leave town within 24 hours we could all be arrested at any time and taken goodness knows where. Besides that, from today onwards we can't even buy food to feed ourselves. What are we going to do?"

"Let's go to America!" my children said in chorus.

I smiled sadly. My wife too and been wanting this for a long time. She was always saying to me: "If they kill you, what am I going to do alone with four children?"

I told them my thoughts earlier, adding: "But I don't have any peace about it. I have always been against brothers who said that the Lord was sending them to America. I'm the one who has always said to them: "I wonder why the Lord doesn't send any of you to Russia, China or Mongolia. Why is the Lord sending you all to America? It would be better if you admitted that you were going to America to fill yourselves up with bananas, oranges, pizzas and hamburgers. Don't come telling me that the Lord is sending you to America!"

Was I now justifying my own actions? We had a church service that same evening. Before beginning my sermon, I told the church about everything that had happened at the Militia office. I had always done this at the Haţeg church as well, on the basis of the text in Acts 4:23: "On their release. Peter and John went back to their own people and reported all that the chief priests and elders had said to them."

"They told me I must leave the church and the town in 24 hours," I reported to them, "and starting from tomorrow, I won't even be able to buy food for my children any longer. One course of action open to us is to go to America. That would be the simplest and best thing for my family. But I know that God had a plan in bringing me here. I want to obey him, and in order not to take a wrong decision, I have decided to do three days of uninterrupted prayer and fasting. That is what I used to do in Haṭeg at difficult times. I used to encourage both myself and the church with Isaiah 49:23. "And kings shall be thy nursing fathers and their queens they nursing mothers; they shall bow down to thee with their face toward the earth, and lick up the dust of they feet; and thou shall know that I am the Lord; for they shall not be ashamed and wait for me." I ask my brothers and sisters who feel the prompting of the Holy Spirit to join me, at least in prayer. I want God to speak to me."

"And if, during this period, you should hear that I have been found drowned in the Bega canal, killed by a train or hanging from a tree in the park, be assured that brother Peter has not committed suicide. If this happens, be assured that someone else is responsible!"

The next day, from 8 o'clock in the morning, we were visited by brave brothers and sisters, one after another, bringing us bread, meat, oil, butter. Our fridge had never been as full as it was then. We knelt down and prayed with every group that came. With tears in their eyes they said to me: "Brother Pete, don't leave. We love you and we are praying for you and for your family and no one can touch you. God is able to guard you. We're will be alongside you, and we will share our food rations with you. Don't leave, brother Pete, because God has blessed us so much during these months!" As Elijah was fed by the ravens, our congregation supplied our needs.

Later, other groups of brothers came with full bags. These ones, and especially the young ones, said: "Brother Pete, you're still a young man, you know some English; you have a wife and four young children. Go! Go as soon as possible, before it's too late. You've got to put these children's safety and future first. We will pray for you!"

But, after each day of prayer and fasting I had more and more peace, despite the difficult situation I found myself in. The children kept attending school. Every day, I was expecting them to be removed from the student roster, but it didn't happen.

During the afternoon of the third day, the last day of my fast, a group of charismatic sisters from the church came with a group of sisters from the Elim Pentecostal church to pray for us. I was not at home, as I had gone to make some pastoral visits. After they had prayed, the sisters left a note for me with my wife. In this message the Lord was telling me to stay in the place where God had put me because I was going to be victorious and the plans of evil men were going to be overturned. I believed that God could do this, but at that point in time I could not see how he was going to do this.

Angels with British Passports

"How precious to me are your thoughts, O God! How vast is the sum of them! ... When I awake I am still with you." (Psalm 139:17-18).

I knew and believed that in the spiritual world God has angels, ministering spirits, spiritual beings unseen by us who protect and help us at difficult times, as the Psalmist says in Psalm 34:7: "The angel of the Lord encamps around those who fear him, and he delivers them."

But I did not know that these angels can sometimes be flesh and blood people like ourselves, and that God could send them behind the Iron Curtain under the protection of British passports. These were those who spoke not only English but also the *agape* language, the universal language of the Kingdom of God.

Baptist pastor Philip Campion from Stockport, England was a close friend of mine. At least once a year he would bring a team from his church to Romania. He usually came at our Easter (Orthodox Easter) and he always gave out chocolate eggs to the children in our church in Hațeg. Pastor Philip would preach and the other members of the team sang or spoke, including two deacons, John Grunding, who married Mihaela, a girl in our church, and Cyril Tuffin, a pharmacist. It was rare for brothers from the West to visit our churches so their presence was a particular blessing for us.

Less than a week after the bleak day when I was ordered to leave Timișoara, I received a call from England. It was Cyril Tuffin telling me that he would be arriving in Timișoara on a chartered plane in a few days' time with Brian Mansfield, and they would be bringing medical equipment for the Timișoara County Hospital. Brian Mansfield was the director of a charity called Protector Trust which collecting medical equipment from large hospitals in England that had been replaced with newer equipment but was still in excellent working order. The equipment was then reconditioned and brought to African and Eastern European countries. Fittingly, their letterhead bore the title 'Born Again Technology."

Cyril asked me notify the airport authorities so that they could have permission to land and take off, and to ask the Public Health Authorities if they were interested in receiving this donation.

I got in touch with Dr. Constantin Luca, the manager of the County Hospital, and Dr. Lucia Anghelescu, the head of the County Health Authority. Both of them were very enthusiastic but told me that I also needed to inform 'channel two', that is, the Securitate.

On the appointed day, we went together to the airport to wait for the charter flight from England. The two visitors were greeted very cordially by their official hosts and a festive meal was even organized at the hospital in their honor. The equipment that was brought included an echograph, the first one in Timişoara. The following year, more equipment arrived, this time for the Children's Hospital and for the Victor Babeş Hospital.

Right from the beginning, our friends in England made it clear that these donations were being made solely through the auspices of the First Baptist Church of Timişoara and Pastor Peter Dugulescu. Further, they made it known that there was much more equipment at the Oxford University Hospital and other hospitals in London which could be obtained via the same route: First Baptist Church and Pastor Peter Dugulescu!

After returning to England, our friends sent an official letter to the Timiş County Public Health Authority, inviting a doctor nominated by that department to come to England with me to collect the equipment. The value of this cannot be imagined. Romanian hospitals suffered – then and now – from dire financial constraints: there is an acute shortage of medicines and medical equipment. Most of the equipment in use at that time was between 30 and 40 years old.

One day, Doctor Anghelescu invited me to her office to ask my assistance, by going to England with Dr. Ene Virgil to collect this equipment.

"I would be delighted to be able to help you, madam, but we must be realistic," I told her. "As long as my ID is not in order, I cannot even dream of getting a passport."

"But what problem is there with your ID?" she inquired.

I told her the whole story of the cancellation of my residence permit by the Miliţia and the fact that I had been ordered to leave the town within 24 hours.

"But you're a good man!"

"It appears that other people have a different opinion, ma'am."

"Will you allow me to present your case to the First Secretary of the County Branch of the Romanian Communist Party, Comrade Ilie Matei?" she asked.

"Yes, of course," I said.

I may never know what happened behind the scenes, but I know that I was left in peace to pastor First Baptist Church and that two weeks later, the Secretary General of the Baptist Union in Bucharest rang to tell me that my transfer had been approved. He explained that, for the moment, this was an oral approval and that he could not give me a written one. But the miracle was that I received a one-year residence permit for myself and my family.

Discussions went on between 'channel two' and the County Health Authority in connection with my possible trip to England with Dr. Ene. At Timişoara, the only Securitate officer who discussed things with me was Major R.T., the deputy head of the Securitate. I gathered that it was being said in official circles that I was a CIA agent and had access to dollars, whisky and Kent cigarettes which I used to corrupt Securitate officers and recruit them for foreign spy services.

The person in Bucharest who took decisions concerning me was Colonel Z.A., who was responsible for all the religious denominations in Romania. An enlightened Transylvanian whose attitudes towards evangelical religious groups were much more positive than those of the other Securitate men, the colonel was literally a 'blue-eyed boy,' and one of those who had interrogated me in Haţeg in February 1985. He never spoke to me unpleasantly or even raised his voice. Probably, he let the other 'boys' handle the uglier aspects of the job.

I felt that he was tacitly sympathetic and was trying to help me. He let me know in a few sentences that he knew everything that was going on towards religion in Romania and was trying to persuade his superiors that evangelical pastors did not represent a danger. On the contrary, they were people who loved their native country, and the contacts they had in the West could benefit Romania.

At the beginning of June in 1987, this colonel rang me from the Continental Hotel in Timişoara and asked me meet him in the hotel foyer to discuss the medical equipment from England. A major who held a senior post within the Ministry of the Interior in Timişoara also participated in our meeting.

We sat down by a small table, and the colonel from Bucharest asked me:

"Mr. Dugulescu, tell us what the English want in exchange for the equipment."

"Nothing," I replied.

Then the other man intervened: "Get serious, Pastor. Who the hell gives you something in this world without wanting something from you in return?"

"There is one person," I said.

"Who?" they both asked at the same time.

"God. He gave his son, Jesus Christ, to die for us without asking us for anything in return. In fact we have nothing to give God in exchange for such a great gift. He only asks us to love him and be grateful to him."

"Let's change the subject," said the Timişoara man. "That's religion."

"No, Major," I continued, "God offers us not a religion, but a personal relationship with him through his Son, Jesus Christ, who said: "I am the Way, the Truth and the Life" (John 14:6).

"Reverend," said the colonel, "we know that you Baptists have many brothers and significant connections in America, in England, everywhere. But we do not want other people to take advantage of your good standing in a way that prejudices the interests of Romania."

"Colonel, I know you are well-informed. You know that we repenters have a peculiar characteristic: we behave like a family because we *are* a family. We help one another on a local, national and international level. The head of our church – Jesus Christ – taught us to love one another with a love that gives without asking for anything in return. Please believe me that our brothers in Great Britain are offering us this equipment without asking us for anything in exchange. I assure you before God, there is no hidden agenda in this donation."

About two weeks the Health Authority informed me that Dr. Ene and I had received permission to go to England. I couldn't believe it, yet, it was true.

I then rang the 'blue-eyed' colonel asked him a special favor: to allow me to take my two older daughters with me, since I was going to be traveling by car and meeting up with Doctor Ene in London. He put in a good word to Timișoara, and the people at the Passport Office told me that I could come and pick up passports for my two daughters, Ligia and Cristina. I was very grateful.

I have said many times, and will always say, that I have great respect for my children, who have paid a steep price for my service to the Gospel. I considered this trip to be an earthly reward for all the many frightening, sad and lonely times they had gone through.

Before we departed for England, we had yet one more surprise: we received authorization for the partial demolition and remodeling of the villa we had bought. While the Communist regime was demolishing Orthodox churches in other places in Romania, we and the Elim Pentecostal church received building authorization. It was the answer to the 30-plus years of prayer and a miracle from God.

After I had met up with Dr. Ene in London, and we received the medical equipment which we had been given, I went to the U.S. embassy in London and was given a tourist visa for America. I rang Dr. Iosif Ţon, who paid for my ticket, and went to the States for two weeks. There I was able to raise over $10,000 dollars towards the construction of our church. Meanwhile, Ligia and Ina returned to Romania by train.

I returned to London, and before I left for Romania Pastor Philip Campion and the brothers from the Romanian Aid Fund and the Christian Medical Association arranged for me to have a hernia operation at the Middlesex Hospital free of charge. Due to my experience, I was afraid to have any more operations in Romania, after the previous hernia was operated on in October 1983. At the county hospital, something very strange had happened to me. My wife had told me her brother-in-law in Târgu Jiu had had a dream indicating that my enemies were going to try to take my life during the operation. When I went to the doctor's office next day to give him a packet of coffee, as was customary in Romania, a dark-haired man in a visitor's smock was there, waiting. I knocked, but the doctor was not in the office. As I returned to the ward, my inner voice told me that the man was from the Securitate in Deva and that he was there on my account. When I returned a half hour later to the doctor's office with the packet of coffee, the suspicious guest was sitting in an armchair in the doctor's office, conversing with him. I apologized for interrupting and left. An hour later, the ward sister, who was a very cheerful, chatty woman, said to me: "Reverend, I think I'm going to die of laughter! D'you know what the doctor told me? He said that a Securitate agent from Deva came to discuss the operation with him of a clergyman, and while they were discussing it, in he came with a packet of coffee." My guess was confirmed.

I believe that the doctor could not reveal to me directly what had happened, but being a person of character, he made sure the information reach me via the head nurse. I then asked the surgeon to give me a local anesthetic rather than a general one. The doctor told me that he would do so and added significantly "so you won't be afraid."

After the operation, at night when the other patients were asleep, a young woman wearing a smock, who I had never seen her before and was not part of the hospital staff, came to my bed. She had a syringe in her hand for an injection. She lifted up the blanket and pulled back my pajamas. I was shocked and asked what kind of injection it was. She said the doctor had prescribed it. I knew what post-operative treatment the doctor had prescribed for me and it did not involve any injections. The mysterious nurse persisted, but I totally refused to let her inject me. She left and returned a few minutes later saying: "I'm sorry, the injection was for another patient in a different ward." That experience, as well as the others following the accident, made me highly suspicious of having an operation in Romania.

Before and after my operation, I stayed with Jim and Ann Clark in their flat in central London. They were among the 'angels with British passports' who accompanied some consignments of medical equipment to Romania. I thank God for these wonderful people. When I returned home, the Securitate officer who received my passport looked at me and said: "So you've come back, despite everything".

"Of course," I said, "my place is in Romania."

"I, for one, was convinced that this time, you wouldn't come back."

I had thought that after this successful trip, I would be appreciated and my troubles would be over.

When the big truck loaded with equipment arrived, it was unloaded at the County Hospital. There were two more echographs and a computerized angiocoronarograph and huge quantities of disposable supplies. The specialists in the Timişoara hospitals said that this angiocoronarograph was an extraordinary piece of equipment, but, for reasons I was not told, permission to install it was never received – even though the English people offered to send specialist engineers to do the work, as they had done with a modern X-ray machine which had been installed in the County Hospital. Rats in the hospital stores eventually chewed through the cables and the equipment deteriorated. Perhaps someone thought it would create too much propaganda for the English imperialists and the Romanian Baptists.

At one of the meals or receptions held at the hospital in honor of the English guests, someone put something in my food or drink. After the meal, I had some very odd symptoms. My blood pressure suddenly shot up, my face was flushed and red, and I began to shiver and have depressing thoughts. I was convinced I was going to die. My wife called Dr. Ene who came to see me right away with another doctor. They were couldn't make a firm diagnosis; they just gave me some blood pressure medicine. I was trembling so violently that the bed was shaking too; I was frightened and kept on saying that I was going to die. The next day, I felt better, but in the evening while I was translating at a church service, I felt my head becoming hot. My face turned red and I felt I was going to fall. My daughter, Ligia, who was a nurse, became frightened for me.

These symptoms returned again during the weeks that followed, and ever since, I have to take medicine for high blood pressure. This time a different method was employed, but I was convinced, and still am, that this was another attempt to kill me;

but I am equally convinced that the word the Lord Jesus gave his disciples as an assurance was fulfilled at that time: "and these signs will accompany those who believe: ... when they drink deadly poison, it will not hurt them at all." (Mark 16:17-18).

Meanwhile, construction work on the new church building had begun and the brothers were working hard. We were renting a house from some of our church members, the Ilie Neagoe family. The church had decided to buy this house as a parsonage with the help of some brothers in America, but the authorities had refused to issue the necessary authorization. The family who wanted to sell the house applied to the court received a positive response: "Yes, the church has the right to buy a house for the pastor, and you may sell your house to whomever you like." But after only a few days, an Inspector from the Department for Religious Denominations came to Timişoara and following his visit, the court overturned the judgement given previously. It said that a church had the legal right to possess a parsonage but that since Pastor Dugulescu was not well regarded by the authorities, the First Baptist Church could exercise this right unless it dismissed that pastor and agreed to a different one. That same Inspector told me that I was living in Timişoara illegally and that it would be a good thing if I left the town in the shortest possible time.

Rebuilding the Walls

At the general meeting of the church, we had pledged before the Lord that every member of the church would contribute two months' income every year for as long as the construction work lasted. The pastor and deacons would lead the way. Every member also promised some of his family's food ration to the site canteen, and to give some of his free time to come and work on the building project.

For a significant part of this time, all my sermons were taken from the book of Nehemiah, who rebuilt the walls of Jerusalem. This was to encourage and motivate the workers and the church. I taught that in spite of the hard times in which we were living, the House of God should be a place of plenty and not of poverty or lack (Malachi 3:10).

I had promised the volunteer workers that they would be fed well, and just as Nehemiah ensured a supply of wine every day for those who rebuilt Jerusalem, I, promised that I would provide plenty of filter coffee every day for those who came to build the Lord's house. Filter coffee could only be bought in the hard currency shops, and one kilo of it cost a week's salary. Those who had afternoon jobs came to work at the church in the mornings. Those who had morning jobs came in the afternoons and went on working until nine or ten at night. Retired people worked as their strength permitted. A group of sisters worked in the kitchen and provided three hot meals a day, plus tea and coffee.

The two and a half years of the building project were a special time of grace in which we saw God's hand every day. It was a time in which we grew closer to one another, got to know each other better and learned to serve one another. Our church services were held in the old building on Romulus Street during this period.

The new building was dedicated on December 10, 1989. Only later did we know that this was the first day of a week which was to begin a new era in the history of Romania. During that week, we celebrated with great joy the dedication of Bethel with evangelistic services every evening by the best preachers in. The 1,100 seats in the church hall were filled and many, many others stood to listen or went to the basement and the side rooms where we had installed speakers. More than 1,500 people attended each service, and each started with people praying fervently for Romania.

Just two months earlier, all the evangelical churches all over Romania had had a Sunday of prayer and fasting for Romania, at the request of Pitt Popovici, the retired pastor of First Baptist Timişoara, the man who brought me to Christ. We prayed specifically that the Lord would have mercy on the people of Romania, bring times of freedom, and heal the Romanian nation from the disease of atheism.

The last sermons I preached in the old building on Romulus Street were from the book of Joshua and were entitled: "Preparations for the Conquest of the Land." We knew that one day the answer would come; but we did not know when it would happen or what form it would take. It came, sooner than any of us suspected, and in a way more mysterious than we could ever have imagined.

"God Exists!"

From this point on, in my narrative, I must describe the events by date, because so much happened in each day. Even to us, who had prayed earnestly for our nation, things moved with dizzying speed.

Friday, December 15, 1989
Although the Reformed Church was just a five minutes' walk from our church, it was from Radio Free Europe that I found out what was happening there. Some two weeks earlier, I had heard a report about the Reformed pastor László Tökes. It was said that some "hooligans" had attacked his family in their apartment in the church building, while they had guests for dinner. The pastor had defended himself by fending off his attackers with a chair and, being a man of some physical strength, had succeeded in throwing them out of his home.

This was an act of intimidation, a warning. The County Inspector of Religious Denominations had repeatedly ordered this dissident pastor to leave Timişoara, but he had not complied. The final straw however was when Dutch and Hungarian television had broadcast one of his denouncing the dictatorship of Nicolae Ceauşescu and the village demolition program. A rumor was now going around that the Reformed pastor would be arrested on the morning of December 15. More precisely, since he was not prepared to voluntarily leave, the Militia and the Securitate were going to force him and his family to move to his native village in Transylvania, where he would be compelled to live.

On that morning, before ten o'clock, I was there in front of the Reformed Church in Timotei Cipariu Street with my son Cristi and a number of Baptist believers from Bethel and the other churches. There we met a number of brothers from the Elim Pentecostal Church, as well as other people we did not know. Several Reformed believers were posted at the entrance and in the corridor to defend their pastor. But when the Militia, the Securitate and the Mayor of Timişoara arrived they could not prevent them from entering, since the authorities had an official arrest warrant and were armed.

Nevertheless the presence of the group in the street meant that the new arrivals hesitated to proceed immediately with their intention of evicting the pastor's family by force. They were waiting for us to leave first. But the group of people in the street kept on growing. I remember the Communist Mayor, M.I., appearing at the window and addressing us, the people in the street, saying "Romanians, go home please! Why are you wasting your time here? If the Hungarians wish to stay that's their business, it's their church. They are chauvinists anyway. But you Romanians, go home!"

Many voices immediately answered him: "We're not leaving, we're not leaving!"

The crowd had been infiltrated by Securitate agents whose job it was to give passers-by false information. A man walking by asked:

"What's going on here?"

One of the disinformation agents, a tall well-built man with an astrakhan hat replied:

"Hell, a priest from the Hungarian church has hanged himself!"

Since I was standing near him I could not let this pass so I called out:

"He's lying. They want to arrest the Reformed pastor. Look, there's the militia truck over there, waiting to take his furniture!"

The Securitate disinformation agent shot me a look of hatred, as if to say "Watch it, your turn will come too!"

After the mayor had left the window, Pastor Tökes took his place and spoke to the people, asking them to behave in a peaceful and Christian manner. Towards afternoon, some young people in the crowd suggested that we should sing hymns that Baptists, Pentecostals and Reformed all shared. We sang "At Midnight" and "We are Waiting for the Lord to Come" in Romanian and Hungarian.

Although it seemed that the eviction of the pastor and his family had been postponed, many remained there through the night. As darkness fell, one of the young men from our church, Dănuț Gavra, asked my permission to go to the Orthodox church nearby in Sinaia Square, to buy candles. I told him to go. He returned in ten minutes, worked his way through the crowd to me, opened his coat and showed me a large packet of candles. I suggested he distribute them among those present, and I returned to our church for an evangelistic service. Dănuț Gavra lit the first candle and the others lit theirs from his. With candles lit, the crowd began to sing and pray, holding them in their hands. It was a fairy-like spectacle, extremely rare in a Communist country.

Saturday 16th December 1989

The next morning I arrived early to find that many others had joined those who had stayed through the night. The group of peaceful fighters was now much larger and was constantly growing.

I kept running between the Reformed church and our church office. About lunchtime Dr. Ionel Rab, an ethnic Hungarian, came into my office. Dr. Rab knew me well, because he had worked on one of the first echograph machines that I had brought from England in 1987 and given to the Victor Babeş Hospital. He had been permitted to visit Pastor Tökes' wife, who was pregnant. During the visit, Tökes spoke with him alone, and had asked him to meet me to ask us to send more brothers, especially young men, to the Reformed church building. Although the only contact I had had with Lászlo Tökes had been via Radio Free Europe, we now felt very close to one another. I telephoned the young men I knew I could rely on in this kind of situation, and all of them agreed to go there.

Before our evangelistic service began, two of the elders of the Reformed church came and asked if they could speak to me privately. Mr. Balaton, a teacher, and Mr. Varga, an engineer had brought a proposal from Pastor Tökes, that I and many of the members of Bethel should go to the Reformed church the next morning, which happened to be the Sunday the Hungarian Reformed celebrated the Lord's Supper, and that we fill the church and take part in the service.

The atmosphere was extremely volatile, and he knew that the hours until he was arrested were numbered. He wanted to prevent this by ensuring the presence of a very large number of people. The two messengers also asked me to send some more young men to stay outside the church building all night singing and praying.

When the pair had left, some of my fellow-workers in the church, guessing what the meeting had been about, said to me: "Brother Pete, don't get involved. It's risky. This is straight politics."

"Yes," I replied, "but it's God's politics against the powers of darkness."

I went into the balcony, which was crowded with young people waiting for the evangelistic service to begin, and signalled to some of them to come outside. I told them to take some of the others with them and go to the street outside the Reformed church. I went up into the pulpit with Pastor Negruţ. That evening, the church was packed including the basement and all the side rooms where TV monitors had been installed. There were almost 2,000 people in the congregation. At the close of the service, all these people set off for Maria or Sinaia Squares to catch their trams and buses home. But many of them joined the crowd of 'revolutionaries' at the Reformed church, where the atmosphere continued to become more tense, and was reaching boiling point,.

This torrent of people coming from our church towards Maria and Sinaia Squares greatly increased the mass of the people that had been holding vigil at the Reformed church. The militiamen started asking each other on their two-way radios: "Who are these people and where are they coming from?" because the balance had changed. The gathering in Maria Square was becoming extremely large and beginning to assume explicitly anti-Communist overtones. Some courageous men, among them the poet Ion Monoran, began stopping trams, climbing onto them and disengaging the connections from the overhead power lines.

After service, my family into the car and set off for the Reformed church. When I reached the traffic signals by the regional railway headquarters, I saw a column of several hundred armed and helmeted militiamen with shields and batons coming over the bridge from the direction of the Cathedral. They were advancing at a steady pace and beating on their shields with their batons, an ominous drumming. To the right two fire engines aimed powerful water hoses and foam cannons at full power at the crowd. Several powerful jets reached our car, cutting off all visibility. I swiftly turned the car around to pass by our church make sure it was safe. I was turning onto 7th December Street, when I heard the sharp crash of breaking glass. The plate glass windows of the Mihail Sadoveanu bookshop on the corner were shattered and a group of young people, among them some from our church, were throwing communist books with out of the shop, pouring gas over them and setting them on fire. I saw piles of one book, an expensively printed one entitled *Respects*, in flames. Pictures of Ceauşescu and his wife were burning. The young people were flagging down cars and asking people to donate gas, which was rationed and very precious at that time; you could only buy 10 gallons a month.

Anyone who refused to 'donate' a liter of gas had his car turned over. The people who initiated the window breaking were provocateurs, ordered to do so to justify harsh reprisals on the pretext that the demonstration was no longer peaceful, but that those taking part in it had engaged in acts of vandalism and looting. Now, low-lifes, thieves and professional criminals stormed the shops on both sides of the central boulevard that runs from the Cathedral to the Iosefin market. Dozens of militiamen poured out of the side streets, beating people savagely with their batons. They arrested many young people and herded them into the waiting buses.

I reached home very late. My little daughter Eunice was waiting up for me to remind me that today had been her birthday. She was just five. I apologised that I had not been there at lunch time, as I had promised, and I prayed for her at our late supper. I told her that from that year on we might be commemorating Romania's re-birthday, as well as her birthday, every December 16.

Romania's Grieving Daughter

Sunday, December 17, 1989

"Oh, that my head were a spring of water and my eyes a fountain of tears! I would weep day and night for the slain of my people" (Jeremiah 9:1).

My people are the Romanian people, among whom I was born and whom I love, people of eventful history and undeserved fate; but Romania's grieving daughter will always be Timişoara.

I set out for the church at eight in the morning. The city was sad and silent. An abandoned fire engine was lying by the Maria Bridge. Its hoses, which had been employed against the peaceful crowed, had been torn off later and thrown into the Bega canal. After being driven away from the front of the Reformed church by the water cannons of the firemen and the clubs of the militiamen, the demonstrators spontaneously formed themselves into four groups that marched off through the streets shouting anti-Ceauşescu and anti-Communist slogans. Others had been captured and were loaded into Miliţia vans and taken to the Popa Sapcă prison, which was overflowing with detainees. Five young men from the Bethel and Bethany churches were among these.

We celebrated a wedding at the church that morning, the first in the new building. Afterwards, there was a reception in the basement room, but my mind was on the demonstrations taking place in the rest of the city. I excused myself and rushed to the center of the city where people had occupied the Town Hall and the County Council headquarters; they were throwing red flags with the hammer and sickle and books written by 'the most beloved son of the people' and 'the world-renowned intellectual' out of the windows and setting fire to them. No one and nothing was going to stop them now.

Peter Dugulescu

They took the national tricolor flag and cut out the Communist hammer and sickle, as if to surgically remove the cancer that had dominated and sickened our beloved country. Everywhere, demonstrators were waving tricolors with that empty hole in the middle. It was clear: the political revolution had now begun.

What the world did not see on their television screens or newspaper pages was the two days and nights of peaceful 'Christian revolution' in Timişoara which gave birth to the political, anti-Communist revolution. What happened on December 15 and 16 was a miracle, something even greater than a revolution.

After all, the revolutions of this world happen when citizens rise up violently against the governing class and seize power through bloodshed. But the people who lit the spark in the Timişoara Revolution had no guns, no ammunition, no tanks – but only hymns, prayers and candles. And they won an amazing victory, a victory like that of Gideon and the people of Israel in the Old Testament. They stood against a totalitarian atheist government, highly skilled in using brute force and tyranny, supported by thousands of soldiers, militiamen and secret police, weapons of war, machine guns, tanks, helicopters and more. Worse still, it was willing to, and did, use these wantonly against its own people. Unbelievable, but true. And yet the strong lost and the weak conquered: "for my power is made perfect in weakness" (2 Corinthians 2:9).

What cannot be shown on the 6 o'clock news are the invisible forces: faith, love, brotherhood, selflessness, and the awareness that God is real. The people who stood shoulder to shoulder for two days and nights to protect an innocent pastor from an unjust arrest and forced exile drew their strength from a source that no political analyst could have predicted. Yet it was their courage, their unity, their example that coalesced a conviction throughout the city. The people of Timişoara first witnessed the peaceful opposition of the government by a handful of faithful Christians, like Gideon's army. Then, they agreed with it, finding in it the voice that had been stifled for 45 long years. Finally, they joined it, and expanded it to a fight against the ideology that had usurped God and enslaved the people.

At 5 p.m. that day, during our final service of the week-long dedication of our new church building, Pastor Paul Negruț was preaching the final sermon, when we heard the first shots. Isolated at first, the shots became more and more frequent and we could hear bursts of machine-gun fire. One of the deacons passed me a note: the government forces had opened fire on the demonstrators simultaneously in different parts of the city and that those who had children should be very careful on their way home from church.

That night, two sisters, Mariana and Silvia Căceu, were walking to our service when they were shot in the head and killed instantly. They were 34 and 36 years of age.

Dănuț Gavra, the 24-year-old man who distributed the candles before the Reformed church lighting the first one and sharing the light through the crowd on Friday was at the head of a group of demonstrators on Sunday, Dec. 17, carrying a Romanian flag with a hole in the middle. His 21-year-old girlfriend, Slobodanca, a member of the Elim Pentecostal Church, was walking beside him holding his arm, as the demonstrators processed along the walkway lined with student dorms, calling to the students watching from the windows to come down and join them. "Romanians, come with us!" the demonstrators shouted to those at the balconies and windows. But the militiamen had locked the main doors to prevent the students from joining them. The column continued its march towards the County Council building, but when it reached the Decebal Bridge near the People's Park it was met by uniformed soldiers and plainclothes secret police, armed with machine guns. The soldiers opened fire into the unarmed group. It was a slaughter. Dănuț's girlfriend, Slobodanca, was killed in the gunfire and collapsed beside him in a pool of blood. Dănuț's left leg was riddled with bullets.

Any wounded were picked up by ambulances. They were not transported to hospitals. They were taken outside the city and shot.

But God's hand protected Dănuţ. A merciful citizen helped him into the trunk of his car and took him to the Orthopedic Hospital where his mangled leg was amputated above the knee.

Indiscriminate shooting began throughout the city: at the Cathedral, in Freedom Square, in Lipova Avenue, in the People's Park, and no quarter was given. Women, children and old people were mown down, along with the demonstrators. Timişoara, the city of flowers, was transformed into Timişoara, the city of martyrs. Shots and screams continued to ring out until long after midnight.

The revolutions that had taken place in all the other Communist countries in Eastern Europe, even in East Germany at the Berlin Wall, had been 'velvet' ones, without the loss of life. In Romania, the price of our liberty was paid with the blood of innocents.

Monday, December 18, 1989

In those morning hours the city appeared calm on the surface. The shots and screams were both silenced. One would think that the gunning down of the protesters, and the loss of human lives would have frightened the people of Timişoara and broken our spirits. Surely, they would not have the courage to take to the streets again. But this was the deceptive calm in the eye of the storm.

Ceauşescu, returned from a state visit to Iran, lost no time in declaring a state of emergency on Sunday evening. A 10 p.m. curfew was imposed for vehicles and pedestrians were forbidden to be in groups of more than two. Ceauşescu spoke angrily of the "acts of vandalism" in Timişoara, the "hooligans" in that city and the "espionage agencies" of the West which had infiltrated Romania to destabilize the Socialist order of our country.

Timisoara was in mourning. People on the trams and trolleybuses were silent and sad, many wearing black as a sign of bereavement. I went to the County Hospital searching for the two Căceu sisters, Mariana and Silvia. Surrounding the hospital was a cordon of militiamen and civilians in leather jackets, carrying automatic weapons. They asked who I was going to see and demanded to see my ID. I told them I wanted to visit an elderly brother from our church operated on the week before. They allowed me to pass but told me I should have left my pastoral visiting to another time. Inside the lobby, I was dumbfounded. The County Hospital looked like a funeral home. Weeping black-clad women and grim-faced men were everywhere, speaking to no one. The doctors and nurses refused to answer any questions from anyone at all. Military personnel were posted at some of the wards.

The top leaders of the Executive Committee of the Romanian Communist Party had been despatched to Timişoara with special orders from the dictator to crush the uprising. At the hospitals where the wounded had been admitted, the Securitate men confiscated all the patient records. Many wounded people were shot dead, right there in the hospitals–in elevators, in wards or in certain doctors' offices that were commandeered by the secret police. People who had been admitted with gunshot wounds in the leg were returned to their families with bullet holes in their heads.

The Securitate were trying to get rid of the evidence of their repressive actions. On Monday night, at the command of Colonel V.I., the hospital lights were turned off at the main circuit board. Then, 45 bodies were removed from the morgue, loaded onto a meat wagon and driven to Bucharest to the crematorium there. The ashes were dumped into the canal at Popeşti-Leordeni.

The Căceu family found Silvia's body in the County Hospital morgue, on Monday afternoon, but could not find Mariana's. When they continued their search on Tuesday they found

Mariana's body – her head had been shaved and there was a bullet hole – but that of her Silvia had mysteriously disappeared. It may have been loaded onto the meat truck with those 44 other victims, or it may have been incinerated on the outskirts of the city together with other bodies, where several sacks of human bones were later collected.

Leaving the hospital through the double cordon of militiamen and leather-jacketed 'heavies' armed with their AKMs, I arrived home in a state of shock. I could not believe that it was real. But I had hardly entered the yard when I heard a rumble of tanks and voices shouting: "Freedom! Down with Communism! No violence! Down with the dictator!" coming from the direction I had just been. I climbed onto the garage roof. I could not see, but could hear the events unfolding. Soldiers were racing the engines of their armoured cars as they headed into town from the Giroc military base, officers were shouting at the crowd to fall back, and the people were crying: "Freedom. Down with Ceauşescu!" It turned out a crowd had stopped the trolleybuses, disconnected them from the overhead power lines and turned them sideways on to block the tanks' route into town. Children picked up iron bars and forced them into the tanks' caterpillar tracks, pulling them off their drive wheels so that several tanks were immobilized. People began throwing whatever they could lay their hands on at the armoured cars, although the soldiers kept warning them that they were loaded with ammunition. There, standing on that garage roof, I heard the voices of men, women and children shouting "Freedom! Freedom!" My heart ached with emotion. The *denouement* was not long in coming.

A long pitiless burst of gunfire rang out. Again the words reached my ears, "Freedom!" but shouted by fewer voices. More gunfire. This was the only response to the cry for "Freedom" that the Communists had: gunshots. After another two minutes, even fewer voices could be heard be heard, but still they shouted: "Freedom! Freedom!" Once more, the tried and tested response. The shouting stopped and silence descended in that place. Those who ran to take refuge in the entryways of apartment buildings were pursued and gunned down. Shots were fired in the stairwells and even into the windows of apartments.

The Giroc Road massacre seared my consciousness. I came down from the garage roof, white and trembling. I could not eat or sleep for many days. My ears were still ringing with the shouts of the crowd, including the voices of children: "Freedom! Down with Communism!" Then, the merciless response of the machine guns. I wrote my tribute to those unknown heroes in my poem *The Giroc Road*.

The Giroc Road

The Giroc Road
Has ploughed furrows across my consciousness
Marking out indeed our Via Dolorosa
Where I baptized my being
Climbing towards history's vantage point

The sky stood blood red then, that evening
Little dogs were trading barks
When the stars fell headlong
Into the wilderness of my soul
There, on the Giroc road

Daily, I go along the Giroc road
A silent pilgrim to the place
Where children had forgotten play
And been playing with fire
For the last time

There, on the Giroc road
Death and childhood met
Tanks and freedom rendezvoused again
And – dying and believing --
The weaker overcame

Long have I journeyed on the Giroc Road
Not yet to know its end
Nor the body count of those innocent lambs
Who, with such clear clear voices
Had (alongside my own heart) cried out, and cried out
"FREEDOM!" "FREEDOM!"

Yes, I will return along the Giroc Road
Towards that tragic Christmas of the lambs
Wanting to know who, and from where, their butchers were
Who threw away the knife so soon
To take up shepherds' staffs

Then, at that Romanian Christmas
They could hear the Virgin Mary's sigh
And how the grieving Bethlehem mothers wail;
Romania was seeing God return again
Entering Timişoara
Along the Giroc Road

Pastor Vasile Taloş called me from Bucharest to ask me if the Radio Free Europe news report that they were firing on the general population in Timişoara was true. I held the telephone receiver aloft and said: "Listen!" The shooting could be heard even from indoors.

During those days of terror, I was expecting the death squads to burst into our home at any moment and shoot me and my whole family. On the day of the massacre, I was called by the head of the Bucharest Department of Religious Denominations, who had come to Timişoara with the other members of the Government to crush the protest. They had set up their headquarters at the offices of the Orthodox Metropolitanate. The County Inspector, M.T., informed me tersely that the comrade minister wanted to speak to me:

"Pastor, I am very angry that you and your flock went to defend that troublemaker Tökes. Please tell your people, especially the young people, not to take to the streets any more and not to join forces with those slogan-shouting hooligans. And don't shelter those hooligans in your church. Keep the doors locked, do you hear me?"

"Sir," I replied trembling with indignation, "how can you ask me to do something like that? You and the Government you support gave the order to fire on the populace, on women and children, even on the steps of the Cathedral. Innocent blood has been spilled in this city, yet you call these people 'hooligans'? Not only that, I am in the same position as Tökes. Three weeks ago the General Inspector of the Religious Denominations Department declared my transfer invalid and threatened that I would have to leave Timişoara."

"Pastor, I can promise you that after things have calmed down, we will sort out your affairs, too."

But he had no chance to deal with my affairs. God dealt with both of our affairs, according to his own methods. Four days later, on December 22, the Minister for Religious Denominations departed the building of the Banat Metropolitanate through a window, leaving his suitcase with his clothes behind. His last message to me, passed months after the revolution was, "Tell Mr. Dugulescu that there have been other troublemakers like him and that their bodies were left cold on the steps of the Cathedral."

Tuesday December 19, 1989

The ELBA battery and lamp factory went on strike. The workers were gathered in the factory yard holding a peaceful protest. A strike in a Communist state was something unforgivable. In a workers' paradise, where the people own the results of all labor, a dissatisfied group of workers exposes the lie. Communists did not know the meaning of the word 'negotiation'. While representatives of the Government were leaving the headquarters of the County Council for the factory to discuss with the union and factory management, the army took up positions at all the factory gates with tanks, and trucks full of soldiers. In other areas of the city there was still sporadic firing, but it was much lessened in intensity. However, a shot fired from one of the armoured personnel carriers at the ELBA factory killed a man in the Iosefin Market.

Wednesday, December 20 1989

We may never know the truth of the last days of Communist power in Bucharest. One thing we do know is that Ceauşescu and the Defense Minister, General Milea, were sharply divided. In Timişoara, it was rumored that at the suggestion of Elena Ceauşescu, her husband wanted General Milea to use biological weapons on Timişoara which would have destroyed all life, but preserved the buildings. Ceauşescu and his wife told the general: "The salvation of socialism is worth the destruction of a city!"

The Minister of Defense was a professional soldier and must have tried to explain to Ceauşescu that he had already gone too far in ordering the army to open fire against its own people, and he delayed carrying out this criminal order.

Among the victims of the bloodbath the government had ordered were the soldiers, the young men of Romania. My daughter was working as a nurse at Victor Babeş Hospital where the wounded were brought following the massacre on Monday. One was a recently drafted soldier who had no bodily injury, but an immense psychological wound. His period of basic training was when his regiment was ordered to quell the "rebels" at the city center. Among the demonstrators, he saw his own relations, friends and acquaintances who shouted to him: "We are your parents, we are your brothers. Don't shoot us!" When the company commander ordered them to open fire he complied, but when he saw the first victims collapse, he threw down his weapon and attempted to flee.

His comrades returned him to the barracks, but the next day he was brought by ambulance to the hospital in a state of delirium and nervous shock. He was sent from Victor Babeş Hospital to the Military Hospital.

Colonel Viorel Oancea, the commander of the regiment in Lipova Avenue, refused carry out any more orders from the army general staff and came onto the balcony of the Opera House to make a proclamation to the people of Timişoara to applause and shouts of joy by the several thousand strong crowd of demonstrators gathered in Opera Square. For several days demonstrators had been meeting continuously day and night in the square in front of the building of the Romanian Opera. After Colonel Viorel Oancea had made his proclamation other military commanders took their units over to the Revolution. That day Timişoara proclaimed itself the first city in Romania to be free from Communism. Five days previously Timişoara had been the only rebel city, and isolated from the rest of the country. Day and night we had been expecting to be razed from the face of the earth.

On December 19, the Romanian Democratic Front had been established, led by Lorin Fortuna, Ioan Marcu, Beniamin Oprea, Professor Ivan from the Polytechnic University, and others.

The leaders of the Romanian Democratic Front installed a powerful public address system on the balcony of the Opera House and, for the next two days and nights, scores of speakers took turns addressing the people. The spiritual dimension became more pronounced, and there was a powerful anti-atheistic, pro-God atmosphere in Opera Square. While the crowd outside the Reformed church numbered thousands, here the crowds were of tens of thousands. At the climactic moment on December 22, there were more than 100,000 demonstrators present, perhaps close to 200,000.

Along with slogans such as, "Down with Ceauşescu!" "Down with the dictator!" or "Let him take the rap – right here in the

Banat!" There were frequent shouts of "God Exists!" Some young Baptists and Pentecostals had brought their guitars and begun to sing various Christian songs; "Glory, Glory, Halleluiah" and "At The End Of The Ages We Live" were sung. The crowd really fell in love with this last song so it became a rallying anthem and became known as 'The Hymn of the Timişoara Revolution.' Hands clasped as if in prayer, their faces transfigured, the people lifted their voices together:

> *At the end of the ages we live*
> *With struggles and hatred and war*
> *But joyfully looking above*
> *To the Lord whose coming is near*
>
> *He is coming again! He is coming again!*
> *What joy beyond telling he'll bring!*
> *Put an end to the night's bitter reign,*
> *The Lord, who is coming again!*

Romanians who were estranged from God for 45 years, systematically taught that God did not exist, were now seeking God, longing for God, calling out to God from the depths of their beings.

I have only seen one thing in my life that can describe that moment.

When salmon return from the ocean to the clear sweet waters of the river from which they came, the river is full, almost black, with the thousands of salmon swimming against the current towards the clear waters in which they had been born – towards their origins. Even when people built dams across the river, they would ascend the salmon ladders, leap by leap, until they reached the top. If one fell back in the waterfall, it would gather its strength and launch itself again at the obstacle until it reached the top. When they encountered the iron grilles they continued to battle against the current. Some had no skin left on their heads, not merely injured but some mortally wounded. Yet, there was no going back for them. They had felt the irresistible call of the clear waters of the springs. They knew that this was their destiny and fought to follow the pattern established by the Creator.

The time had come for the people of Romania to return to the wellspring--whatever the price. So, they had set themselves against the stream. In Timişoara, they had faces the hoses and water cannon of the firemen, and then the clubs and bullets of the militia and army, crying: "Without violence! Freedom! God is with us!"

After December 21, this spirit of denying athieism and upholding God was felt in Bucharest, Arad, Sibiu and throughout the country.

Thursday, December 21, 1989

This entire week, my time had been divided between the church, the Opera Square and my family. I slept two or three hours per night, fitfully, expecting thugs to come and kill us at any moment.

On Thursday, I took my three older children, Ligia, 19, Ina, 17, and Cristi, 15, to Opera Square. There, Professor Ivan from the Polytechnic, issued a challenging invitation to the city's clergy.

"We need a priest or a pastor to come to this microphone and to speak to us about God. After 45 years of atheism, we need to hear about God."

Some men in the square went off to the Cathedral to invite one of the priests to come to speak. To their disappointment they found the doors of the Cathedral locked and nobody would talk to them. When the Romanian Democratic Front leaders on the balcony heard this Professor Ivan spoke, his voice full of indignation:

"We are very sorry that the clergy of the churches in our city are compromised; the priests and pastors have sold out to the Securitate. We need a man of God to come to this balcony and bring us a message of encouragement from God. We are only three days away from Christmas, and Christmas has been a forbidden festival to us for 45 years. We need a priest or a pastor to speak to us about God, about Jesus Christ, now in the time when we are preparing to celebrate His Birth.

I said to my children and the friends from the church:

"I'll go. Here is an opportunity to present Jesus Christ to these tens of thousands of people."

Ligia, my eldest daughter, said to me:

"Dad, please don't go. They will kill you. You know how they've tried to on other occasions. We need you. Don't go!"

"Ligia," I said, "don't break my heart. Can't you see that nobody is willing to go? If, tomorrow, Romania is free it will be easy to preach the Gospel, but I would never forgive myself if I were not to be courageous enough to make a stand for God at the critical moment. Today that balcony is my pulpit."

I spoke to my children these words, which I am sure they will never forget:

"Our God is the God of history and he uses ordinary people like us to write the history of every nation. Now is God's time for Romania. We have heard on the Voice of America and Radio Free Europe about the spectacular changes in East Germany, Poland and Czechoslovakia and now it is Romania's turn. God wants to open a new chapter in the history of the people of Romania and He wants the first page to be written here, in Timişoara, today. It seems that God wants me to represent him from that balcony before all these people. Pray for me!"

My children understood that God had called me to obey Him and they promised to pray for me. Ligia wrote out a note that a brave young man delivered to the people on the balcony of the Opera. Hours passed but my name was not called. A battle was going on behind the scenes, on who should control and influence the crowd from the microphone on the Opera balcony. The Romanian Democratic Front were there, but were also infiltrated by Securitate agents who were still swarming around and seeking ways to impose their will. Ceauşescu was still in power in Bucharest and the top representatives of his government were still in Timişoara.

At that moment, the balcony of the Romanian Opera House was the most strategic and the hottest place in all Romania. The outcome of the Revolution and the future of the entire nation hinged on what happened there. If the spirit of Timişoara could have been broken on that balcony, Romania might have remained under Communism indefinitely.

Many people had offered to guard the people on the balcony, to sift through the messages and announcements they received and to select the speakers to address the crowd. It was obvious that some were trying to dilute the spirit by giving very slippery talks, promoting a different goal. When demonstrators realized the motivation of such speakers, that they were not on the side of the Revolution, they were booed and interrupted.

On the same day that I waited to speak at Timisoara, Ceauşescu was holding a rally of his own in Bucharest at the Romanian Communist Party Central Committee Square. His goal was to mobilize the citizens of Bucharest to condemn the population of Timişoara. Tens of thousands of workers were summoned from the factories, students from their lectures and administrators from their offices. It was reported that if Nicolae Ceauşescu had won the approval of this captive audience, the

Peter Dugulescu

planes were ready to take off to attack Timişoara blowing it off the map of Socialist Romania.

He told the large crowd that in Timişoara, bands of hooligans supported by secret agents from the West, were attempting to disturb public order and the Socialist destiny of our country. These hooligan bands had attacked the forces of law and order and military units. His final, guaranteed crowd pleaser was announcing to pensioners that a few minutes before, at a meeting of the permanent office of the Central Committee of the Romanian Communist Party, he had raised their pensions by 100 lei per month.

Imagine his shock when, instead of applauding and shouting their approval, the crowds began to boo and to hiss at him. Only those in the front rows, all carrying red banners and placards with pictures of him and his wife, dutifully shouted "The Party, Ceauşescu, Romania!"

When the booing began, his entourage and guards tried to pull him back into the building and to persuade him to stop speaking, but he took no notice. Something like this was inconceivable for him. He tried to continue speaking, but it was impossible. The volume of the booing and hissing became even more intense and then, the people began to chant: "Timişoara! Timişoara!"

At this moment, the spirit of Timişoara had indeed conquered. Conquered, because it was not the spirit of Timişoara alone, but that of liberty, dignity and most importantly, faith in the Living God.

The shouts of freedom from those shot down in Timişoara had not been silenced by death. Instead, their prophetic words had come true: "Today in Timişoara, tomorrow in the whole country!"

Now, five days later, the echo of that shout resounded in the heart of the capital. Angry at his disastrous reception, Ceauşescu ordered the army onto the streets of Bucharest in tanks and armoured personnel carriers to put down any anti-government demonstrations.

That day, the poet Ioan Alexandru, university professor, stood in University Square in front of the tanks, with a crucifix in one hand and an icon of the Mother of the Lord in the other. Young students around him undid their overcoats and shirts and bared their chests shouting: "Pull the trigger! Shoot us. We will die and then we will be free!"

And the soldiers fired.

Mihaela, a young woman of 17, fell in a pool of blood beside the poet, and he had knelt down in the blood flowing warm from her young body and prayed for her soul. He prayed also for her murderers and cried out to God to have mercy on Romania.

One of the officers asked him: "Are you a priest?"

Spontaneously, he replied: "Yes, I am a priest." So they left him in peace.

"In that moment," he said, "I was thinking like an evangelical believer, who believes in the principle of the priesthood of all believers."

The people of Timişoara took courage when they heard what happened in Bucharest, and the spirit of the Revolution spread to the other large cities in Romania as well.

Friday, December 22, 1989

On the night of Thursday, December 21, I again slept very little.

Between the church duties and my vigil in Opera Square, I had arrived home at midnight. My wife and children were worried about my health because I was having frequent attacks of high blood pressure. I fell asleep around 1 a.m. The telephone rang at 2, but I did not hear it. Ligia told me that young people from our church had called to tell me that my note had been read from the balcony of the Opera House and that I had been called to the microphone. Perhaps those arranging the order of the speakers had tried to ensure that few people would hear my message about Jesus Christ. Ligia had not wanted to wake me and told them I would come very early the next morning.

At 7 a.m., was called by BBC Radio in London to interview me about the situation in Timişoara. At eight, I went to the square, after passing through the security screen I reached the balcony. At the entrance I met Father Borza from the Orthodox parish of Mehala who had come to speak to the demonstrators. Because he represented the majority church, I asked him to speak before me.

Professor Ivan, who had issued the appeal for a priest or a pastor to address the crowd, took me on one side to ask me what I was thinking of saying to the demonstrators.

I shared with him the main thoughts of my message. He said that it was very good but he asked me to urge the crowd to shout "Down with Ceauşescu, down with Ceauşescu!" at the beginning and end of my message, and to give the thumbs down sign.

At that time, Ceauşescu was still in power and there was no knowing what might happen in the future. But I accepted these conditions because I sensed that this was their method of screening speakers in order to be sure that no Securitate men or supporters of Ceauşescu could have access to the microphone.

By this time, there were over 100,000 people in Opera Square. Since the army had gone over to the side of the Revolution, people had been pouring in every day from surrounding towns and villages. They came in cars, in trucks, in tractors and trailers, on motorcycles and bicycles. The COMTIM Company and other grocery stores were supplying the crowd in the square with free supplies of fresh bread, salami, tea and mineral water. This helped the demonstrators to stay together day and night and to keep the flame of the Revolution burning.

From the balcony, I could see that it was not just the central square of the city that was full; all the neighboring streets were thronged too. As far as the eye could see in any direction there stretched a sea of people waving tricolor flags with that famous hole in the middle and anti-Ceaușescu and anti-Communist banners.

Someone made the following announcement from the microphone. "Pastor Peter Dugulescu from Bethel Baptist Church has responded to our invitation to address us from this microphone. Let's listen to Pastor Dugulescu!"

At that moment the crowd broke out into applause, chanting:

"Good for him! Good for him!"

I came to the microphone feeling moved and in accordance with the promise I had made, I began with the slogan "Down with Ceaușescu!" and the thumbs down sign. The crowd did the same.

Then I began: "I am Pastor Peter Dugulescu from Bethel Baptist Church and after 45 years of Communism – my own age, unfortunately – I have come to bring God back to you. The Communists confiscated God by taking him out of our minds, our families, our schools and our society. The Communists hated God and they have tried to kill me in various ways. But, I am alive today--because my God is alive!"

At that moment, a cry burst from the crowd, which then erupted, as if from a volcano, from the lips of everyone there. It was a cry from the heart, authentic and uncensored.

"God exists! God exists!"

It was an impressive, overwhelming moment. This was the most revolutionary cry possible for Romania.

"God EXISTS!"

We had all been systematically taught, every day of our lives since kindergarten, that God did not exist. Now, instead of the mandated slogans ordered by the Party, a single slogan was shouted, written in the depths of our hearts:

"GOD exists! God EXISTS!"

We shouted these words over and over, without stopping.

These were the Romanian people returning to the original springs of their birth, who had pitted themselves against the powerful current, seeking their home. Like the salmon overcoming every dam, every obstacle, every iron cage, they were unstoppable. When the shouts proclaiming the existence of God diminished, I proclaimed that there were certain absolute principles upon which the Romania of tomorrow must be constructed:

- Free elections
- A free, democratic society
- A free-market economy
- Religious liberty
- The Bible and prayer in schools
- Co-operation between all Christian faith communities for the spreading of the gospel and the proclamation of Jesus Christ
- Freedom for pastors, such as Lászlo Tökes

Suddenly, while I was speaking, an urgent news bulletin from Bucharest was announced on the television: the Minister of Defense, General Milea, had committed suicide. It is believed that he was killed because he refused to carry out the orders of a demented dictator who would do anything to maintain power.

The next item was even more stunning: the dictator and his wife had fled by helicopter from the roof of the Romanian Communist Party Central Committee Building.

Hearing this announcement, the crowd began to chant:

"Ole, ole, ole, Ceauşescu's gone away!"

"Let him take the rap, right here in the Banat!"

When the crowd's shouts of joy had died away, I asked the entire crowd for a special request: that we join our hearts and voices together in the Lord's Prayer. "I hope you still know this prayer. On this historic day which sees the liberation of our people from under the yoke of atheistic Communism, let us honor God with this prayer. Everyone, absolutely everyone."

And with that, more than a hundred thousand people knelt down on the ground and repeated the Lord's Prayer aloud.

It seemed as if the whole city shook as the last vestige of communism crumbled. Hundreds of thousands praying to God again after a half century of enforced silence, in a single voice. It was more than impressive; it was heart-stirring.

After the flight of Ceauşescu, the Romanian Television building in Bucharest was taken over, and various people spoke in the first uncensored broadcast in the country's history. The first speech was by the actor Ion Caramitru, who began with the words: "God has turned his face towards the people of Romania."

A New Government

That afternoon, the National Salvation Front was formed. It was made up of political dissidents and personalities from Romanian political and cultural life. Ion Iliescu, a former Secretary of the Central Committee of the Romanian Communist Party, who had fallen into disgrace and been marginalized by Ceauşescu for his more liberal and democratic sympathies, was nominated President of the National Salvation Front.

On that same day the National Council of the NSF moved on to the organization of a provisional government. Ion Iliescu was named as President of the country and Petre Roman, a university professor at the Bucharest Polytechnic and the son of Valter Roman, a former general in the Soviet army, was named as Prime Minister. It was rumored around the country that Ion Iliescu was a friend of Mihail Gorbachev, and that Gorbachev had helped him to assume power so that he could implement *glasnost* and *perestroika* in Romania – something that Ceauşescu had stubbornly refused to do for years.

I for one, as an ordinary Romanian, had regarded the dissident Ion Iliescu sympathetically and would have been glad to see him take over from Ceauşescu at any time in the latter's period of dictatorship. Now, after a revolution which had such a pronounced Christian and anti-Communist character, which had paid so high a price in human life and innocent blood, I would have preferred Romania's new political leaders to have been people with no connection at all with Communism. But it was not to be. Anyway, whatever open or hidden nostalgia some of the new leaders might have felt for the old ways, the Romanian people no longer wanted anything to do with Communism or its institutions. One thing was becoming ever clearer: there was no going back.

Shortly after the presidential helicopter had taken off, reports began to circulate around the country: that Ceauşescu had given orders for his presidential airplane to be made ready so that he could flee to China with his family; that the helicopter pilot had requested a landing at Snagov to drop off some people because the chopper was overloaded; That allowed Ceaușescu to pick up some personal documents and details of his foreign bank accounts; that he was heading towards Constanța to flee the country in his personal yacht; that the presidential airplane had been grounded by the revolutionaries. One thing is certain: on his way towards Constanța, he was ordered by radio to land on the Bucharest-Pitești freeway. There, he was arrested, handcuffed and taken in an armoured personnel carrier to a military base in Târgoviște.

On the evening of December 22 the first publication of the Romanian Democratic Front appeared with the headline 'The Tyranny has Fallen!'.

After the arrest of Ceaușescu and his wife, a new set of announcements were made from the balcony: that the forces of the Securitate still loyal to the former dictator were likely to launch terrorist attacks throughout the country to wage a life and death struggle to free the Ceaușescus. The revolution's leaders--those who had addressed the people from the balcony of the Opera-- might be targeted by these rogue forces, so they should take measures to protect themselves.

At the urging of some of my friends, we went into hiding at the home of Petrică and Ibi Stanoievici for two days. My family was guarded by two strongly-built young men from the church, armed with clubs and knives. There was no shooting around my house, but near the place where I was taking refuge, the tanks from Giroc fired on what we were told were the terrorists. Several times, I had to lay flat on my stomach in the apartment as the walls of the room were struck by bullets flying above me. Indeed, in the evening of December 22, fighting broke out between the 'terrorists' and the army, which had the Civil Guard on its side. This happened simultaneously in Timișoara, Bucharest, Sibiu and other towns.

Up till now, December 2002, when we are commemorating 13 years since the Revolution, this mystery of the 'terrorists' has not been solved. Who were they? Where did they come from? Where did they disappear to? I doubt we will ever find the answers to these questions. Some of them were arrested, or admitted to a hospital when wounded, but it seems that they came in by one door and went out by another. In this climate everyone was really paranoid about the 'terrorists'. They would open fire from the roofs of blocks, from the windows of apartments , from cars with false number plates. They shot at civilians queuing for milk and bread and then sped away.

It is now known that in some cases, they used cannon fire simulators mounted on apartment blocks to which the army and the Civil Guard responded with live rounds, as they were convinced that they were fighting with the 'terrorists'. In many situations the soldiers were firing at each other. One thing is certain: after the arrests of Nicolae and Elena Ceauşescu, there should have been no more shooting or victims, but in fact, the number of those who died after the revolution on December 22 was much greater than that of those killed up to that time.

It is hard to say who had an interest in creating this scenario and in giving the Romanian people the impression that they were rescuing us from people belonging to the former Securitate and loyal to the former dictator. We were innundated with the dark imprecations that these sinister people were haunting us like ghosts, and that the true Revolution had only begun after December 22.

What began as a Christian revolution and then a popular revolution was now being re-packaged as a political one. One could be cynical, but in the long run, this is how God allowed it to happen. The changes which began in Romania after December 22, have been major and positive ones; the people who I did not like at the time have changed greatly as a result of tens of thousands of prayers, mine included, and as a result of the European and international socio-political context. May God be praised for this.

If Nicolae Ceauşescu had retained power, we later learned, some 50 people would have been publicly executed in Opera Square, on December 23rd as a warning to others. The list of those to be executed was found at the County Council headquarters. My name appeared on that list.

While waiting out the storm in Stanoievici family apartment, I followed the television reports of the National Salvation Front leaders in the capital. They were making desperate appeals, some of them confused, for people to come and defend the national television station in Dorobanţi Street in central Bucharest. That night there was also talk of Arab terrorists who had illegally entered the country, and of unidentified military units converging on the capital.

The massacre of 54 soldiers who were guarding the Bucharest International Airport, shot by comrades from another military unit on December 24, is a disturbing example of how the 'terrorist' rumors unleashed violent bloodshed – even though not one terrorist was ever shown on TV or brought to justice. This manhunt continued almost up until the New Year.

In Timişoara, the Civil Guard were checking all road traffic very closely, inspecting documents and searching trunks. It was rumored that some people had been caught transporting arms and ammunition. I was checked at least twice on my way from home to church. Once my briefcase was also searched and they opened my notebook of preaching outlines at a sermon which I had preached in September entitled "Preparing to Conquer the Land". The text was from Joshua Chapter 3. Immediately I was told to pull my car off the road for a more thorough search.

"You are a terrorist," they said to me. "Which subversive group do you belong to? What preparations have you been making to conquer the country?"

"Gentlemen, this was a sermon I preached in September when we were praying that God would have mercy on Romania and bring about a change, and, now, He's done it. We also prayed that he would use us and I believe that he has done so."

"But how did you know what was going to happen?"

"We didn't know, we believed. And look, it has happened."

"Ah...you're that repenter pastor who was on the balcony of the Opera."

"Yes, I am."

"Fine, fine, you can go."

The new police force had not yet been organized and the old militiamen were afraid to wear their familiar uniforms, towards which the population bore a deadly hatred. In some parts of the country people beat them up just because they were wearing the old uniforms, and some were even killed.

Sunday, December 24, was Christmas Eve and Monday, the 25th was Christmas Day. Ironically, this was the only year when there were no church services because automatic gunfire was still going on around the city.

On Saturday night, long after midnight, the trial of the Ceaușescus was broadcast on TV. It had been held inside the military base at Târgoviște where they had been held since their arrest. It was unbelievable to see the man who, for almost a quarter of a century, had been the most powerful person in Romania, with the title 'the most beloved son of the Romanian people,' standing in the dock, sleepless, with dishevelled hair, having his blood pressure taken by a military doctor before the trial and being addressed by the judge merely as "Citizen Ceauşescu Nicolae."

He refused to answer questions and stated he would only answer them before the Grand National Assembly. The judge told him that this no longer existed, but he refused to accept it.

Finally, he was convicted of genocide and sentenced to death by firing squad. This sentence was carried out on Christmas Day, Monday, December 25, 1989.

It may seem incredible, but it is true. On national television, the opening words of the evening news bulletin on that day were: "Today the Antichrist died and Jesus Christ was reborn in Romania!"

After the news bulletin I heard the sound of a group of Christmas carol singers. It was the first time in 45 years!

One of the junior officers who had been part of the firing squad, and who had tied Ceauşescu's hands and escorted him to the execution site, later told me what happened.

"He was a fanatical Communist, perhaps the only one out of 23 million Romanians who really believed in Communism. He walked to the wall singing the *Internationale*. As for Elena, she struggled as hard as she could against the soldiers who were trying to tie her hands and kept saying: "I've been like a mother to you. How can you shoot your mother?" in her attempt to appeal to their feelings.

"He died quickly. After the first volley he pitched forward onto his knees and then collapsed onto his back.

"It was with mixed feelings, of simultaneous pity and anger, that one saw the man who had never knelt before God, the man

Peter Dugulescu

with the most unbending knees in the world, who had hated and denied God and his children, collapsing on his knees in that final moment before falling on his back.

"Unlike him, she was hard to kill; she thrashed around in a pool of blood and didn't want to die. Then I emptied all 30 rounds from my automatic pistol into her body.

"But after that I suffered from great pangs of conscience and nightmares. I kept seeing them in my dreams, lying there beside the wall writhing in that pool of blood. I tried to justify myself to my conscience by reflecting on the fact that I had carried out a patriotic act, that I had freed the country of those tyrants, but it was in vain. I tried drinking more and more alcohol in order to forget, but it was still no use.

"One day when I was discussing my pangs of conscience with a neighbor in my block, he made me a proposal: "Captain, come with me on Sunday to the Baptist church that my wife and I attend!"

And I went. The sermon exactly described my need for forgiveness. I came to understand that only the holy blood of the Lord Jesus Christ can cleanse our consciences from dead works so that we can serve the Living God. (Hebrews 9:14). Then I received Jesus Christ into my heart and asked him to cleanse me of all my sins with his blood. Very shortly afterwards I bore witness to him in baptism."

How wonderful that the love of Christ can reach out and heal the soul of the executioner of the man who tried to eliminate his existence in the hearts of a nation. Truly, we can see that no walls, no prisons, no tyranny can stand against the unyielding love of God.

On Christmas Day, there being no services at the church, I went to visit Dănuț Gavra at the Orthopedic Hospital, the young man who lost his fiancee and his leg during the student demonstrations. I found him in the same ward to which I had been admitted with a broken arm after that attempt on my life in September 1985. Dănuț's left leg had been amputated above the knee and he was on an intravenous drip.

In the next bed, was a 21-year old man named Cristi whose right arm had been amputated at the shoulder as a result of a shooting on December 17.

When Dănuț opened his eyes and recognised me, his face immediately lit up and he said: "Brother Pete, you haven't forgotten me?"

"No, Dănuț, I haven't forgotten you for a moment and I've been praying for you all the time. I heard that you had been wounded and I've come to see you."

"Brother Pete, do you remember the evening of December 15, when I asked your permission to buy the candles? After you had set off for our church, I stayed there and gave everyone a candle. I lit the first one and they all lit theirs from mine. On Sunday, I lost both my left leg and my girlfriend, but I am glad that it was not in vain! The light has overcome! The light has overcome in Romania!"

As he said these words two tears ran down his pale face from his moistening eyes.

I gave these two young heroes some Christmas presents and prayed for them. Dănuț has remained in my heart as one of the dearest and most precious people I have ever known. Last year he got married to Ema, a girl who also belonged to the Elim Pentecostal church, and God has blessed them with a baby daughter.

Jesus, the Hope of Romania

"Happy is the people whose God is the Lord" (Psalm 33:12).

January 12th was declared a Day of National Mourning. Timişoara and the whole country mourned its dead and everywhere the national flag, with its now-famous hole in the middle, flew at half mast.

At the interdenominational memorial service in front of the Orthodox Cathedral, I was asked to speak on behalf of the evangelical churches, and our church band was invited to join the procession as it went to the Heroes' Cemetery.

I told the Metropolitan of the Banat and the members of the organising committee that I wanted to give my place to a dear friend of Romania, the evangelist Steve Wingfield, an American. He had come to Romania for the first time in January 1989, replacing evangelist Sammy Tippit who had been blacklisted.

During his one-week visit with our church, Steve had witnessed the arrest of Kevin Ford (son of Leighton Ford and a grandson of Billy Graham) outside the Continental Hotel in Timişoara and together had prayed for him. After we had succeeded in getting him released by the Miliţia, we had rejoiced together over a meal.

Steve had concluded the week of evangelistic services in our church with a talk on Ezekiel: Chapter 37, entitled "The Valley of Dry Bones."

"So I prophesied as he commanded me, and breath entered them; they came to life and stood up on their feet – a vast army." (Ez: 37: 10)

After that message, there was a powerful spirit of brokenness and repentance. Steve was weeping and so was the entire church.

I learned the reason for his tears. He had had a warning from the Holy Spirit that before his next visit, we would be passing through a time of great trial and that the dead bones in the valley of despair would come to life.

While translating the sermon, I was surprised when Steve said to the church:

"I promise that in February, next year your pastor will be invited to the National Prayer Breakfast with President George Bush."

I stopped translating and asked: "Who are you talking about?"

"About you," he said. It seemed too good to be true.

In the midst of the Revolution, the borders were closed and it seemed impossible that Steve would still be able to come for the evangelistic services in January 1990. I looked much more likely to end up in the cemetery than in America.

But, the borders were re-opened immediately after Christmas, and Steve came, bringing an invitation and airline tickets for me to go to Washington.

It seemed absolutely right to me that the man of God who had brought that prophetic word in Timişoara, one year earlier, should be the one to bring a message of encouragement now that, figuratively speaking, the dry bones had come to life and on the day that, literally speaking, we were mourning those whose bones were decaying in the ground. The memorial service was televised and broadcast nationwide. It was the first time that the Gospel was preached on television in Romania.

In his message Steve said:

"When you faced the tanks here in Timişoara on December 17, you cut the Communist emblem out of your national flag and left a hole. All around me, I can see Romanian flags with that hole in the middle. My friends, that hole speaks to me of a spiritual void which Communism has left in your souls. Atheistic ideology was not able to fill that void, and capitalism with its free-market economy will not be able to fill it either – because it is a spiritual vacuum. Only Jesus Christ, who said: "I am the Way, the Truth and the Life" can fill the empty place in your hearts. Call on Jesus, receive him into your hearts, because: "Blessed is the nation whose God is the Lord".

At that moment, God put a desire in my heart, and a vision in my mind, to found an interdenominational evangelistic organization, and to call it "Jesus, the Hope of Romania."

Right from the beginning I decided that this organization would not be an entity completely separate from the body of the church, but rather be an arm of the church reaching out beyond its walls into society. It would be a serving team formed of people from within the church. Its work would be based on the Great Commission and on the church's vision to involve itself in evangelistic campaigns, discipleship, church planting and social projects.

At the same time, my fellow-workers and I have a responsibility to remain under the authority of the church, to remain always accountable.

In June 1990, I began a nationwide evangelistic ministry. I knew that my gift and calling from the Lord was that of an evangelist. I had served the Gospel as a pastor for 15 years under the Communists and, because my fellow pastors in Romania honored my evangelistic calling, I was asked to evangelistic services in all parts of the country. This was the reason for many problems and much persecution from the authorities.

At that time, the Communist government, represented by the official Department of Religious Denominations, did not even want to contemplate the existence of the job of an evangelist as part of the staff make-up of evangelical churches.

Now that government and the Romanian Communist Party were no more. At last we were free, glory to God Almighty! We are free!

I couldn't believe that I was no longer being called in to see the Inspector of the Department for Religious Denominations on Monday mornings to account for my sermons, or to the Securitate to explain about the Americans or other visitors who had preached in my church. It was hard for me to get used to liberty.

While I was learning to live in liberty and to serve God in freedom I said to myself: "Now is the time! I will dedicate myself to the work of evangelism, because Romania needs to be evangelized!"

Although the regime and the Romanian Communist Party no longer existed, there still remained that hole in the flag of the nation and in the hearts of Romanians. I knew very well, and still know today, that the only thing that can fill it is the Truth, the Love and the Hope of the One who died and rose again for us and is alive for evermore!

"Christ in you – the hope of glory!" (Colossians 1:27).
The new association, which was significantly called 'Jesus, the Hope of Romania,' chose as its mission statement: "We serve by contributing to the moral and spiritual regeneration of Romania!"

Of course, such a regeneration requires leadership, and a new generation of leaders requires new training. In February, less than two months after the Revolution, I was in Chattanooga, Tennessee, with my friends from Precept Ministries, Mia and Costel Oglice. They introduced me to Don Jennings, the President of Tennessee Temple University, who asked me to address the more than one thousand students at their chapel service and to speak to them about the Timişoara Revolution. My eldest daughter Ligia was also there with me. I had been praying that I would be able to obtain a scholarship for her to study in the United States. After my message, the President of the University thanked me and said that he would be honored for my daughter to become a student at the University. I was pleasantly surprised at this swift answer to my prayer. In my speech of thanks, I told the president that I would like to help him to an even higher place of honor by giving more scholarships to Romanian young people.

"You Americans," I said, "are blessed in having had Christian Universities and educational institutions for over two centuries. In Romania, for many decades now, we have had only atheistic education in schools and universities. In our new-found freedom, as we try to fill the void left by Communist ideology, we need to train pastors, evangelists, university teachers, high school teachers and people who can work in business and in the mass media. Please help us!"

This man of God shared my vision for Romania and was generous enough to grant scholarships for 23 young Romanians, including my two elder daughters and Andy, a young man who was to become my son-in-law.

I wanted our work to be modeled on the earthly ministry of the Lord Jesus Christ: "Jesus went through all the towns and villages, teaching in their synagogues, preaching the good news of the kingdom and healing every disease and sickness" (Matthew 9:35). That vision has never wavered.

The Lord Jesus Christ's ministry had two main aspects: evangelism (meeting spiritual needs) and charity (meeting people's physical and material needs). The apostles of the Lord Jesus understood very well the importance of this balance in the Gospel. See, for example, Galatians 2:9-10: "James, Peter and John, those reputed to be pillars, gave me and Barnabas the right hand of fellowship when they recognised the grace given to me. They agreed that we should go to the Gentiles, and they to the Jews. All they asked was that we should continue to remember the poor, the very thing I was eager to do."

In April 1990, on what the Romanians call 'Thomas Sunday' – the Sunday after Easter – Pastor László Tökes and I, together with all the other evangelical churches in Timişoara, organised a big evangelistic service in the Rose Park. Over 5,000 people attended. Every year since then, 'Jesus the Hope of Romania' has organised a Resurrection March on Easter Monday. More than 10,000 people from all the churches in Timişoara and all the ministers of both traditional and evangelical churches. Jesus, the Hope of Romania has been a catalyst in bringing all the people of God around the personage of Jesus Christ.

We preach from the same Holy Scriptures and we worship the same God in our churches all through the year, although according to our unique traditions. Just once a year, we call all the churches, with their ministers taking the lead, to come outside the walls of their buildings so that, together, we can be no longer the churches of Jesus Christ, but the Church of Jesus Christ – so that we can proclaim the Resurrection of the Lord Jesus Christ in the place where the Revolution began. We then set off in procession with brass bands and choirs from outside the Metropolitan Cathedral towards the Rose Park amphitheater, where we hold an evangelistic service. Along the way we stop twice – once outside the Town Hall and once outside County Hall – so that we can pray for those institutions. The evangelistic service in the Rose Park is followed by a youth concert of contemporary Christian music and a meal for the town's clergy and their wives.

In the same way we organize evangelistic crusades in sports stadiums, in Cultural Halls, sports centers and parks. We also organise evangelistic and revival services in churches. Since 1990 we have helped in the planting of over 100 churches.

In the field of charitable work, we became involved, after December 1989, in meeting the needs of orphan children in Recaş – a village near Timişoara. Ironically, we knew nothing about the poverty and the miserable conditions of state orphanages in which these unwanted children lived. It was only when we saw on our TV screens the heart-rending images filmed by visiting French, American and Canadian reporters that I felt guilt that although I was Romanian, I had not known a single thing about the lives of these unfortunate beings who were living on our doorsteps.

Immediately after the 1989 Christmas of mourning, I went to the Recaş Children's Home, where there were 250 boys, ages 6 to 18, all of whom were considered to be mentally handicapped.

There was a powerful smell of urine in the dormitories. The sheets and blankets were torn. The children had rat bites on their fingers and their ears. Cooking was done on a primitive stove whose fuel consisted of scraps from the leather factory in Timişoara.

We took a love offering in our church and bought stoves and wood. Many of the large number of trucks bringing food, clothes and furniture which had started arriving at our church from England, Holland, and Germany were directed to this orphanage.

Teachers from our Sunday school went every week to teach these children the Word of God at an appropriate level. On Sundays, we would bring groups of the children to church by minibus. After church, they were hosted at lunch by different church families in whose homes they could receive affection and play with the children.

Soon Doru and Rodica Racovicean began to dedicate themselves fully to this work of Biblical and musical education. They began a similar work at the girls' home in Lugoj, which housed over 200 children.

In April 1992, I was invited to Blackpool, England as the main speaker at the 75th anniversary of the Rotary Club, with whom we had been collaborating for three years in the distribution of aid to hospitals and orphanages in Romania. After my speech the chairman ceremonially presented me with a diploma and a special Paul Harris Fellow medal for "Meritorious Service In Humanitarian Work".

I felt unworthy when I read in the local papers: "A Labor of Love" and "A Romanian Pastor gives 18 hours of his time to orphans and those in need." The articles went on to say that the four previous recipients of this medal and diploma had been Ronald Reagan, Margaret Thatcher, Mother Teresa and Princess Anne. I was moved to tears and I could not believe that someone had taken such appreciative notice of my ministry. I thought "If, here on earth, someone is counting my hours of toil, and analyzing and evaluating my work, how much more is Someone in heaven doing this all the time?"

"Therefore, my dear brothers, stand firm. Let nothing move you. Always give yourselves fully to the work of the Lord, because you know that your labor in the Lord is not in vain." (1 Corinthians 15:58).

A Public Servant

In the Spring of 1992, a group of friends in faith, especially poet and parliamentarian Ioan Alexandru, urged me to become a candidate in the September parliamentary elections. I had already been involved in the struggle for religious liberty and many brothers encouraged me to take a more public role. I was accepted as a candidate for the National Christian Democratic Peasants' Party (PNȚCD).

Despite the feelings of some that as an Orthodox country, Romania had never had a high office holder who were repenters, I was elected on September 22, 1992 and was re-elected in November 1996. During my first term, I served on the Standing Committee for Human Rights, Denominational Affairs and National Minorities.

My colleague, Viorel Pavel, the member for Giurgiu, and his wife Mihaela came to the Lord through our relationship. They started a Bible study group which at first met in their apartment but then increased to a size where they had to hire the Cultural Hall. Thus was born the Giurgiu Baptist Church. Now it has its own building, and is growing to the glory of God.

On another front, Senator Ioan Alexandru and I began the first Senators' and Deputies' prayer group, which we held in Elena Ceaușescu's former office, the place where the wife of the former dictator had discussed reprisals against Christians and gave orders for the demolition of church buildings, and the confiscation of Bibles. Every Wednesday morning, a group of approximately 25 senators and deputies now rested their Bibles on her old desk and studied the Word of God. Senators and Representatives from different political parties, both in government and opposition, left their political and denominational labels at the door of the meeting, where we meet together around the person of the Lord Jesus Christ,

U.S. Senator Dan Coats and Congressman Frank Wolf prayed with us in this office and played an active role in the first National Prayer Dinner. As I had been invited to the Washington National Prayer Breakfast every year from 1990 onwards, Ioan Alexandru and I pioneered a Romanian National Prayer Dinner, with Doug Coe as our mentor. First held at the National Army Center, in subsequent years, this National Prayer Dinner has always been held in the Palace of Parliament during the first week after Easter. Nicolae Ceauşescu, constructed this palace for his glory; it is the largest building in the world, after the Pentagon, and was designed along the lines of megalomania and opulence. But the dictator did not manage to make use of this palace for even a single day, because the Revolution intervened. In this palace, every year, hymns of glory have resounded to the One who is alive forever and ever, sung by every kind of choir: Orthodox, Baptist, Pentecostal and Greco-Catholic.

I think that while Nicolae Ceauşescu was building this palace, on the scale of the monuments of the Pharaohs and the Tower of Babel, God must have been smiling in heaven because he had other plans for it.

We have been honored to have John Ashcroft (then Governor of Missouri), Pat Robertson and the astronaut Charles Duke as special guests at our prayer group and at our prayer receptions.

In 1994, former Secretary of State James Baker visited Romania. He stayed in the Ceauşescu's former villa in the Spring quarter of Bucharest. Since the Revolution, this has been official accommodation used to house special guests of the Government. Having met him at the Washington National Prayer Breakfast, Congressmen Frank Wolf and Doug Coe asked me to organise a prayer and Bible study breakfast in Nicolae Ceauşescu's living-room that Sunday morning. The meeting was attended by members of the Government, and of Parliament, and I, Peter the Repenter, received the guests and played the host in Ceauşescu's house.

To really bring the power of God into the nation, I initiated a move to have every parliamentary session each morning begin with the recital of the Lord's Prayer.

I pushed for this to be accepted by the Chamber of Deputies while my brother Ioan Alexandru did the same in the Senate. One of the atheist senators spoke from the dais and asked the senators not to approve Senator Alexandru's proposal because, as an atheist, he would feel offended to hear this prayer in the Romanian Senate.

Brother Alexandru returned to the microphone and responded as follows:

"The Holy Scripture, in Psalm 53:1, says: "The fool has said in his heart: 'There is no God.' I hope, colleagues of the Senate, that this Senate is not a house of fools. At the last census, it was established that the population of our country is 98 percent Christian. Which Romanian population does the honorable gentleman represent?" The poet Ioan Alexandru not only made his point with humor, but he won a majority of the votes on the issue.

In the Chamber of Deputies the house president, Adrian Nastase (now the Prime Minister) treated my proposal seriously and asked me to present it before its twelve members of the standing committee. Two vice-presidents of the House spoke derisively, dismissing it as a joke. One said: "This is the House of Parliament, not the House of God. This is where we pass the country's laws. If Deputy Dugulescu wants to pray he should walk over to the Orthodox church, and then when he's said his prayers, he can come back here for the session."

Another said: "'Let us Pray' – eh? But we are the supreme forum of the country, we are the legislative authority – the highest institution of the State. How can we take it upon ourselves to pray? That would mean that, if they followed our lead, all lectures in schools and universities would start with the 'Our Father', and even shifts in mines and factories. Where would it end, gentlemen?"

Shocked by their thinking, I responded by reminding them of the following:

In December 1989, in Timişoara, in Bucharest and in many other cities, hundreds of thousands of Romanians had knelt to pray the Lord's Prayer. They had shouted "God exists!" and many had lost their lives for the right to assert the existence of God. It was their blood, their sacrifice, I reminded my colleagues, that had put us into parliament – and we were under a debt to fulfill their deeply felt longing. They had died hoping for a future where a new Romania would welcome and honor God in every part of its existence, and as the the legislators and supreme forum, we should ensure that it happened.

A second indication was in the many times in our parliamentary discussions, that we would cite the example of such successful nations such as the U.S. and Great Britain, trying to learn from their legislation and experience. Why would we not learn this from them also? In both the British parliament and in the U.S. Congress, the sessions begin with prayer.

My third point was that our authority is delegated by the people, but the people's rights come from God. The U.S. Declaration of Independence says that these are inalienable rights, endowed by the Creator. The Holy Scriptures tell us, in Romans Chapter 13: "All authorities are from God and they bear the sword of the law so that they can punish evildoers and defend those who do good." If we, as the elected representatives of the Romanian people, stand reverently and declare together "Our Father, which art in heaven, hallowed be thy name ..." we will represent the Romanian people here before God, which would bring our whole nation under the authority of God. Through this, we would be affirming the divine authority by which government is established and from which authority derives, and God will bless Romania."

Of the twelve members of the committee, four voted against my motion and eight in favour, thus I could bring the proposal before the whole House. There, it passed by a majority vote, and became the new tradition to begin government deliberations in Romania.

"I am a Baptist, but the majority of the members of the chamber of deputies are Orthodox," I said, after the vote was final. "I would propose that the Lord's Prayer be led each morning by Deputy Emil Roman, from Arad, who is an Orthodox priest. I would only wish to lead the prayer when he is not present."

This gesture gained the respect of some who opposed me, because they realized that I was not doing battle for the sake of myself, but for a larger principle.

My motivation, when I agreed to become involved in politics, came from the Great Commission of the Lord Jesus Christ: "Go and make disciples of all nations ..." (Matthew 28:19). It was my earnest desire, during my eight years of service in Parliament, to make disciples, to testify to God to serve my brother Christians of all denominations. I have been inspired to meet others living a life of faithful discipleship within public service.

Former member of the German parliament Rudolf Decker has been inviting me to the Prayer Breakfasts of the Bundestag for 8 years now. I also attended the Berlin conference: "Responsibility before God and People." Doug Coe in Washington has not limited his work to the annual National Prayer Breakfast, but has created a network for discipleship in the political world.

Since my term of elected service in the Romanian parliament came to an end, I have continued to serve the gospel in this political realm. I was honored in March 2001 to meet with former President George Bush, in his Houston office, in order to present to him – ten years after the fall of Communism – a commemorative scroll and medal on behalf of the martyr city of Timişoara. He played an immense role in that period, when not merely the Berlin Wall but the entire Iron Curtain was coming crashing down, and the nations of Eastern Europe were looking for a new way forward in their history. Once again, I am amazed that I was able to be an eyewitness, or even a participant, in a dramatic unfolding of events in which God once again demonstrated to humanity His awesome love and his ready blessings.

A Letter from my Executioner

Near the end of my term in Parliament, in June 2000, my secretary handed me a letter, which disturbed me, and yet explained so many things. At that time all our children – including Cristina who presently lives in North Carolina with her husband and son – were at home. So that evening, after supper, I asked our eldest, Ligia, to read it aloud. Total silence descended in the room, as she read the letter to us, and by the end, we all had tears in our eyes.

Highly respected Pastor Peter Dugulescu,

After almost three years, I have found the courage to contact you again. This may or may not be upsetting to you. I would like to tell you a little bit of truth which you do not yet know. Even though you may not believe me, I am doing this to fulfill a responsibility before God.

Are you aware that, 22 years ago, the Romanian Secret Services decided to create a file on you with the intention of placing you under close surveillance and physically eliminating you? I believe you may not know the whole truth about your past and nobody is in a position to tell you more than I can.

Following the miners' strike in the Jiu Valley on August 3, 1977, the Hunedoara County secret services department, led by Colonel G_____ S____, in conjunction with Colonel D____ G____, the head of the Securitate for the whole county, were trying to come up with various 'missions' in order to improve their standing with their superiors in Bucharest. You were suspected of

*having close links with many Christians abroad. The
decision to physically eliminate you was made in Bucharest
in September 1977.*

*I do not know how well you know me, but I was
selected and trained in Bucharest to fulfill this mission. It
had to be carried out without the knowledge of the Hațeg
Securitate, to be more specific, without Captain N_____
knowing. At the county level, the only person informed of
this decision was Col. D____ G____, the head of the
Securitate. Those concerned all knew that I had been
chosen to carry out the mission and that the chosen method
of physical elimination was to be by shooting.*

*With this in mind various possibilities were evaluated
taking into account the local terrain. The action plan was
drawn up by Colonel N___ of the Securitate, who went with
me to study the area. On arrival, we established the best
possible locations as your route from your home to your
church in Hațeg, or to the church in Bucium. At that date,
you were driving a red Dacia station wagon.*

*Besides the possibility of your execution by shooting,
one other option we considered was placing explosives
under the bridge that you had to cross on your way back
from Hațeg to Bucium. This would have had to be done
with an electric wire allow us to control it from a distance.
The plan was to leave one or two large rocks on the bridge
to make you slow down just where the explosives had been
planted, thus maximising our chances of success. There
was a very large price on your head at that time.*

*The option of shooting you was to be used either while
you were crossing the bridge towards Bucium or while you
were crossing the wooden bridge towards Sântămăria-
Orlea and Subcetate at a place called Lower Orlea.*

Now, I stand before God and confess the truth, because I initially accepted the mission with a great deal of inner conflict, given the fact that I had attended your church services in Bucium and Hațeg many times. Of course I left the services before the end, after watching you and listening to the Word of God, but every time I left the church building I felt as if someone was touching my heart and urging me not to do what I was supposed to. I tried to avoid executing this mission, even though nothing bad would have happened to me. In fact I would have been decorated and rewarded, as I has been after many other missions.

I felt a great affinity towards you. I had begun to like you as a person, through listening to your messages in church. Satan was at work, too, and I fell in love with a very beautiful girl who was a Christian. We had a long-term romantic and adulterous relationship. It was my friendship with this girl that inhibited me from acting against you, and in order not to attract suspicion, I worked extra hard on other missions in other areas.

Then came a point when, after attending many churches, I became convinced that God exists.

On September 15, 1979, I took part in a hunting expedition with President Ceaușescu in the Ghiurghiu mountains. That evening, there was a discussion about repenters. The people under discussion were you and a Dr. Vass from Târgu Mureș who was even more closely monitored by the Securitate than you were. Anyway, if God helps me to get out of here, I will show you a copy of the plan for your physical elimination, which was code-named as Operation Lame Man.

I remember two people I met in Bucharest in September 1977, who were members of a Baptist Church

Peter Dugulescu

and knew you very well. They were informers for the secret services department. Their names are Nicolae C_____ and Ioachim – I don't remember the latter's first name. They were aware of the fact that you were under surveillance, but did not know about the plan to physically eliminate you.

You and your wife, Mărioara, were being very closely watched including on all your trips to Arad and to Timişoara.

The reports turned in by the informers in Haţeg were exaggerated and did not match the truth. I know this because four or five times I recorded what you were saying word for word and when I looked at the reports we received they did not correspond with what you had said. Several of us agents were working on this case, following your every step without knowing of each other. But I was the only killer recruited for this project. This was because of the trust the General in charge of the mission had in me. He was co-ordinating this activity in a highly secret manner. One word from me would have meant my liquidation, and I came very close to making a big mistake on another death mission.

Even though over a period of many years I kept promising that I would accomplish this mission – I gave the excuse that I kept having to change some of the details – the truth is that every time I saw you my heart would beat very fast. Here I want to explain to you another of Satan's devices. During Ceauşescu's regime all the people with leadership positions at the national level had to agree to work with the secret services. It was like a commitment. From 1980 onwards Mr. H_____ would help me accomplish missions if he rated their chances of success at or above 90 percent. Your situation became more dangerous in 1984-6, when Colonel D_____ G_____ took the decision not to delay your killing any further. You were envied for your great *popularity and also for the acquisition of that Mercedes. The former secret services chief in Timiş County, Colonel T____ S___, also opposed your move to Timişoara. He insisted that Colonel G____ must 'take care of you' in Hunedoara County. After you moved to Timişoara without permission in the Fall of 1985 there were a few frantic days before the actual attempt to kill you during which strenuous efforts were made to 'get' you, but without success. You did not drive at night along the route where they had planned to shoot you, and they were unable to use a firearm in the daytime.*

At this point Colonel D____ G____ in Deva decided that you were going to be liquidated in a car accident. You were going to be rammed broadside on. This attempt failed because you were not killed. Do you know the identity of the driver of the 'death bus' that September 30, 1985, at the intersection of Mărăşeşti Street and Lazăr Street? Do know who planned the attempt and where? Do you know that in March or April 1986, I don't remember exactly but it was about the time when the disaster happened in Chernobyl, there were further discussions about you and a few days later your every step in Timişoara was followed so that you could be liquidated?

Pastor Peter, I acknowledge before God that I was a contributor to making those years of your life hard ones. Many times I looked into your eyes and thought to myself that you were not even aware that you were standing face to face with a state-hired killer. My purpose in telling you all this is not to make a profit or to obtain a favor. All that motivates me is a wish to obtain your forgiveness. I would like to be able to rejoice in the salvation offered by Jesus Christ, and I want to ask you for just one thing: to FORGIVE ME!

Because I accepted the mission to liquidate you although you had never done me any wrong, I consider myself guilty of a great sin, besides the many others I have committed.

I ask you again to FORGIVE ME, and I want to follow the Savior – Jesus Christ. If God allows me to get out of here, I will put my Xerox copy of that shocking document, the liquidation plan, into your hands. (At that time nobody had a Xerox machine except the secret services.)

On the afternoon of September 30, 1985, when your accident took place I went to Timişoara with Colonel D___ G___. I believe it was a Monday and we got there at around 5:20 pm to do the follow-up to the business.

Please try to contact Colonel D___ G__, the former head of the Deva Securitate, and maybe he will have the courage and dignity to tell you the truth. I know you will certainly forgive him.

If you are able to forgive me, please write to me in a few words telling me that you have done so.

I would like to join the Baptist Church. God bless you!

With respect and consideration,

Jianu Beniamin
May 3^(rd)

This confirmed what the alleged bus driver had also told me in 1990 after the Revolution: that the bus that hit my car was not driven by him, but by a Securitate agent. The Securitate had not been confident that the bus driver could accelerate powerfully enough to kill me and had given that job to one of their men – a Securitate agent. The agent had disappeared immediately after the accident and the driver had handed over his papers and taken the responsibility on himself. But they had promised him that nothing would happen to him and had kept their promise.

This explanation seems plausible to me because it has been confirmed by two people independently of each other and because in the normal course of events, a bus driver, however great his obligations to the Securitate, would not be able to do something like that. Such a deed could be accomplished only by a Securitate agent for whom murder was a profession.

Now, years later, we read the letter attesting to the deliberate attempts to end my life. I broke the silence and said to my wife and children: "In the Fall of 1977, when Operation Lame Man was meant to have been carried out, when you were all meant to have been left fatherless and your mother widowed, you, Ligia, were seven, Ina was five and Cristi was only three. This murderous plan of Satan's came to nothing, and now you are grown up and we are still together. The only reason I am alive is that we serve a living God who was able to overturn the plans of evil and bloodthirsty men." We knelt down prayed in deep, fervent thanks for the mercy and protection God had shown us.

Through this letter, my own personal Angel of Death asked me to forgive him and to visit him in prison, to help him become free of the enormous burden that was weighing on his conscience. I decided to visit him the next Friday, as I returned to Timişoara from Parliament in Bucharest.

I had seen the news report of this man's arrest in Deva in 1995 for shooting five people with a hunting rifle in less than 24 hours. Those he shot had refused to reveal the hiding place of his second wife, who had deserted him and gone off with another man. At that time he had been described as the most dangerous criminal in Romania. I had heard him declaring over the TV networks: "I haven't killed anyone. I have executed people. I have no regrets at all."

I called the Governor of the Arad Penitentiary from Parliament and told him that I would be flying to Arad from Bucharest on Friday, July 5, to see Beniamin Jianu. The Governor sent one of his deputies, a colonel who was a very cultured and God-fearing man, who was in charge of the prison Education Department.

After we met, he said: "Sir, I have to inform you that Jianu is regarded as the most dangerous detainee in any penitentiary in this country. He is the VIP of detainees. He is constantly saying: "I didn't kill; I executed." He also says that he still has 17 people on his list whom he is going to kill as soon as he gets out of here. I am afraid to leave you alone with him. With your permission, I want to ensure your safety."

I said that I had no secrets and that he could stay with me. When Jianu had been brought into the prison library, his handcuffs were removed. Four armed wardens and the colonel I first met stayed to guard me. At my request, a friend of mine from Timişoara had brought his video camera to film this rare event.

Jianu was very moved, and after I had shaken hands with him, he thanked me for coming to see him. I asked him what had made him write me that letter, and whether everything it said was true. He told me that he had been wanting to speak to me for years but had not had the courage to do so. Three years previously, he had written to me from prison in Craiova to ask me for a Bible, but without revealing his story. I had read that letter out from the pulpit and a young woman in the church had sent him a Bible. He told me that he had received it and that he read it eagerly every day.

I asked Beni how he had been drawn into the net and become a professional killer for the Securitate. He told me that when he was 18, he had shot a girl of his own age with a hunting rifle, out of jealousy. This has been at a wedding in a village near the Orthodox Church and all the wedding guests had flung themselves face down on the ground. Beni was arrested on the spot and taken to the County Militia Headquarters in Deva where an officer told him: "You have two options before you. Either you stand trial and serve a long stretch in prison, or you agree to go on some training courses for 'special missions' and work for us. You're a good shot and we need you."

"Later," said Beni, "I found that these 'special missions' were, in fact, murder missions. I took the offer and didn't spend even one day in prison. From the age of eighteen, I was taught to kill, to show no mercy, to feel no remorse. They trained me like a robot." He related to me how on his first murder mission he worked in a team with three colleagues, using weapons disguised as umbrellas. With these they carried out the cold-blooded killing of two Serbs who were political opponents of Tito in the lobby of the Hotel Dorobanți in Bucharest. They then handed over the corpses to the Yugoslav secret service at the Iron Gates border post. This crime received extensive coverage on Radio Free Europe, but the murderers were never found.

Then he told me how, on a solo mission, he had shot a young man in the head in the center of Cluj. He did not know much about the young man except that he was a repenter. He carried out the orders of those who had been trailing him.

His next victim was a forest ranger whom he killed by driving an awl into his ear during one of Ceaușescu's hunting expeditions in the Gurghiu Mountains. At that time, he too wore the uniform of a forest ranger. (Among the photographs I later found in his parents' attic was one of him wearing this uniform.)

He told me that at the meal that followed that hunt, Ceaușescu had expressed great hatred against sectarians and repenters.

Lastly, he told me in great distress, that in 1988, he had shot Pastor Vasile Gherman in the head on the highway between Orșova and Drobeta Turnu Severin, and had then pushed the pastor's Trabant underneath a large truck so as to fake a road accident.

The he repeated what he had said in his letter about the contract he had signed in Bucharest to kill me too, and how God had stopped him: "Before killing you I had to come to church to tape your preaching. I sat down in the back row on the men's side with a mini-cassette recorder in one pocket and a loaded pistol in the other. When I saw you, Bible in hand, gesturing, smiling and explaining the Word of God, a voice said to me: "Have nothing to do with that man!" That sermon and that voice still pursue me even now. I kept putting off the execution of this mission while demonstrating my commitment and great zeal to my bosses by the way I carried out the other missions they ordered."

He told me that after General Mihai Pacepa, Nicolae Ceauşescu's Secret Service chief, had defected to the USA, the Securitate forgot about me for a time. A very large number of Romanian spies working in the West were arrested, and very many special military bases were relocated. At that time it was said that Pacepa's flight to America had cost Romania much more than the devastating earthquake that took place in March 1977.

"After 1982, the plan to physically liquidate you was moved back onto the front burner," asserted Jianu.

I was surprised to discover how many things he knew about me relating to my years in Haţeg. These were odd events that I had only shared with my family and some close friends in the church. After so many years I had thought that they were totally forgotten and that they only existed now in a little secret drawer of my memory. There were places, dates, times, chance names that had raised many questions in my mind – questions to which I had found no answer at the time. I was aware that I was being hunted, that evil forces were concentrated around me, but I had not known who was working behind the scenes.

Beni asked me if I remembered the mysterious 'hospital nurse' who had come one night to give me an injection that the doctor had not prescribed. This had been while I was in hospital in Hunedoara in October 1983. Did I remember the compromising trial in Hunedoara? Did I remember the road accident that had taken place in Timişoara at 2:20 p.m. on September 30, 1985 at the corner of Mărăşeşti Street and Gheorghe Lazăr Street? He told me that at about 5 p.m. that day he took part in the 'evaluation meeting' about the accident. "Because you had resolved to ignore the veto of the Communist authorities and the Baptist Union and move to Timişoara, the secret plan to physically eliminate you was transferred to Timişoara. All the officers present at that evaluation meeting were very angry that you had escaped with your life. Everything possible had been done to ensure that the impact of that bus hitting the driver's door of your car at full speed would be fatal. So because you had not died, they asked me to put on a white hospital gown, go into the operating theater with the medical team and kill you on the operating table. I told them I was afraid that your wife would recognize me from the church in Haţeg and that my cover would be blown."

Another of his questions brought back a very painful memory: "Do you also remember, Pastor Pete, the time you almost died on the operating table when the oxygen supply ran out? I was the 'Angel of Death' working as a hospital technician and I cut off the oxygen. That time I couldn't get out of it. I had to carry out my orders! And still, you escaped with your life. Then they tried to poison your food one morning; do you remember that incident when you refused to eat the meal you were brought?"

That was the final straw! I had thought that no one but myself could possibly know about that incident, and after all it could just have been an exaggerated fancy of my own.

Then he looked at me and said: "Pastor Pete, for a long time I have wanted to contact you and speak to you, especially since the Revolution. I have no peace. I am carrying a heavy burden. When I pray in my cell, I ask God to forgive me, not only for the five cold-blooded murders that I committed out of jealousy in 1995, but also for the five other murders that I carried out on the orders of the Securitate.

"No one, except God and those who ordered me to commit those murders, knows of my involvement. I have not been able to sleep properly for years. When I close my eyes and fall asleep, all I see around me is corpses. The blood of those innocent people cries out against me from the ground like the blood of Abel.

'Pastor, can I still be forgiven? All the wardens and guards tell me that I'm a killer, a murderer, a piece of dirt and that I deserve to be shot. I know they're right. My conscience tells me the same. First Timothy 1:15 is literally true for me: "... among sinners, of whom I am the worst." Pastor Pete, I signed a contract to kill you as well, I cut off your oxygen and you were only a step away from death. Can you forgive me? Can you accept me? Because no one wants me; all I get from everyone is rejection and curses."

He told me that two years before, when he was in the maximum security prison in Craiova, they had once sent an older warden to handcuff him and take him out of his cell. This man, who knew from his workmates that Jianu was the most dangerous prisoner there, came up to him in great terror, was taken ill and fainted.

"That was a moment of decision for me. I asked myself: "What have I become? An animal, a wild beast, so that even an armed warden is afraid to come near me?" Then I remembered the first sermon of yours that I heard in the Fall of 1977, a sermon that has stayed with me all these years."

The he looked at me and said: "Please tell me, brother Pastor Pete, can you forgive me?"

At that moment I knew that as a Christian and a pastor I must forgive him – but how was I going to tell my fellow parliamentarians and other people who knew from the television who Beniamin Jianu was, and who hated and despised him? Could I tell them that from now onwards Jianu was my brother and my friend? I knew that Jesus Christ had been the friend of sinners, but this was extreme.

Pondering this, I said: "Beni, I want to tell you that as Jesus Christ was dying on the cross for our sins he forgave a man like you. That thief had been condemned to death by crucifixion for murder. I don't know how many murders it was, but he was a murderer too. Because he repented of these murders and acknowledged his guilt, and because he believed that Jesus Christ is the Son of God, the Lord said: "Truly, truly I say to you, today you will be with me in Paradise!" If you confess your sins before the Lord and ask him to come into your heart and wash you with his blood, you can be forgiven." And I read him 1 John 1:7. "but if we walk in the light, as he is in the light, we have fellowship with one another, and the blood of Jesus his Son cleanses us from all sin."

Then we prayed, Beni first and myself after him. The deputy governor and the four wardens were witnesses of this scene – unprecedented in their experience. When we finished praying, I hugged him and, overcoming my last resistance, I kissed him like a brother on the cheek. When I left the prison, Beni and I were brothers.

As I was leaving, the Governor met me and invited me to have coffee in his office. Then he said: "Mr. Dugulescu, I hope you haven't been taken in by Jianu and his fantasies. He is insane. I hope you haven't been taking him seriously."

Surprised by his attitude, I replied: "Governor, I don't know whether this man is mad or not, but he has told me of certain incidents in my life and given me names, places and dates that only

I knew. These fit with what actually happened. What he said makes sense to me, Governor."

The deputy governor, who was walking along with us, confirmed this by saying: "Yes, Governor, Mr. Dugulescu is right. It appears that the things Jianu is always talking about are not imaginary fantasies, but factual and consistent".

Governor B's statements were typical of those who, like him, had worked in the prison system for many years under the Communist regime, before the Revolution, and did not want certain facts to become known. I have met the same attitude in other prison officers who had worked for years under the old system. Their former colleagues, who were veterans of Ceaușescu's Securitate were now working for the new information services. It was not in their interests for Jianu's story to be taken seriously.

"Governor, if this prisoner should happen to die in an 'accident' here in the prison, you are going to have problems. The case would go as far as the U.S. Congress! Please ensure that Jianu is kept safe. Don't let some other prisoner kill him during the evening exercise time."

I visited Beni many times in the Arad high security prison and took him food, Christian books, a cassette player and sermon tapes. But my visits disturbed the 'old torturer' as Beni used to wryly call him. The Governor insisted that, once I was no longer in Parliament, I would never set foot inside the prison again.

But Beni had become a different person. He prayed and read his Bible systematically, and has read the Bible from cover to cover every month, since. On November 5, 2000, with the permission of Mihai Eftimescu, the Director General of Romanian Prisons, I baptized Beniamin Jianu in the prison yard, assisted by pastors Zaharia Ioan from Arad, Eugen Groza from Timișoara and Pavel Petruț from Eftimie Murgu. Pastor Petruț too had been followed by the 'Angel of Death' for some time, although, in his case, without being the subject of a liquidation plot.

The day after the baptism, one of the wardens said to Beni: "Jianu, you've committed the greatest sin of your whole life by being baptized into the repenters and abandoning the religion of your forefathers!"

Beni replied: "If this is a sin, I am sorry I didn't commit it long ago, because then I wouldn't have ended up here. Religion did not change me, but Jesus Christ has."

There are two interesting footnotes to this testimony, of the salvation of Beni Jianu.

About two weeks later, in another maximum-security prison in Bucharest, a group of murderers serving life sentences killed two of their cellmates. In the Interior Ministry magazine 'For Our Country,' The Director General of Romanian Prisons wrote an editorial in which he tried to respond to the question: "How can these beasts in human form, who kill so cruelly, be educated and socialised? Is there any chance that they can be recovered and integrated into society?" He gave the following reply: "There is just one way in which these dangerous murderers can be recovered and changed: if they could have a good spiritual counsellor like Beniamin Jianu has had, someone to explain the message of the Gospel to them and lead them to Jesus Christ. If a man like Jianu has been able to change so radically, this means that the others can change too."

The amazing thing is that the same wonderful grace of the Lord Jesus Christ which changed the life of a murderer, Beniamin Jianu, had also changed the life of the Director General of Romanian Prisons, Mihai Eftimescu. Two years earlier he had come with me to a seminar in Indianapolis on the "Character" held by Bill Gotherd. There, the word of God pierced his heart. We became friends at that time and after we had returned to Romania we met up again, had meals together, prayed together, and I told him how God had worked in my life.

To my great joy, four weeks before I wrote this, he called to tell me that he and his wife were attending Holy Trinity Baptist church in Bucharest and that he was soon to be baptized.

The Brothers of Onesimus

The letter of Paul to Philemon tells an interesting story, about a runaway slave named Onesimus. "I appeal to your for my child, Onesimus, whose father I have become in my imprisonment. (Formerly he was useless to you, but now he is indeed useful to you and to me.) I am sending him back to you, sending my very heart. I would have been glad to keep him with me, in order that he might serve me on your behalf during my imprisonment for the gospel, but I preferred to do nothing without your consent in order that your goodness might not be by compulsion, but of your own free will.

"Perhaps this is why he was parted from you for a while, that you might have him back forever, no longer as a slave, as a beloved brother, especially to me but how much more to you, both in the flesh and in the Lord. So if you consider me your partner, receive him as you would receive me. If he has wronged you at all, or owes you anything, charge that to my account. I, Paul, write this with my own hand, I will repay it—to say nothing of your owing me even your own self. Yes, brother, I want some benefit form you in the Lord. Refresh my heart in Christ. Confident of your obedience, I write to you, knowing that you will do even more than I say."

In the sewers and train tunnels of Romania, the throwaways, the children of the streets, eke out a miserable life. Unloved, unfed, and unwashed, they scrabble to survive, and numb their wounded hearts with the anaesthetics of drugs, alcohol or other agents. These are the modern-day runaways and slaves, the brothers of that long-ago runaway slave, Onesimus.

When we began the Brothers of Onesimus Project, my colleagues and I in 'Jesus the Hope of Romania' embarked on a joint venture of faith. City Hall asked us to get involved in this work and gave us a building which was in a state of serious disrepair, lacking both water and lavatories. We renovated the house with a gift of $10,000, contributed by American churches to pay for materials but the labor, both skilled and unskilled, was done by willing volunteers from evangelical churches in Timişoara. At the dedication, there were just seven children rescued from the underground heating and sewer tunnels of the city, but soon their number grew to 43. For the dedication ceremony, the orphan children's choir from Recaş sang, and representatives of political and media were on hand. Some of the journalists asked me why I was working with street children. *"If we do not help these children to come to know the Lord Jesus and to become the Christians of tomorrow, they will become members of the criminal class of tomorrow's Romania,"* I was quoted in the articles.

Others asked me whether or not we had a secure operating budget for the coming year. At that point in time, I didn't really know what such a budget meant, but I told them that we had funds enough to feed the seven children for two months.

"But of course you have a large church in the United States that will support you?" was the next question.

"I wish that were the case, but it isn't," I replied.

"Then you are probably relying on charities in England or Germany."

"I wish I could rely on such organizations but nobody has promised us help. But I have someone that I can rely on absolutely."

"Who?"they asked, immediately.

"God, who said "I am the Father of orphans and the defender of widows". He always identifies himself with the poor and abandoned."

They gave me a tolerant smile and said I was "naïve." I think they were right. I was naïve, and I still am. I believe that the men of faith in the Bible were not normal people, but neither were they abnormal; they were supernatural people in the way they rose above mere logical reasoning.

I also believe that when faith and love meet in someone's heart, the result will not be speculation but action. If my little daughter or someone dear to me falls into a river and is in danger of drowning, I am not going to start thinking about whether I am going to get my clothes wet or the coldness of the water. I am going to leap in and save her. True love is not a subject for vague discussion but the stuff of action. If these urchins and glue-sniffers, these unfortunate beings, these dwellers in sewers and trash dumps are not dear to you, you will not be motivated to sacrifice yourself for them. But I know that Jesus loves them, and we in JHOR cannot help but love them.

When the first seven urchins were gathered from the underground tunnels on December 22, they were filthy, infested with lice, they smoked and they were sniffing glue. Their vocabulary was as filthy as they were. When they discovered that this home was run by repenters they shouted in the yard: "We don't want to become repenters, we don't want to become repenters!" They were like the man possessed by demons whom the Jesus loved and wanted to set free. We had prepared a Christmas tree for them on which we had hung decorations and chocolate candies. Within 30 minutes, the Christmas tree had been wrecked and they had broken several windows.

We told them that nobody was going to force them to become repenters, but that we wanted to help them to begin a new life: clean, warm beds to sleep in, clean clothes to wear, shoes on their feet, good food, nice toys and to go to school. They were fascinated by the video films we were able to show them on the large-screen multisystem TV we had been given by brother Isfan's organization in Chicago.

These 43 unwanted children, akin to the runaway Onesimus, are cared for at a cost of just $150 per child per month, including the salaries of their caretakers. But that's a lot in Romania.

So, for the eight years in which I served in the Romanian parliament, I used every parliamentary vacation to travel to the U.S. to preach in various evangelical churches and raise money for the needs of the children. Some of my colleagues and seniors in the Chamber of Deputies said to me: "Mr. Dugulescu, you are a public office holder in Romania and it is beneath the dignity of your office to beg for money for Romanian orphans!"

Perhaps, but I am also the pastor of a church, and it says in my Bible: "I am the Father of orphans and the defender of widows." God identifies with those who are orphaned and abandoned. He has delegated to us the privilege and responsibility of being fathers and mothers to them in His place. If I have to choose between my pride of position as a member of Parliament and the needs of these children without dignity or defense, I would rather forget my dignity and choose theirs. I want these children to know themselves worthy human beings, created in the image and likeness of God, and to have a future and a hope.

I thank God for all these children's caretakers, who have filled, and continue to fill, the role of parents for them and who have loved them as if they were their own children. I thank God for my former and present co-workers: Eugen Groza, Lorena Rusovan, Cornel and Viorel Târziu, Doru and Rodica Racovicean and my daughter Ligia Niculăeş Dugulescu.

I cannot adequately express my gratitude to Alec, Patty and Kenny Woodhull for their work in collecting funds for these children when they served our branch association in Knoxville, Tennessee. And how could I ever thank Bob and Charlene Pagett of Scotts Valley, California, for their love and unfailing support through all these years? Since 1993, Bob Pagett has been organising all my fundraising tours in America through his humanitarian organization, Assist International, which channels financial and material resources to Romania.

I thank him for modern medical equipment he provided to dozens of hospitals in my country, and for the countless containers of food and children's clothes. Bob and Charlene Pagett helped bring John Ashcroft, the then-Governor of the State of Missouri and now, the U.S. Attorney General, to Romania in October 1992, with his wife. The meetings with the President and Prime Minister of Romania and the presidents of the two houses of parliament contributed to official respect for evangelical denominations in Romania.

In the letter to Philemon, Paul commends his spiritual child Onesimus, who now has a new identity in Christ and a new social status, to his former master. In Philemon verses 18 and 19 we read: "And if he has done you any wrong or owes you anything, charge it to me. I, Paul ... will pay."

We see in Paul's words:

A great commission of preaching the Gospel and making disciples. He uses the conversion of Onesimus to demonstrate that there are no circumstances which prevent a true follower of Jesus Christ from fulfilling the Great Commission, even if he is in chains and in prison.

A deep compassion. In the kingdom of God a mission without compassion is only an obligation. Jesus Christ sees and serves people with love and compassion. "When he saw the crowds, he had compassion on them, because they were harassed and helpless, like sheep without a shepherd" (Matthew 9:36). Paul's words reveal great love and sincere compassion for this former slave, a child of the Roman streets, who had stolen some money or goods from his master and had thus ended up in prison.

A powerful promise: "If he owes you anything ... I, Paul, will pay for him" (Philemon 18-19). When I present our work with these unfortunate children of the streets and sewers, whom nobody loves, and who will continue in hell if no one shows them love and shares the Gospel with them, I expect Christians to rise and say: "I will pay for him! Brother Pete, take one more child from the sewers and make him a brother of Onesimus in the Bible, because I will pay for him!"

So many have made this great and sacred promise to the Lord. May God bless the honorable Congressman from Pennsylvania, my dear friend and brother in Christ, Joseph Pitts, who inspired the management of the New Holland company to large-hearted and generous donation of a large tractor and combine harvester for the farm starting this autumn at Buziaş, not far from Timişoara. The farm will provide jobs for these children and they will learn to support themselves as they produce food and generate financial resources for other children in need.

Like Onesimus, the love of God has changed the lives of these children and made them useful. Many have invited Jesus into their hearts, and have been baptized. For the older boys who are now aged 18 or over we have bought two apartments and rented another two. Thirteen children who belong to the 'My House' project live in these four apartments. They have all learned a trade and are working for Christian-owned companies. Houseparents teach them how to manage their money, do their shopping, cook for themselves, clean the apartment and do their laundry.

The transformation that has taken place in these children's lives is striking. Besides the fact that they are properly clothed and fed and attend school and church, they feel loved and valued.

It's very inspiring to see these former street children going out every day in the minibus, two at a time, to take hot meals to the 45 elderly people included in our MANNA project. These are people who are sick, lonely and elderly and have no one to care for them. They inhabit those grey concrete blocks, the ghettos of Communism, and receive only tiny pensions. They cannot pay their electricity or gas bills and haven't enough money to buy bread or medicine. For these people, the regular hot meal that the 'brothers of Onesimus' bring them at lunch time every day, with love, is a real hand from heaven.

Once, our children rang and rang at the door of an old man who lived alone but he didn't come and answer it. The children then went and told the neighbors, who forced the door, only to find the man had died in the night. That was when we started providing them with regular medical check-ups and free medicine.

Even though older people (their parents) abandoned them when they were small, our children are taught to have a spirit of love and compassion for older people. So, in addition to the funds to the $5 a day to raise these abandoned children, we are looking for $2 a day so that hot MANNA can regularly arrive on the tables of forgotten, abandoned elderly people.

One Orphan's Story
(A testimony by Milly, Onesimus caretaker)

"I started working at the Brothers of Onesimus House in April 1993. Among the five children in my care was a boy called Corneluş who was very sweet and likeable Everyone got on well with Corneluş until he got upset. The boys called it an 'attack' because it would begin without any particular reason and cause fits of crying that could last for hours on end. Sometimes he would even beat his head against the walls or the furniture.

"He had run away from a children's home in Oltenia and his great sorrow was that he had never known his parents. Though all the staff showed him more love and patience than I could have believed possible, his sadness continued. Cornelus only that he had been born in a maternity unit in Sânnicolau Mare, abandoned by his mother and transferred to the children's home in Drobeta Turnu Severin, it was time for him to start school. At that point he had been moved to the orphanage in Patule, where there was a girl who had the same surname as him (Avădanei). Because one caretaker told him they were brother and sister, Daniela was the only person in the world with whom Cornelus felt a bond. Daniela secretly looked up her records in the orphanage office and copied down an address in Timişoara. She gave it to Cornelus, saying it was where their parents lived.

"Cornelus made his way to Timişoara in Spring of 1992, to find the address she had written down. On the door was the name Avădanei, but the woman living there was cold and sharp with him, and said that she was Daniela's mother, but not his.

"Confused, hungry and feverish from a bad cold, Cornelus wandered through the streets of Timişoara until he finally found the police station, where he recounted everything that had happened to him. The police insisted the Avădanei woman take responsibility to bring Cornelus back to the orphanage in Patule. However, Cornelus ran away when her back was turned, ending up back on the streets of Timişoara, until winter 1993, when he was taken to the Brothers of Onesimus center.

"I understood how much he was suffering as a result of not knowing his parents, especially his mother, and that this was the reason for his unusual behavior.

"One day, when Corneluş was again in deep sorrow, my brother was visiting. He was deeply moved by Corneluş's suffering and asked him what could help. Corneluş replied that he wanted to see Daniela, his "sister." My husband and I and a colleague, Codruţa P. visited that children's home with him, and seeing it helped me to understand why Corneluş had run away.

"Everyone who knew Corneluş, even the psychiatrists, were doubtful about his prospects. But something major happened in his life that was to overturn all their expectations and fears. As a result of attending church every Sunday with the other children and their caretakers, Corneluş decided to become a Christian and enrolled in the catechism class at Bethel Church. I talked with him at length and explained to him the seriousness of the decision he was taking. He told me that he was fully aware of what he was doing and that he was determined to be faithful to God whatever it cost. On April 24, 1994, Cornelus was baptized at Bethel. He was the very first child take this step. For me, it was an incredibly special day because my daughter Cristina and my colleague Marcel were both being baptized too. I cannot forget how Pastor Dugulescu held Cornelus up in his arms while he was testifying to how he had met the Lord Jesus because he was too small to be seen over the side of the baptistry.

"After his baptism, the children began calling him 'repenter' – a name which has stayed with him to the present day. I can testify that his life has changed radically. After finishing his eight years of compulsory schooling Cornel attended a vocational school, and graduated with two friends. At 18, an apartment was rented where they could live together in the future. Fearing that all the work we had invested might have been in vain once they were no longer under our fulltime supervision, many of us were anxious, but our fears turned out to be groundless.

"Cornel has two jobs and is taking high school classes at night school. Busy though he is, he never misses church or choir practice. Of all the boys who have left the home, Cornel has remained the closest to it. He always finds time to come and visit, as he considers this place to be the only home he has ever had.

"Before writing these lines I invited Cornel to my home to ask his permission for me to tell his story. He laughed and asked: "My name in a book?" The smile disappeared when I asked if he had learned anything about his parents. He has no answers, but he still hopes to find them one day. His mental pain was every bit as great as when he cried out in such dispair, but his attitude is different."

The Orphan Nation

I am frequently asked "Why are there so many orphans in Romania? My beautiful Romania, which was once a prosperous, flourishing country, has ended up being known all over the world as a country of orphans, handicapped children and street children. This is a national shame and a cause of reproach to us when we knock at the doors of the European Union, NATO or the IMF.

I think there are several reasons. First, during the dictatorship of Ceauşescu, abortion was forbidden because Ceauşescu desperately wanted the birthrate to rise. It was falling every year, while emigration, both legal and illegal, was constantly increasing. Ceauşescu wanted Romania to be a big, powerful nation worthy of its Great Leader. An abortion was a serious criminal offense both for the woman who requested it and for the gynocologist who performed it. So women who experienced unwanted pregnancies, particularly young, unmarried women would give birth but then put the into the hands of one of the children's homes which came to fill the country.

This led to the second reason: Ceauşescu 'sold' orphans to some Western countries for hard currency. A steady supply of orphans could be trained as terrorists in certain Arab countries or became bodyguards working for the dictator or for Securitate officers. Their loyalty to Ceauşescu and to the system knew no bounds. For them, the Romanian Communist Party was both father and mother.

Under Communism, homes for orphaned and handicapped children were institutions that were closed to the wider public. It was only in December 1989, via our TV screens, that we discovered the lot of these unfortunate human beings.

Children living in these houses of horror had to endure hunger and cold, were sworn at and beaten by the staff and sometimes sexually abused by their elders, so many chose to run away from these institutions when democracy came, to live in freedom. But the freedom they longed for had a higher price than they were able to pay. The street, the station or the sewer system became their home. When the weather turned cold, their only source of warmth was the underground network of the towns' utility tunnel systems – and the sewers. To survive, they began to steal and beg. All too easily, they became slaves to tobacco, alcohol and solvent abuse.

Sadly, the first 'victory of democracy' that the Romanians received, just days after the execution of Ceauşescu, was the legalization of abortion. For less than $10, any woman could have an abortion any time she liked. Between then and now, according to the Pro Vita statistics, over 7,000,000 unborn children have been butchered. And yet the number of orphans and street children is not decreasing.

Another factor that needs to be understood is the economic one. As long as the average monthly income of a family stays below $100, many parents with five, ten or twelve children, with anguish of heart, will go on abandoning their children. Also, children who lack sufficient food or who are subjected to abuse, will runaway to seek a better life.

The moral factor is the number one cause of child abandonment. Parents who themselves have not had any moral or religious education, do not give their children the upbringing they need. Those 50 years of atheistic education and the elimination of the sacred from the minds of the Romanian people is still taking an enormous toll.

Every day, the media reports murders, rapes, incest and violence within the family. The headlines of the papers scream the unthinkable—and it's happening every day.

In one typical example in my own experience, two policemen came to the Brothers of Onesimus home one night, with two boys of about 6 and 8 years. They were from the town of Deva and had come to Timişoara on the train without any tickets. The ticket collector handed them over to the police, who knew our home, and brought them to us. After the policemen left, I asked the two brothers why they had run away. They told me that they barely knew their father, because he was usually in prison, and that their mother was an alcoholic and used to beat them every day. She would send them out to steal or beg for money, so that she could buy herself another bottle of vodka. The older one said: "We don't want to steal or beg any more, and we've had enough of beatings and hunger. That's why we ran away from home."

In Romania, alcoholism has reached terrifying proportions, fueled by poverty and dispair.

Traditionally, the people of Romania are 86 percent Orthodox Christians and they now take pride in their 2,000-year old Christian heritage. But this 'Christianity' is largely in name, not in life. Priests who preach the gospel and explain its application to their congregations are few in number. Not many carry out pastoral visits to nourish their congregations or give an example to their flocks. The priests who are the most Godly and conscientious in their ministry are those who belong to the spiritual renewal movement within the Orthodox Church known as the Lord's Army.

For the great majority of Romanians, their connection with the church is limited to attending the Holy Liturgy and rituals, and most only go to church at Christmas and Easter.

One controversial observation, made by a television interviewer, pointed out that countries with a predominantly evangelical population have achieved the highest level of development, with the Catholic countries in an intermediate level and the Orthodox ones poorest. "Is there a direct connection between the religion of a nation and its level of civilization?" The featured guest responded that the evangelical ideal is for the individual to take personal responsibility before God on the basis of a personal faith; in the Orthodox tradition, salvation is received through the church and is communal. The church is the disseminator of grace and truth.

This is not to say that the Protestant and evangelical churches are fine: they are in great need of revival and of a return to the springs of Holy Scripture. Yet the difference is clear and bears further investigation.

If we examine this idea on a smaller scale, in evangelical communities in Romania, though hardly perfect, cases of these families abandoning their children are extremely rare. I personally know many families with ten, twelve or sixteen children. They live on the same income as families with two or three children, and yet all their children are properly fed, clean and well-raised. What these families have that makes the difference is personal faith in God, which is expressed in Bible reading, family prayer and Christian education.

In contrast to that, four teenagers whose parents were highly educated business people who seemed to lack nothing, decided to celebrate a birthday by getting drunk, high on drugs, and then seeking out street children to bully, armed with baseball bats. One boy, who declared himself a Nazi, was extremely cruel. They forced the street children out of their sewer shelter by tossing in flaming objects, and then pounced on them with their heavy bats as they emerged. Three escaped, but one was trapped by the group at the river, and the desperate boy jumped into the Bega, and unable to swim, drowned. Though apparently lacking nothing in the material sense, these young people lacked something even more essential: the fear of the Lord that is the beginning of wisdom. They had parents, homes, clothes and food while the four urchins had only the sewers for their home, but rather than having compassion and reaching out to serve them, they used them as prey for vicious sport. Without God in the home, evil can take root and flourish.

And finally, Romania has many desperate people so that we can love them. Before his death, Jesus told his disciples: "The poor you will always have with you, but you will not always have me" (Matthew 26:11). Orphans, street children and poor people in Romania provide a challenge for us, so that through them we may show genuine love for him. He identifies with them and for that reason the greatest commandment that Jesus gave us in Matthew 22:37, "Love the Lord your God with all your heart and with all your soul and with all your mind," is confirmed in the second commandment he gave, which is like the first in importance: "Love your neighbor as yourself." (Matthew 22:39).

Jesus is in Heaven does not need our checks, money or aid, but he has left us those who represent him on earth so that they can be the recipients of our genuine love. One day he will say to us: "I tell you the truth, whatsoever you did for one of the least of these, my brothers, you did for me." (Matthew 25:40).

God's Sense of Humor

"Why do the nations conspire and the peoples plot in vain? The kings of the earth take their stand and the rulers take counsel together against the Lord and against his anointed saying, "Let us

Peter Dugulescu

break their chains," they say "and throw off their fetters." He that sits in heaven laughs; the Lord scoffs at them." Psalm 2:1-4

As I trace the events of Romania's history under communism, and as I see the events of my own life, I realize that God must have a sense of humor. Although many Christians would never associate the Holy, Righteous, All-Powerful and Sovereign God with the idea of humor, I believe that there are times when God enjoys confounding the plots of men, and turning things around to serve his Will. Thus, I see a God who laughs.

When Pharaoh decided to exterminate the people of Israel by killing all their sons, God laughed at his plans. "You intend to destroy my people? Okay, then, you yourself are going to raise the future liberator of my people in *your* own house and sit him on *your* knee while he's a child. You will have him educated by the best Egypt can offer, and one day he will come before you and say: 'Let my people go!'"

The Lord Jesus showed the same heavenly irony when asked if it was right to pay taxes to Caesar. He asked whose image was the coin, and when they replied "Caesar" Jesus taught them with humor, saying: "Then give to Caesar what is Caesar's, and give to God what is God's!"

Seeing through the attempts to entrap him when asked by what authority he acted, he turned the question around: "As long as you first tell me whether John's baptism came from Heaven or from men". They replied: "We don't know" because to commit themselves either way would have landed them in trouble. Then Jesus Christ looked at them, knowing their quandary, and said to them: "Then I won't tell you either." The divine mind sees through the pathetic machinations of those who seek earthly power and authority, and asserts the truth despite every attempt to deny it.

During all the years I served the Lord, teaching the Gospel under the oppressive rule of Communism, they ordered my death many times, only for me to escape "like a bird out of the fowler's snare" (Psalm 124:7). I did not see any humor in these at the time, but now, looking back on my life, I see so many reasons to smile and laugh, realizing how cleverly God guided me, like a Father does his beloved children.

"Why would God use me, a child of poverty, without great education, born into communism?" I ask myself. But God's wisdom is greater: by living in poverty, I understand the suffering and needs of others, and my heart has remained linked to theirs.

When the time came for my military service, I would have chosen as low-risk a branch of the army as possible, but God sent me to the riskiest, a special battalion trained to parachute deep behind enemy (NATO) lines. There I was forced to start learning English, get intensive physical training and overcome fear. I did not understand that God's unique sense of humor. These things prepared me uniquely for the demanding work I would later perform for his kingdom. The communists actually trained me to be a guerrilla fighter for God, and to help topple their false government.

As I found the Lord, Nicolae Ceauşescu became head of the Romanian Communist Party. When I graduated from the seminary, Ceauşescu became President of Romania declaring 'ideological war' on religion and 'mystical and reactionary attitudes.'

After the miners' strike in Jiu Valley on August 3, 1977, Ceauşescu sought scapegoats, so the state secret police decided to kill me, since I was high on the list of suspect persons in that area.

But when the paid killer received orders to come to my church to record me preaching, God spoke to his heart. Although he had signed a contract to kill me, he deceived his superiors and kept procrastinating. Nicolae Ceauşescu himself called him into his office and asked him: "When are you going to liquidate that Dugulescu?" According to his testimony, that sermon in

September 1977 was the seed that fell into his heart, and some 23 years later, grafted him on the true olive tree, the Lord Jesus Christ.

Ceauşescu was the most powerful and the most feared person in Romania. I was a poor Baptist preacher in a tiny town no one ever heard of. He had every means at his disposal to kill me, and indeed, tried many times. And yet he did not succeed—not in the carefully planned bus collision, not in cutting off the oxygen during my later operation, not by the poisoning of my food, or injection by a state agent posing as a nurse. So many traps were laid for me—the abduction attempt on that night in August 1986, the invitations at the health spa, the searches of my home for illegal Bibles. Yet, all these clever plans failed.

I believe God heard their threats and watched their attempts on my life, laughing at them from heaven. He wanted these blue-eyed boys to realize "Peter's life is in my hands, not yours. I don't operate according to your calendar. I have a different agenda for the life of Peter Dugulescu."

Once, before the Revolution, a Pentecostal sister had a word of prophecy for me in a prayer meeting: "Behold, your enemies are relentlessly pursuing you and desire to take your life, but I have put my hand between you and them and I will not permit them to touch you. Behold, I will bring fire and judgement on their heads and I will bring them to your feet and they will ask for your forgiveness. You I will raise into a place of honor where you will exalt my name!" I told the sister after that I doubted God spoke through her, but that sister just looked at me in disappointment and said: "We will speak again, Brother Dugulescu."

Not only were attempts made on my physical life, but upon my name, my legal status as a resident, and even my right to purchase food or drive a car. Using the vast mechanism of the state agencies, my enemies took my driver's license, refused approval to pastor the church I was called to, cancelled my residence permit, fabricated false charges to put me on trial, and offered my congregation the church building they prayed for for 30 years, if they would renounce me as pastor. Through all these attacks, God protected me and my family.

When the Timişoara Revolution began, my name was on list of the 50 people to be executed on December 23, but instead, those who wrote that list were removed from power, the day before. On December 25, Christmas Day, Ceauşescu was shot in Târgovişte by his former Party colleagues and the one who refused to kneel to God fell to his knees at the hands of his former minions.

One week after the Revolution, I had a visit from the wife of one of the former Timişoara Securitate commanders entrusted with the task of crushing the demonstrations in Maria Square and outside the Reformed church. He had been arrested and sentenced to many years in prison for genocide. Now, he wrote to me from prison, asking for my forgiveness and requesting my help, because he was innocent.

"Brother Peter," he wrote in the letter, which I found ironic in terms of the history, "I declare to you before The Truth (thus avoiding the word 'God') that I never gave orders to open fire and that I did not shoot a single person. It was others, who are now in high positions in Bucharest, who did that. I am the scapegoat. Brother Peter, I have watched you closely over the last several years and I want to tell you that I admire your uprightness. You have endured so much from us, particularly from my colleagues in Hunedoara County, yet you are not using your sufferings as a claim to fame, while others who didn't suffer at all are setting themselves up as martyrs. Speak to Art Curry, the political attaché at the U.S. Embassy, whom I arrested on December 16 when he was intending to visit Pastor L T. I took him to the airport and made him get on the Bucharest plane. As between colleagues, I ask him to forgive me. Please make sure that this letter reaches him." I carried out his request in the course of the next few days.

I then remembered the prophecy that the sister had given me, when I read this letter. "I will bring them to your feet and they will ask your forgiveness." It was being fulfilled down to the smallest detail.

When, barely a month later, I was participating in the National Prayer Breakfast in Washington D.C. with President George Bush, sitting in the Hilton Hotel with U.S. senators and political leaders from all over the world, with the President of the United States speaking a few tables away, the Holy Spirit reminded me of those words that I clung to and nourished my churches with: "Kings will be your foster-fathers and their queens your nursing mothers" (Isaiah 49:23).

Then I saw, in amazement that God fulfilled this promise completely. "A poor child from a tiny Romanian village, 'Peter the Repenter,' a pastor persecuted by an athieist regime, sitting to a meal with the President of the most powerful country on earth and political leaders from 130 countries?"

I thanked God for this honor, as well as Steve Wingfield, who had not only encouraged us through the dark days preceding the Revolution, but who arranged my invitation and paid for my plane ticket. Since then, I have been invited to every year, and subsequently, was able to bring delegations of members of the Romanian Parliament. I am grateful God could use me to awaken my government's leaders to the realization of how important belief in God, the Bible and prayer are in the personal lives of the leadership of America.

So when President George Bush, declared, in a ringing voice, "I desire that my country, America, should become truly a nation under the authority of God, One Nation Under God," I prayed in my heart: "Lord, I pray that my country, Romania, which has denied and rejected you for so long, may also become a nation blessed under the authority of God."

In May of 1998 I was invited to a European Christian Conference in London, England which was held at Windsor Castle, where Queen Elizabeth and her entourage were in residence at the time. "Queens shall be your nursing mothers," I remembered, spontaneously breaking into a prayer of praise and thanksgiving, knowing how God loved me and fulfilled every promise, even that I would stay in the castles of kings.

Yes, my enemies arranged my death, time after time. They prepared a bullet with my name on it, they prepared a bus to crush me, an injection to kill me, a plate of poisoned food and many other things I may never know about. But God in heaven, saw their plans, and laughed at them. In his ultimate joke, Peter the Repenter not only lived, but became a means of their forgiveness.

A Letter to America

My Dear Friends,
It will surprise no one to learn that I wrote this book as a result of the insistent urging of the Holy Spirit. I have asked myself why this very Romanian story would be important for American people to hear.

For one thing, because this is as much the story of America as it is of Romania. As I look back, I realize that in every crucial moment of our history, America was our key partner. At some times, such as in the fateful mistake made at the conference at Yalta, America unwittingly put us in the hands of those who would become our slavemasters. At other times, such as through the years of struggle for the Christian peoples of Romania, it was the support of American brothers and sisters that brought us Bibles, provided cars, taught us the Scripture, and shielded us from reprisals.

My own life was protected in a thousand ways by the efforts of Americans: by Radio Free Europe and the Voice of America, by

Ambassador David Freudenburk and by Pastor Guy Davis. Had it not been for the presence of American Congressmen in Romania, who courageously used their influence to hold Ceaucescu accountable for his treatment of Christians and ordinary citizens, our circumstances would have been even more dire.

Not only that, but so many Romanian patriots and persecuted Christians were welcomed in America, refugees from the repressive system that gripped our beautiful country. In America, they found a home where they could practice their faith and put down economic roots, which then helped sustain those back in Romania. Only this nation has held out the door of welcome to all the oppressed peoples of the world.

Even the fact that America existed, free and strong, held back the whip hand of those who would have carried out far more heinous crimes. America was the one asserting the importance of human rights, as a basis for international relations. America was the one supporting NATO forces, providing a bulwark against expansion. America was the one proving, day after day and year after year that communism was wrong, that athieistic materialism was a false ideology, that freedom and democracy and religious liberty were the pillars of a successful nation.

So, in a way, the story of the Christian revolution in Romania which resulted in the overthrow of Communism, is as much the story of America's effort as it is of Romania's.

America is, and will always be, recognized in history as the greatest and the most richly blessed nation on earth. "Blessed (or 'happy' we say in Romanian) is the nation whose God is the Lord." (Psalm 33:12).

In history, there have been two nations through which God has chosen to work and to teach other nations of the world. Two nations have followed in obedience to God, and fulfilled the promise of Deuteronomy 28:10: "All the peoples of the earth will see that you are called by the name of the Lord and they will fear you".

Long ago, he chose Israel as his people, to bear his name and to reveal His nature to the entire world. Whenever Israel obeyed God and followed his commandments, she was blessed with political sovereignty, economic prosperity, strength of arms and national defense, and powerful families. Other nations looked on Israel with envy and admiration, and sought her favor. As promised by God: "You will be the head, and not the tail" (Deuteronomy 28:13).

But when the people of Israel turned their backs on Jehovah, by forgetting His laws, and by seeking after false idols, they were invaded by other nations, were poor and oppressed in their own country – because they had broken the covenant with God.

In our this age, which are known as "the last days," God has selected America because of a covenant made by the founding fathers, who built the foundations of this nation on the Judaeo-Christian values which emanate from the Word of God.

For more than 200 years, America has been the brightest beacon of civilization, of liberty, democracy and prosperity on the whole planet. This is what happens to a nation whose God is the Lord, and which called itself "One nation, under God!"

America's faith in God has been its fortress and its shield for the American people for more than two hundred years. Unlike that long ago coin of Caesar, America even printed on its money the pledge, "In God We Trust." A nation that trusts in God will have its economy blessed too.

But just as America has helped Romania with the works of faith, I feel "America the Beautiful, American the Blessed" is in great danger.

America needs to consider what happened to Romania, and learn this lesson before it falls into the same pit.

Before the Second World War, Romania was considered the breadbasket of Europe. Endowed with fertile soil, blessed by God, and populated by hard-working people, Romania was not only able to feed herself but to export grain, meat and vegetables to the countries of Western Europe. Romanian young students could pursue their studies in Vienna, Paris, Berlin and London. God was taught freely, prayer was heard in our schools, Christmas and Easter and religious observation days were the festival days of our country.

Then, on August 23, 1944, a government that denied the existence of God came to the helm of Romania and declared it a land without God.

Overnight, Romania became the poorest country in Europe, an impoverished people in a rich land. We had the same fertile land, the same natural resources, the same hardworking people – but we worked harder and harder only to earn less and less.

It lost its freedom, becoming a puppet of Stalin's Soviet Union. Even worse, it deprived its own people of freedom for almost half a century.

The book of Haggai (1:5-7) warned, "Now this is what the Lord Almighty says: 'Give careful thought to your ways. You have planted much, but have harvested little. You eat, but never have enough. You drink, but never have your fill. You put on clothes, but are not warm. You earn wages, only to put them in a purse with holes in it.' This is what the Lord Almighty says: 'Give careful thought to your ways'."

As for the faithful, those followers of Jesus Christ behind the Iron Curtain, they carried the cross every day for many years. Stigmatized, condemned and marginalized, even put to death in some cases, these Christians fulfilled the words of Hebrews 11:38: "The world was not worthy of them. They wandered in deserts and mountains, and in caves and holes in the ground".

I grew up like most children in my country at that time: hungry, without sufficient clothing, and barefoot. We were always hunting through the house for any dry crust of bread, never finding one. But the newspapers and radio were constantly giving glowing reports about the joy of the peasants who were working the collectivized farms, such as the one which had impoverished our village.

The Bible and prayer were excluded from school and the teachers were charged with teaching us in every lesson that God did not exist. On Christmas Day and Easter Sunday, the children of the Christians were singled out and summoned to school for special lessons in atheism, ironically called "The Friends of the Truth."

Christmas was secularized into the "Winter Tree Festival" and St. Nicholas or Father Christmas became Old Man Winter.

Sundays were turned into community labor days. School students chanted to the Communist leaders to thank them for their food. Those who dared to put God first were mocked, slandered, had their goods confiscated and their rewards withheld.

The true patriots of Romania were slandered and painted as evil. Truth was called false, and false was called true.

Now, in America, I am seeing this same process taking place. Every year, there is some new advance in the march of secular dominion.

In many places, the nativity scene and the menorah are forbidden. The Christmas tree has been re-named "The Community Tree." Schools can teach Santa Claus and Easter

Bunnies and Tooth Fairies, but not the historical personage of Jesus of Nazareth.

The original ideals and writings of America's Founding Fathers are ignored. Revisionist histories of them, pointing out flaws and convicting them of crimes they are supposed to have committed have supplanted these. The pilgrims are thought to be witch-hunters. The framers of the Constitution are painted only as slave owners. The devout patriots who risked life and fortune to purchase freedom are called hypocrites and despots.

In the public school classrooms, prayer is forbidden, and the one book that cannot be read is the Bible. Yet, nearly every important figure and event in American history drew inspiration from that single forbidden text.

Now, in public buildings, parks and courthouses, plaques inscribed with the Ten Commandments, the origin of all laws, are forbidden by the courts of the land. Judges who seek to protect these reminders, which are guaranteed by the First Amendment of the U.S. Constitution, are thrown out of office.

Romania had her pictures of Stalin and Lenin and Ceauşescu in every public place, as the shrines to the false gods of athiest religion. America fills its billboards and television screens with celebrities whose immoral example, selfish ambition and materialistic message lead millions into wrongdoing.

Romania's youth were sacrificed to the secular gods, turning their hearts cold and their bodies to addiction. America's youth are being sacrificed to the need for economic survival, so the homes are empty, and they are alienated from parents, God, and turn to drugs instead.

Romania's underground and streets are filled with runaways and abandoned children. America's inner cities teem with homeless, gangs, and drug dealers.

Even within the churches, there is a tendency for Americans to put material growth ahead of spiritual growth and Christian service. When I look at huge churches, designed with every comfort and technology, I can't help but think of the millions of souls in the world that could be nourished with the Gospel, if the congregations had different priorities. I think of those who work tirelessly among the poorest places, to extend the love of God to those who cannot repay them, and I cannot help feeling that American churches could do so much with that money they spend on gorgeous architecture and beautiful furnishings.

In the true church of Jesus Christ, as taught from the earliest days of Christianity, the church functions as a body in which the different parts serve one another, and that when one part suffers the whole body suffers with it.

This needs to happen within the community, but also on a national and international level, "so that there should be no division in the body, but that its parts should have equal concern for each other. If one part suffers, every part suffers with it; if one part is honoured, every part rejoices with it. Now you are the body of Christ, and each one of you is a part of it." (1 Corinthians 12:25-27)

Revelations 3: 17-19 says: "You say, "I am rich: I have acquired wealth and do not need a thing." But you do not realise that you are wretched, pitiful, poor, blind and naked. I counsel you to buy from me gold refined in the fire, so that you can become rich; and white clothes to wear, so that you can cover your shameful nakedness, and salve to put on your eyes, so that you can see. Those whom I love I rebuke and discipline. So be earnest, and repent."

At a meeting of evangelical pastors in Roanoke, Virginia, where I spoke shortly after the Romanian Revolution, a Wesleyan minister came to me with tears in his eyes. "Peter," he said to me, "our train is about to draw into the station which yours has just left. Pray for us!"

I will never forget the sadness in that pastor's eyes, nor the seriousness with which he begged me to pray. It has stayed with me, urging me to pray for your country. Because I have seen it, and I can testify: A powerful and prosperous nation can become poor and oppressive overnight when it turns its back on God.

My dear friends, my brothers and my sisters, I hope you understand from these words my concern, my love and my pain for America. I come to tell you that throughout the world, America is synonymous with civilization, liberty, democracy, prosperity, honor. The ideals of the Statue of Liberty that guards the gate of this great country still draw millions of people to seek freedom and religious liberty within, and to create it in their own lands.

I want America to remain America until the coming of the Lord Jesus, who will bring in a world that will be even better than America. We need America; the whole world needs her, not for her economic riches and military power, but as a moral and spiritual reference point, a lamp upon a stand, a city on a hill.

But in every great empire, collapse begins on the inside. A nation becomes vulnerable when it is rotten within. When we replace the love of God with the love of self, when secularism and hedonism become the defining traits of a society – these things mean that a nation has come out from under God's authority and, it follows, out from under the umbrella of his protection.

In 2002, I was honored to be asked by the American Freedom Foundation to participate in their July 4 Independence Day festival at Provo, Utah to receive their Freedom Fighter Award, which had previously been given to Lech Walesa, the former union leader who became President of Poland. Looking out upon some 300,000 people who love America, and love freedom, and who saw fit to name me as a protector of liberty, I felt more than ever how much God loves this nation.

Two thousand years ago Jesus Christ said to his disciples: "You are the salt of the earth, you are the light of the world" (Matthew 5:13-14). I believe that the state of darkness and breakdown of a nation is inversely proportional to the church's spiritual power, to salt and illuminate that nation with the Gospel.

One last story: it was Sunday August 26, 2001, when after preaching at an interdenominational service in Pennsylvania, I was interviewed by journalists on the controversy about atheists suing to have the Ten Commandments removed from a local courthouse, because they found them offensive.

"If you Americans pull down the Ten Commandments," I said to the journalists, "you will be spitting on your God, spitting on your history and your Christian heritage, because America was built on the Judaeo-Christian values of the Ten Commandments.

"America has become the most powerful and blessed nation in the world because it has honored God and chosen to be 'one nation under God'! The greatness of America comes in the first instance from the Lord, but America has departed a long way from God. If the nation does not repent and turn back God will judge it."

And then I said to them: "I am not a prophet, but I tell you in the Name of the Lord, in less than ten years other, pagan nations will attack and humiliate this country and America will no longer be America."

Several nights after that interview, sleeping in the missionary cabin where I was staying I had a dream, or rather a nightmare. I was in a large American city and two enormous airplanes appeared over the city, horrible and threatening, and the sky turned dark. A voice inside me said that these airplanes were going to attack

America. They seemed to be passenger aircraft. I woke up, terrified, and couldn't go back to sleep.

I asked myself if it would be possible for a war against America to start. The international political climate didn't seem to point that way. The Iron Curtain had come down, the Cold War was over. Russian-American relations seemed pretty good. How could such a thing happen?

I returned to Romania, and a few weeks later on September 11, a friend called me and said to turn on the TV immediately. To my shock, I saw the two enormous towers of the World Trade Center crashing to the ground, after being struck by two large airplanes. It seemed impossible—a horror movie—a nightmare. But it was real.

A few minutes later, a third plane struck the Pentagon, and another that was headed for the White House crashed in Pennsylvania, not far from the very spot we had been meeting. America had been attacked. America had been humiliated.

When I returned to America in February, some of the people who had participated in that open-air service where I spoke said to me: "Peter, you were a prophet for us."

I told them that you didn't have to be a prophet to predict these things, just to see the direction America is taking. Yet, less than a year later, in June of 2002, a judge in San Francisco wanted to take the expression 'One Nation under God' from the pledge of allegiance.

I believe that America faces a challenge today more desperate than she has never experienced before. These times are unique and in times such as this Americans will be those who will decide whether, in the next ten years – or less – America will or will not still be America.

It is not right for those who receive the benefits from America to cut America off from its Godly heritage. If a guest comes into your home, and you feed and clothe and lodge him, he should honor the laws of your home. He shouldn't say "I don't like the way that you pray each day, and I don't think you should speak about God freely, and I think you should take all the photos off the wall of your grandparents, and I don't want you reading that book anymore."

I hope that you will allow me to be a different kind of guest in your home. I hope you will allow me to say to such an ungrateful person "How dare you? This home is one that is sanctified to God, and in this home, God must be honored. Those grandparents suffered and sacrificed so that this home could be built. Their sacrifice must be honored for all time, not forgotten. And that book, the Bible, which you don't like, is the textbook that was used to provide the food you eat and the clothes on your back. If you do not want to live in this home, by all means, go and live in the home that you would build, where there is no God, no Founding Fathers, no religious freedom, and no Bible. And you see how much freedom and prosperity you will enjoy, without those things."

My dear friends, America is a great home, a great family, and it has a great legacy from its forebears. As Israel was challenged by Joshua, America is now under a challenge: Who will be your God?

"And if it seems evil to you to serve the Lord, choose this day whom you will serve; whether the gods which your fathers served that were on the other side of the flood, or the gods of the Amorites in whose land you dwell; but as for me and my house, we will serve the Lord."
(Joshua 24: 15)

I pray, with all my heart, that America will choose wisely.

Whenever I speak to American audiences, I take questions at the end. At one such speech, a woman asked "If you had just one message to give to America what would it be?"

My answer was simple, and it is the plea I would make today.

My message would be:"America! Wake up!"

May God bless America!
May God bless Romania!

Yours in Christ,

Peter the Repenter

Final word

I, Peter the Repenter, have spent many years of my life making many choices along the way. However, of all of these decisions, major and minor, most of them were about things that were of a temporary nature. I can say, however, that there were four decisions which I made in my life, which I can now look back on, and say were decisions of an eternal nature. I would like to share those with you.

First, I made the decision for Salvation. I decided to open my heart to God, to receive the grace of Jesus Christ, and to allow my sins to be washed away through God's love and Christ's sacrifice and victory. I will forever be grateful that I chose salvation.

Second, I decided to Serve. I prayed to know God's will, and I felt the calling to minister to people with the word of God. I entered the Seminary, and I took on the mantle of a pastor, a preacher, an evangelist. I believe that God calls each of us to a special type of service, but it is up to us to decide to follow the calling or not. I am grateful I chose to serve.

Third, I decided to Suffer for God. This was another level of decision for me, when I began to realize that the price that Satan would extract from me was great, especially in an atheistic nation. I had many opportunities to avoid the suffering, with invitations and urging to move to America, or to another free nation, and to carry on my ministry under friendlier circumstances. However, I believed then, and still believe now, that by undergoing the suffering together with God, I was able to open new territory. The suffering of many faithful men and women of God in our nation, some in jails, some under torture, and some who were martyred— eventually laid the foundation for the end of a Godless system of repression that enslaved Romania. Thus, I am grateful I chose to suffer.

Fourth, I decided to Stand for God. First, when my brother in Christ, Lazlo Tokes, was being targeted for arrest and removal by the government forces, I felt that I must make a stand. I knew that what the government was doing was wrong, and although it may have endangered me and my family, I felt I had to act in solidarity with my brother pastor.

My second test was in Opera Square, when the outcome of the revolution was far from certain. I knew that to align myself with the people on the balcony would surely spell my death, if Ceausescu's forces repeated their bloody reprisals of a few days earlier. However, I also knew that as a man who had given my life to God, I would never forgive myself for not standing for Him at that crucial moment in our nation's history.

Then, once more, after the Revolution, when things became externally easier, I could simply have continued my pastoral work, freed from the repressions of the past. However, I felt that we needed leaders of faith in the Parliament. I chose not only to seek election, but once I was there, I chose to stand strongly for God in our newly emerging government. I stood for prayer in our deliberations, for Bible study among legislators, and for religious freedom in our Constitution. I felt that I must take a strong and courageous stand, even within the secular government body, to bring God's blessing into my country.

I also chose to stand for the orphans and street children that had no voice in the society, to give them the dignity and decent life that Jesus would want to have for them. For this purpose, I have been coming to the very blessed land of America twice a year since 1990, to speak for those who are destitute. Proverbs 31: 8-9 says "Speak up for the mute in the cause of all who are appointed for destruction. Open thy mouth, judge righteously, and plead the cause of the poor and needy."

I am grateful I chose to stand for God.

Peter Dugulescu

I invite those who may hear the story of my experiences to think about the decisions of their lives. If I can give any encouragement, it would be this: seek out, from God, the bold and unique step of faith which will allow you to be more fully his instrument. Although that step may seem daunting, once you decide, you will feel the hand-in-hand relationship with God growing each day. You will also be able to look back, without regret, on the choice that you made. The important decisions of our lives are the ones that will matter for eternity. I pray that in each life, God will be the ruler, and that we may all know the wise and wonderful guidance that will bring us to total joy with Him.

Appendix

Translations of reports on Pastor Peter Dugulescu
(Ed. Note: The following are translations of the state security agency documents obtained after the revolution, showing the degree of surveillance and the reports being circulated that were used to justify the various execution orders.

Various names were blocked out of the original reports before they were released to the public, so these have been replaced by the characters ########.)

TELEGRAM

to the Ministry of the Interior, First Directorate

for the attention of comrade Lieutenant-Colonel Ioan Banciu

B U C H A R E S T

= = = = = = = = =

PERSONAL FILE on PETER DUGULESCU

PETER DUGULESCU is the son of Peter and Irina. He was born at Helmac, Arad County, on 18 August 1945. He is a Romanian citizen. He received an elementary education and attended the Baptist theological seminary. He is pastor of the church in Hateg. He appears in the 'problems' file. He is not known to have any history of political activity or criminal offences. He is married, with two children, and lives at no.1 Aurel Vlaicu Street, Hateg.

The information we have on him shows that while he was studying at theological seminary he was taught by ######. Ever since this time he has been a close

295

friend and convinced follower of this person, both embracing his opinions and supporting his actions.

The subject started acting on a larger scale during 1976, when, taking as his pretext the unfavourable attitude of the local authorities towards the projected construction of a new religious building in Hateg, he began making threats with the aim of putting pressure on certain authorities. He stated that if this matter was not resolved in his favour he would write to Jimi [sic] Carter, who was about to be sworn in as President of the USA, and to the United Nations. More recently, after the Baptist Congress which took place in February, he stated that it had been a farce and that he was going to have to take action. For this reason he would be writing to Radio Free Europe saying that "on the table at this year's Belgrade Conference there was going to be a report from him demonstrating that the rights of Baptist believers were not being respected in Romania, and that he had ways and means of ensuring that this report reached its destination abroad".

In the course of the countless interviews he has had with the regional representative of the Religious Denominations Department, he has made threats that his name and the names of the secretary of the People's County Council and of other office-holders will become a byword abroad for persecution of believers and refusal to respect their rights.

He has also threatened ###### of the Religious Denominations Department, his attitude being one of defiance.

With reference to the network of our authorities he has stated that "he will do whatever it takes, whatever risks are involved, and will not retreat from his position, because you can never succeed unless you persevere. If the communists see that you are weak they will never help you or deal with your complaints".

In late 1976 he made a number of trips to contact ######, who gave him some booklets the content of which is hostile. These were written by ######

himself, who illegally sent the work entitled "The Christian's Place Within Socialism" out of the country to be printed in England. It was then brought back into Romania, still secretly, under the name of "The Christian Manifesto".

Booklets of this kind have been distributed by PETER DUGULESCU to ###### and ###### and to some people in Hateg who belong to his immediate circle, such as ######, etc.

The booklets were distributed in January 1977 and our organs have prepared preliminary documents.

The Party organs have been informed in due time about the activities of PETER DUGULESCU and I have sent reports to the First Directorate (see reports number 0013076 of 17 January 1977 and 0013287 of 3 March 1977).

Head of the Inspectorate
Colonel Gheorghe Simon
[handwritten annotation, indecipherable]
No.140/jL/0013.445.of 01.04.1977
rd.00594/908

MINISTRY OF THE INTERIOR   TOP SECRET
  HUNEDOARA COUNTY   Copy no.2
    INSPECTORATE
     Securitate

No.0013076, Jan. 17 1977

To,
the County Committee of the Romanian Communist Party
Comrade First Secretary
H U N E D O A R A

= = = = = = = = =

In connection with the distribution of booklets with hostile content by the Baptist pastor PETER DUGULESCU of Hateg, I wish to bring the following matters to your attention:

PETER DUGULESCU arrived in this county in 1974, since when he has been working as a Baptist pastor, his salary being paid by the Baptist authorities in Brasov.

The aforenamed is known to be a follower of ###### -presently a pastor in Ploiesti – whose student he was in seminary.

In the course of the past two years PETER DUGULESCU has had frequent meetings with ######, each visiting the other.

With regard to ######, he is the person responsible for xxxxxxxxxxxxxxxxxxxxxxxxxxxx, which is thoroughly hostile in its content, and has also engaged in other activities aimed against the State.

As a consequence of his hostile activities, the security organs began criminal proceedings against ###### in 1975. He was arrested and held for questioning for some time. These criminal proceedings against him came to an end in 1976, since the relevant authorities decided that he should not be put on trial.

It is known that the aforementioned ###### sent this work abroad illegally. It was published in booklet form and brought into the country secretly. ######, who has a history of [????? indecipherable] in the distribution of his writings, gave copies of the booklets entitled "THE CHRISTIAN MANIFESTO" and "WHOEVER LOSES HIS LIFE" to PETER DUGULESCU to distribute among elements of the Baptist confession.

We can add that the booklet called "THE CHRISTIAN MANIFESTO" is in fact ######'s earlier work "The Christian's Place Within Socialism" which circulated in the country in the 1975-1976 period in the form of tape recordings, typed copies and handwritten fragments.

In view of PETER DUGULESCU's activity in distributing these booklets, our organs recommended the taking of measures including home searches, bugging, etc, with the aim of making it possible for him to be sent for trial.

Thus on 15 January this year legal authorization was obtained for a search and for the element then to be interrogated regarding offences against the Press Law, article 90.

When the case was reported to the central authorities, we were instructed not to undertake the measures in question, given the present situation, but instead to concentrate on surveillance.

As a consequence, we intensified our surveillance of PETER DUGULESCU. Our aim was to establish exactly who he had given the booklets to, whether he was still in possession of any such materials and what his future plans were, all with the aim of preventing the spread of these ideas among the rank and file of believers.

In this connection we need to keep in mind the meetings he had with ###### in Bucharest in December 1976, a meeting in Sebes planned for January 17, the Baptist Congress scheduled to take place in Bucharest this February and the subject's fanaticism. He has made a variety of threats when interviewed by officials. For example, while he was being interviewed by the County Authority for Religious Denominations on 20 December 1976 he stated that "if the situation of the Hateg Baptist Church was not resolved, he would send reports to the UN and to the President-elect of the United States".

So far, a total of 5 booklets have been obtained. 4 of them had been passed on to two pastors and one had been given to the regional representative of the Department for Religious Denominations by PETER DUGULESCU himself.

We have to report that this man's status of authorised pastor with no other occupation makes it possible for him to travel freely anywhere in the country, to contact different elements and to act without fear of administrative consequences.

Head of the Inspectorate
Colonel Gheorghe Simon
rd.00165/146

       MINISTRY OF THE INTERIOR   TOP SECRET
       HUNEDOARA COUNTY   Copy no.1
INSPECTORATE
       HATEG SECURITATE

Received by: Lieutenant-Colonel Damaschin Salistean
Source: Informer "Titus Florea"
Date:21.01.1977
Personal dossier no. 3887/0027

              A G E N T   M E M O

              = = = = =   = = = =

     Your agent informs you that on January 18 he met
the aforementioned Peter Dugulescu at his home and
asked him if he had been to Deva and what he had
done. The aforementioned replied that he had met the
Inspector and that they had completed their
arrangements. He also said that he had been summoned
to the People's Council and had been questioned about
some books which the aforementioned ###### had had
printed in England, brought into the country and
distributed among the believers. When your agent
asked what kind of books these were, the
aforementioned said that they were books that
explained that the new man can only be produced by
Christ, through the Holy Spirit, and not by
communism.

     These books were written in Romania but printed in
England.

     Your agent asked whether he himself still had any
books of this kind. The aforementioned replied that
he had not a single one left. Your agent asked him
why he was involved in these kinds of forbidden
things. The aforementioned replied: I'm not afraid of

Peter Dugulescu

what they'll do to me, they won't throw me into
prison. For if they do, all the believers in the
country will rise up in protest and even people
abroad will hear about it, and our country doesn't
need that kind of thing. But I am determined to keep
following the path that Ton has taken.

The discussion ended at this point.

Hateg, 21 January 1977
"Titus Florea"

OBSERVATIONS

This memo was provided on the basis of the
briefing carried out by our organs. Its content
demonstrates P.Dugulescu's hostile attitude
towards the regime, and the discussion the subject
had with our agent shows that he thinks just like
######, whom he supports and idolizes. It is clear
that he would like to be arrested so that the
believers could protest and so that this could
become known abroad.

MINISTRY OF THE INTERIOR   TOP SECRET
   HUNEDOARA COUNTY   Copy no. [none given]
     INSPECTORATE
      -SECURITATE -

Received by: Lieutenant-Colonel Avram Mihut
Source: "Sandu"
Date:11.12.1973
Place: "Tower" House, Deva
Dossier:3504

                    AGENT MEMO
                    ==========

On Friday 7 December, your agent set out towards
Sebes to collect ###### at 1 p.m.. ###### was at the
home of his brother-in-law ###### in Sebes with his
wife, his daughters and a girl from Bucharest.

Your source collected [him? original blanked] and
his family and took them to Deva, to ######, where

stayed until 9.30 p.m., when he set off for the station.

During the journey ###### told your agent that ######, the President of the Baptist Union, had arrived back in Romania from Germany (he had been to Hamburg for some medical treatment). ###### had had a conversation with ###### in Oradea in which he had told him that RONALD GONLDIND [sic], the Secretary of the European Baptist Federation, had come by aeroplane and had had a conversation with him concerning his report. ###### had confirmed that there were realities [sic] that this report must have been written by the Union and even by him personally. As a result of this discussion, the World Baptist Alliance had sent delegations to the Romanian Embassies in Washington and London, where the situation had been discussed. ###### had been very intrigued by what the leadership of the Union had done regarding him and his report.

told your agent that on the previous Saturday evening he had been at the church in Oradea and everyone had been expecting that he would be asked to speak, but this had not happened; he had only been invited to pray. On the day after, he had gone to a church in a village in response to an invitation. On the following Thursday there was a choir practice and the choir director had asked him to say something to the young people. While ###### was developing his theme, the church's cleaning lady had come and told him that the church committee were having a meeting next door and that they wanted him to stop speaking and leave. ###### had asked the people and they had told him to go on. When he had finished his talk he had gone to the committee and had explained to them that he had been invited and that it was his practice to go wherever he was invited. His idea of liberty was that you should not negotiate to obtain 50% or 60% liberty. You had full liberty to witness to what you believed and to tell others too. There had been a stage in which the arrangements with the Department had been misunderstood. We should be open about our beliefs and should refuse to be deprived of our rights, "whatever the consequences, death not excluded. The

Peter Dugulescu

people have been greatly led astray with various "arrangements", but there must be no secrecy about who we are or about the fact that we are ready to endure any suffering, if necessary – if we are indeed followers of the one who calls us to take up the cross." As your agent was on duty he had to leave immediately. When he reached home that evening he found a group on ####### who were discussing the same issues. ###### was very angry that ###### was becoming embroiled in politics and taking ###### attitudes.

Deva 11.12.1973   ss/ Sandu

N O T E :

The agent's memo and oral reports show that ######'s position is still very rigid – fanatical – and that he hopes that his grievances will be redressed with the help of support from outside, if need be.

The informer has been given new duties, both with regard to ###### and in connection with other matters which will be sorted out along the way.

A further consequence of this report is that ###### will be returning to Deva at the end of December. The result obtained will be reported.

Agent checking continues.

One copy of this memo to the First Directorate.

Lieutenant-Colonel A.Mihut

rd.345/3279 third copy

MINISTRY OF THE   TOP SECRET
   INTERIOR   Copy no. 1
HUNEDOARA COUNTY
INSPECTORATE
140/JL/06.08.1974
   "IOAN LASCU"
Dossier no.10241/42

AGENT MEMO

==========

Your agent informs you that the ordination of PETER DUGULESCU as pastor of the Baptist church in Hateg and of the surrounding churches took place on 04.08.1974. The service, which was led by ###### from Deva and the Vice-President of the Baptist community from Brasov, commenced at 9 o'clock. The Hateg church choir and a men's choir sang. Pastors ######, ###### and ###### spoke as representatives of his colleagues, and pastor ######, who also presided over the ordination panel, spoke representing the community.

PETER DUGULESCU was then invited to speak. He related his life story. Next came theological questions posed by members of the panel. DUGULESCU answered these well. Pastor ###### then had the report read. Once the panel had signed this, he pronounced DUGULESCU suitable for the pastoral ministry.

The service ended at 11.30. From 11.30 to 12 the Seminary professor gave some advice on behalf of the Baptist Theological Seminary, He said: Even though we are going to give [sic, should be 'gave'] you advice at the end of the Baptist theological service [sic, should be Seminary?], we now want to give you some advice regarding what a pastor should be like in the future. His message focused on the price a pastor has to pay. He must be patient in all circumstances and show great self-restraint, he must give his life for his fellow-men just as Jesus did, he must endure criticism, he must give up personal ambition, he must lead a quiet life, he must make his contribution to the society in which he lives and be the first in any good work, he must train men of hope, the new man of tomorrow, his life must be so blameless that no-one can charge him with anything, he must love his country and his people.

Everything was finished at 12. ###### set off for Clopotiva where he is staying on holiday with the ###### family with his wife and their little girl.

The inspector from the ###### was also present throughout the proceedings.

There was a large congregation because people had come from the neighbouring churches which wanted PETER DUGULESCU to be recognised as pastor.

ss/Lascu

Officer's memo:

PETER DUGULESCU is the newly-appointed Baptist pastor at Hateg. We hold no records on him. ###### is being watched by the First Directorate.

The informer has been instructed to communicate to us any problems or aspects which arise in connection with ######, both while he remains within this county and after he leaves. This should include friendships he forms, visits received, conversations, etc.
Details regarding his behaviour in the village of Clopotiva can be obtained via the officer in Hateg. The local network in the village has received the necessary instructions.

Copy of memo to the First Directorate.

ss/Capt. L. Jakab

rd.361/2371
fourth copy

MINISTRY OF THE INTERIOR   TOP SECRET
HUNEDOARA COUNTY INSPECTORATE   Copy no. 1
        HATEG SECURITATE
Received by: Lieutenant -Major
        Alexandru Bicazan
Source: Informer "Titus Florea"
        Date:24.02.1977
        Place: Hateg
        No.0027/3887/

AGENT MEMO

==========

   Your agent informs you that on 12.02.1977 he met the aforementioned Peter Dugulescu in Hateg and asked him how he was, and the aforementioned replied that he was occupied with church business. He told him that on Monday 11 February he had been to Deva, where he had had a meeting with the County Inspector for Religious Denominations and with ###### from Bucharest. He said that he had told the two of them that they should send him to the County First Secretary so that he could sort out the issue of the church building in Hateg as swiftly as possible, because he had drawn up another report for Mr Nicolae Ceausescu on this subject. If things were not resolved, he would draw up a report which would be placed on the table at the Belgrade Conference scheduled for June of this year.

   He added that he was determined to pursue this course of action whatever happened. He wanted people outside the country to hear about him. He was not afraid, because his family were not going to be allowed to suffer from hunger. He saw this as the only way of resolving the problem in Hateg. Your agent asked him: But how have these problems been sorted out in other places? Hasn't it been through patience and perseverance? The aforementioned replied: I cannot see any alternative to my way. Your agent told him not to do anything so foolish, because he wouldn't succeed and things might turn out even worse both for him and for others who supported him. Your agent advised him to calm down and to look after his own affairs.

   The aforementioned replied that he was not going to back down and that he was going to pursue this course of action to the limit, whatever the risks, because you can never succeed unless you persevere. If the communists see you are weak, they will never help you or satisfy your grievances.

   The conversation ended at this point.

   Hateg 13.02.1977   "Titus Florea"

Officer's memo

The abovementioned Peter Dugulescu, Baptist
preacher in Hateg, appears in the 'problems' file. He
has come to our notice in connection with certain
hostile activities he has carried out and with
suspicious links with the abovementioned ###### who
is being investigated by the First Directorate.

This memo was requested for the purpose of
discovering the abovementioned Peter Dugulescu's
concerns and intentions. He has stated more than once
that he will resort to any measures to resolve the
issue of the Baptist church building in Hateg.

Duties assigned

To continue to inform us of Peter Dugulescu's
concerns, intentions, contacts and circle.

If he possesses or distributes writings with
hostile content, written by ######.

Measures

This memo is to be forwarded to the Hunedoara
County Inspectorate Analysis-Synthesis Section so
that relevant aspects may be made use of in the
intelligence update.

Copy of memo to First Directorate

Lt-Maj.ALEXANDRU BICAZAN

**The issue mentioned in this memo was the
subject of information laid before the County
Committee of the Romanian Communist Party on the
basis of material from the First Directorate.**

Cpt.DANCILA Copy   Given before us, today
5.04.1977

CPT. T Nicolescu

The following photos illustrate some of the highlights of this true story. Many thanks to the individuals who contributed these. Some are taken from home video footage or television broadcasts, so the quality is not as clear as one would like. However, the images still tell the story of the brave men, women and children who risked everything for freedom.

Above, the tiny village of Chelmac where Peter was born and raised. Below, communist organizers sign up the villagers for the first collective farm, which rapidly became a source of poverty and corruption.

Above, Cicio Pop Castle which was turned into a boarding school that Peter attended. Below, the communist "trinity" adorned every household and public place.

Peter's paratrooper training prepared him for a life of stepping out in faith into an uncharted void. Right, Peter's group, and below, his platoon.

Three important moments: Peter's baptism, his wedding to Mary, and below, his seminary days with Pastor Iosif Țon.

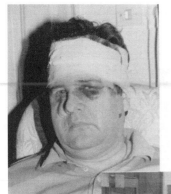

Peter's near-assassination at the hands of the Securitate left him seriously injured but alive, thanks to the sturdy construction of the used car he drove. Below, Ambassador David Funderburk who kept an eye on Peter's trial for fraud.

Rev. Petru Dugulescu
with admiration and
appreciation for your courage

David Funderburk
US Congress Feb '95

Pastor Gherman, with his wife and two sons. Gherman was shot by the Angel of Death, Beniamin Jianu, after givng him a ride. Beni testi•ed that he covered up the killing by putting the minister's corpse back in the car and running it under a truck, to simulate an accident.

Above, Peter's congregation volunteered and built their
new church by hand, consecrating it Dec. 10, just days
before the prayer vigil which swelled into the revolution.
Below, the flag with the communist symbol removed
from the center which became the symbol of Romania
removing communism and replacing it with God.

Pastor Láslo Tökes, whose impending arrest sparked the spontaneous prayer vigil which started the revolution. Below: tanks used to quell the crowds.

Opera Square, Timisoara, where thousands kneeled and proclaimed "God Exists!" despite the threat of military reprisals. After 45 years of mandatory atheism, it was the most revolutionary cry possible.

The Bucharest crowds, assembled by Ceausescu to rubber stamp a planned attack on the demonstrators, refused to cooperate, and instead chanted "Timisoara!"

Above: The former dictator, Nicolae Ceauşescu, is taken from his air-craft, (right) on trial with wife, Elena, and finally, falls to his knees as he is executed, on Dec. 25, 1989.

Left, one of Romania's many street children receives a nourishing meal, and below, the orphans who become the Brothers of Onesimus pray before bedtime, and sing in the choir.

Two baptisms: (left) the young orphan Cornelus baptized with his teacher, and (below) Beniamin Jianu, who transformed from an angel of death to an angel of light, being baptized by Peter at the Arad prison.

Above, the prayer group formed among the post-communist Parliament, where (right) Peter votes on a bill under consideration by the legislature. Below, King Michael, the beloved former monarch and his family share an Easter celebration with Archbishop Nicolae Corneanu, Pastor Peter Dugulescu and other clerics.

Above, Pastor Peter proclaims God's existence to the crowd in Opera Square. Below, hope dawns on the faces of the Romanian people, held too long by the atheist/materialist dictatorship.